THE FLETCHER JONES FOUNDATION
HUMANITIES IMPRINT

The Fletcher Jones Foundation has endowed this imprint to foster innovative and enduring scholarship in the humanities.

The publisher and the University of California Press Foundation gratefully acknowledge the generous support of the Fletcher Jones Foundation Imprint in Humanities.

The publisher also gratefully acknowledges the generous support of the Director's Circle of the University of California Press Foundation, whose members are:

Stephen and Melva Arditti
Shadia Kanaan
Susan Magee
Donald Mastronarde
Alejandro Portes
The Leslie Scalapino - O Books Fund
Meryl and Robert Selig
Sharon Simpson
Marc Singer
Lynne Withey

Ways of Eating

California Studies in Food and Culture

DARRA GOLDSTEIN, EDITOR

1. *Dangerous Tastes: The Story of Spices,* by Andrew Dalby
2. *Eating Right in the Renaissance,* by Ken Albala
3. *Food Politics: How the Food Industry Influences Nutrition and Health,* by Marion Nestle
4. *Camembert: A National Myth,* by Pierre Boisard
5. *Safe Food: The Politics of Food Safety,* by Marion Nestle
6. *Eating Apes,* by Dale Peterson
7. *Revolution at the Table: The Transformation of the American Diet,* by Harvey Levenstein
8. *Paradox of Plenty: A Social History of Eating in Modern America,* by Harvey Levenstein
9. *Encarnación's Kitchen: Mexican Recipes from Nineteenth-Century California: Selections from Encarnación Pinedo's* El cocinero español, by Encarnación Pinedo, edited and translated by Dan Strehl, with an essay by Victor Valle
10. *Zinfandel: A History of a Grape and Its Wine,* by Charles L. Sullivan, with a foreword by Paul Draper
11. *Tsukiji: The Fish Market at the Center of the World,* by Theodore C. Bestor
12. *Born Again Bodies: Flesh and Spirit in American Christianity,* by R. Marie Griffith
13. *Our Overweight Children: What Parents, Schools, and Communities Can Do to Control the Fatness Epidemic,* by Sharron Dalton
14. *The Art of Cooking: The First Modern Cookery Book,* by the Eminent Maestro Martino of Como, edited and with an introduction by Luigi Ballerini, translated and annotated by Jeremy Parzen, and with fifty modernized recipes by Stefania Barzini

15. *The Queen of Fats: Why Omega-3s Were Removed from the Western Diet and What We Can Do to Replace Them,* by Susan Allport

16. *Meals to Come: A History of the Future of Food,* by Warren Belasco

17. *The Spice Route: A History,* by John Keay

18. *Medieval Cuisine of the Islamic World: A Concise History with 174 Recipes,* by Lilia Zaouali, translated by M. B. DeBevoise, with a foreword by Charles Perry

19. *Arranging the Meal: A History of Table Service in France,* by Jean-Louis Flandrin, translated by Julie E. Johnson, with Sylvie and Antonio Roder; with a foreword to the English-language edition by Beatrice Fink

20. *The Taste of Place: A Cultural Journey into Terroir,* by Amy B. Trubek

21. *Food: The History of Taste,* edited by Paul Freedman

22. *M. F. K. Fisher among the Pots and Pans: Celebrating Her Kitchens,* by Joan Reardon, with a foreword by Amanda Hesser

23. *Cooking: The Quintessential Art,* by Hervé This and Pierre Gagnaire, translated by M. B. DeBevoise

24. *Perfection Salad: Women and Cooking at the Turn of the Century,* by Laura Shapiro

25. *Of Sugar and Snow: A History of Ice Cream Making,* by Jeri Quinzio

26. *Encyclopedia of Pasta,* by Oretta Zanini De Vita, translated by Maureen B. Fant, with a foreword by Carol Field

27. *Tastes and Temptations: Food and Art in Renaissance Italy,* by John Varriano

28. *Free for All: Fixing School Food in America,* by Janet Poppendieck

29. *Breaking Bread: Recipes and Stories from Immigrant Kitchens,* by Lynne Christy Anderson, with a foreword by Corby Kummer

30. *Culinary Ephemera: An Illustrated History,* by William Woys Weaver

31. *Eating Mud Crabs in Kandahar: Stories of Food during Wartime by the World's Leading Correspondents,* edited by Matt McAllester

32. *Weighing In: Obesity, Food Justice, and the Limits of Capitalism,* by Julie Guthman

33. *Why Calories Count: From Science to Politics,* by Marion Nestle and Malden Nesheim

34. *Curried Cultures: Globalization, Food, and South Asia,* edited by Krishnendu Ray and Tulasi Srinivas

35. *The Cookbook Library: Four Centuries of the Cooks, Writers, and Recipes That Made the Modern Cookbook,* by Anne Willan, with Mark Cherniavsky and Kyri Claflin

36. *Coffee Life in Japan,* by Merry White

37. *American Tuna: The Rise and Fall of an Improbable Food,* by Andrew F. Smith

38. *A Feast of Weeds: A Literary Guide to Foraging and Cooking Wild Edible Plants,* by Luigi Ballerini, translated by Gianpiero W. Doebler, with recipes by Ada De Santis and illustrations by Giuliano Della Casa

39. *The Philosophy of Food,* by David M. Kaplan

40. *Beyond Hummus and Falafel: Social and Political Aspects of Palestinian Food in Israel,* by Liora Gvion, translated by David Wesley and Elana Wesley

41. *The Life of Cheese: Crafting Food and Value in America,* by Heather Paxson

42. *Popes, Peasants, and Shepherds: Recipes and Lore from Rome and Lazio,* by Oretta Zanini De Vita, translated by Maureen B. Fant, foreword by Ernesto Di Renzo

43. *Cuisine and Empire: Cooking in World History,* by Rachel Laudan

44. *Inside the California Food Revolution: Thirty Years That Changed Our Culinary Consciousness,* by Joyce Goldstein, with Dore Brown

45. *Cumin, Camels, and Caravans: A Spice Odyssey,* by Gary Paul Nabhan

46. *Balancing on a Planet: The Future of Food and Agriculture,* by David A. Cleveland

47. *The Darjeeling Distinction: Labor and Justice on Fair-Trade Tea Plantations in India,* by Sarah Besky

48. *How the Other Half Ate: A History of Working-Class Meals at the Turn of the Century,* by Katherine Leonard Turner

49. *The Untold History of Ramen: How Political Crisis in Japan Spawned a Global Food Craze,* by George Solt

50. *Word of Mouth: What We Talk About When We Talk About Food,* by Priscilla Parkhurst Ferguson

51. *Inventing Baby Food: Taste, Health, and the Industrialization of the American Diet,* by Amy Bentley

52. *Secrets from the Greek Kitchen: Cooking, Skill, and Everyday Life on an Aegean Island,* by David E. Sutton

53. *Breadlines Knee-Deep in Wheat: Food Assistance in the Great Depression,* by Janet Poppendieck

54. *Tasting French Terroir: The History of an Idea,* by Thomas Parker

55. *Becoming Salmon: Aquaculture and the Domestication of a Fish,* by Marianne Elisabeth Lien

56. *Divided Spirits: Tequila, Mezcal, and the Politics of Production,* by Sarah Bowen

57. *The Weight of Obesity: Hunger and Global Health in Postwar Guatemala,* by Emily Yates-Doerr

58. *Dangerous Digestion: The Politics of American Dietary Advice,* by E. Melanie DuPuis

59. *A Taste of Power: Food and American Identities,* by Katharina Vester

60. *More Than Just Food: Food Justice and Community Change,* by Garrett M. Broad

61. *Hoptopia: A World of Agriculture and Beer in Oregon's Willamette Valley,* by Peter A. Kopp

62. *A Geography of Digestion: Biotechnology and the Kellogg Cereal Enterprise,* by Nicholas Bauch

63. *Bitter and Sweet: Food, Meaning, and Modernity in Rural China,* by Ellen Oxfeld

64. *A History of Cookbooks: From Kitchen to Page over Seven Centuries,* by Henry Notaker

65. *Reinventing the Wheel: Milk, Microbes, and the Fight for Real Cheese,* by Bronwen Percival and Francis Percival

66. *Making Modern Meals: How Americans Cook Today,* by Amy B. Trubek

67. *Food and Power: A Culinary Ethnography of Israel,* by Nir Avieli

68. *Canned: The Rise and Fall of Consumer Confidence in the American Food Industry,* by Anna Zeide

69. *Meat Planet: Artificial Flesh and the Future of Food,* by Benjamin Aldes Wurgaft

70. *The Labor of Lunch: Why We Need Real Food and Real Jobs in American Public Schools,* by Jennifer E. Gaddis

71. *Feeding the Crisis: Care and Abandonment in America's Food Safety Net,* by Maggie Dickinson

72. *Sameness in Diversity: Food and Globalization in Modern America,* by Laresh Jayasanker

73. *The Fruits of Empire: Art, Food, and the Politics of Race in the Age of American Expansion,* by Shana Klein

74. *Let's Ask Marion: What You Need to Know about the Politics of Food, Nutrition, and Health,* by Marion Nestle, in conversation with Kerry Trueman

75. *The Scarcity Slot: Excavating Histories of Food Security in Ghana,* by Amanda L. Logan

76. *Gastropolitics and the Specter of Race: Stories of Capital, Culture, and Coloniality in Peru,* by María Elena García

77. *The Kingdom of Rye: A Brief History of Russian Food,* by Darra Goldstein

78. *Slow Cooked: An Unexpected Life in Food Politics,* by Marion Nestle

79. *Yerba Mate: The Drink That Shaped a Nation,* by Julia J.S. Sarreal

80. *Wonder Foods: The Science and Commerce of Nutrition,* by Lisa Haushofer

81. *Ways of Eating: Exploring Food through History and Culture,* by Benjamin A. Wurgaft and Merry I. White

Ways of Eating

EXPLORING FOOD THROUGH HISTORY AND CULTURE

Benjamin A. Wurgaft and
Merry I. White

UNIVERSITY OF CALIFORNIA PRESS

University of California Press
Oakland, California

© 2023 by Benjamin A. Wurgaft and Merry I. White

Library of Congress Cataloging-in-Publication Data

Names: Wurgaft, Benjamin Aldes, author. | White, Merry I.,
    1941- author.
Title: Ways of eating : exploring food through history and culture /
    Benjamin A. Wurgaft and Merry I. White.
Other titles: California studies in food and culture ; 81.
Description: Oakland, California : University of California Press,
    [2023] | Includes bibliographical references and index.
Identifiers: LCCN 2022055958 (print) | LCCN 2022055959 (ebook) |
    ISBN 9780520392984 (cloth) | ISBN 9780520393004 (ebook)
Subjects: LCSH: Food—History.
Classification: LCC GN407 .W87 2023 (print) | LCC GN407 (ebook) |
    DDC 394.1/209—dc23/eng/20230105
LC record available at https://lccn.loc.gov/2022055958
LC ebook record available at https://lccn.loc.gov/2022055959

Manufactured in the United States of America

32 31 30 29 28 27 26 25 24
10 9 8 7 6 5 4 3

For Gus

Contents

Acknowledgments   *xiii*

	Introduction	1
VIGNETTE 1	Duccio's Eden	8
CHAPTER 1	Nature and Culture in the Origins Of Agriculture	11
VIGNETTE 2	*Akashiyaki* at Nishi-Akashi	27
CHAPTER 2	Staple Empires of the Ancient World	30
VIGNETTE 3	Coffee and Pepper	62
CHAPTER 3	Medieval Tastes	67
VIGNETTE 4	Before Kimchi	89
CHAPTER 4	The Columbian Exchange, or, the World Remade	92
VIGNETTE 5	The Spirit Safe	107
CHAPTER 5	Social Beverages and Modernity	110
VIGNETTE 6	Authenticity in Panama	129
CHAPTER 6	Colony and Curry	133
VIGNETTE 7	The Icebox	147

CHAPTER 7   Food's Industrial Revolution   150

VIGNETTE 8   Bricolage   168

CHAPTER 8   Twentieth-Century Foodways, or,
             Big Food and Its Discontents   171

VIGNETTE 9   *Nem* on the Menu   190

CHAPTER 9   Ways of Eating   194

             Conclusion   205
             Notes   211
             Bibliography   223
             Index   231

Acknowledgments

Many cooks in the kitchen, many people to thank. We bang spoons on pots and pans for our colleagues and friends in food anthropology, food history, and food studies broadly writ: Rebecca Alssid, Elizabeth Andoh, the late Mary Beaudry, Warren Belasco, Katarzyna Cwiertka, Joanna Davidson, Darra Goldstein, Rafi Grosglik, Barbara Haber, Ursula Heinzelmann, Rachel Laudan, Jill Norman, Heather Paxson, Stephen Shapin, and Bee Wilson. Corky (a.k.a. Merry) would also like to acknowledge the support of her early mentor, Julia Child, and Elizabeth David, who helped her along the way.

Adam Simha introduced us to knifemaking. Josh Berson helped us come up with our title over dinner, and generously read our book in draft. Carlos Noreña and Thomas David DuBois both read our chapter on ancient empires and offered their expertise, Paul Kosmin made valuable suggestions about Rome and Persia, and Jeremiah Dittmar read a very early draft of our chapter on the industrial revolution. Thanks, too, to our anonymous readers, and Ben would like to thank his summer school students at Wesleyan, who gave this work a trial run as a textbook.

Gus Rancatore, Shannon Supple, Lewis Wurgaft, and Carole Colsell patiently listened as we discussed this book over years of meals and offered their thoughts.

We're so lucky to work with our skilled and thoughtful editor Kate Marshall at the University of California Press. Many thanks as well to Chad Attenborough, Catherine Osborne, Francisco Reinking, Alex Dahne, Kevin Barrett Kane, Ramón Smith, and the whole UC Press team. We dearly miss Sheila Levine, Corky's editor on past UC Press projects, and a force in shaping the academic study of food. Shannon Supple generously contributed illustrations.

This book is dedicated to Gus Rancatore, in gratitude and love.

Lastly, we acknowledge each other. It is sometimes a challenge for a parent and child to work together on a project like this one, to argue over interpretations and to edit one another's words. We feel lucky to have emerged enlivened and unscathed, and to have learned a great deal from one another in the process.

Thank you, each other!

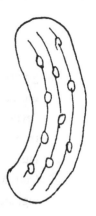

Introduction

EATING COMES BEFORE WORDS. A baby takes nourishment before it can speak. Eating and drinking establish our relationship with the surrounding world. We explain that world with words, but we remain dependent upon, and vulnerable to, the world that feeds us. When conditions are good, we have enough. We become accustomed to finishing a bottle of milk, a cup of coffee, a bowl of rice, and feeling satisfied. But we are never done learning about food. Learning lacks the quality of finality. There is always more to know. Our curiosity reappears like hunger returning. Why does an egg scramble as it does; how does grain ferment into beer; what makes a cookie crumble?

The first-ness of food in our lives is an understandably old story. "First we eat, and then we do everything else," runs a widely quoted remark made by the food writer Mary Francis Kennedy Fisher. This is true enough. Eating doesn't just come before words; it comes before all other human activities, within the narrow frame of an individual's life. But beneath this simple statement lies an intricate relationship between sustenance and "everything else." "Everything else" means everything from grinding corn into masa to breeding pigs, from creating agricultural subsidies for Japanese rice farmers to defending Ethiopian cattle-grazing land. In other words, there is a great deal of agricultural and food work that prepares the way for eating. And some of this work is not toil in the fields, or in kitchens. The "everything else" in Fisher's line includes the operations of culture, from Greek myths about the origin of the world out of an egg, to Dutch still-life paintings depicting opulent oysters and decaying fruit. Many kinds of human activity set the table (as it were) for eating, including creating images and descriptions of what we eat.

Representations of food aren't just stories and images. They touch what they represent. Consider a burning fire on a beach in ancient Greece, upon which the hero Odysseus and his men have arranged pieces of sacrificial beef. The heroes of Homer's epics, the *Iliad* and the *Odyssey*, sacrifice, roast, and eat a great many animals, but all this carnivorousness was not the reality for ancient Greeks. It was hard to raise so many animals on rocky terrain. Rather, Odysseus's larger-than-life diet reflects aspiration and the prestige ancient Greeks associated with meat.[1] To talk about meat was to describe luxury and high social status, or to connect great deeds with prestigious roasts. In the *Odyssey*, a number of servants and slaves serve Odysseus's family, raising pigs and goats and cows for the nobles to eat, and a complex social hierarchy determines who enjoys what. But stories about meat helped to maintain meat's prestige, not just in stories told by poets but also in the daily lives of the gathered audience members. We must reverse M. F. K. Fisher: first we do everything else, from planting crops to telling stories, and then we can eat.

This book is an invitation to be curious about food, and especially to think about food in new ways. The history and anthropology of food show us the strange tales of origin behind familiar tastes and illuminate mysteries within commonplace rituals. But we have to be willing to dig. A ripe strawberry, bursting in your mouth, tells you nothing about the experience of bending down to pick that strawberry in a sun-baked field. It says little about the history of the strawberry's breeding, the emergence of the modern plant from a now-forgotten ancestor through generations of domestication. In a certain sense, a plate of food is the coming-together of natural history (the evolutionary stories of the plants and animals we cook) and human history (the ways in which we "guide evolution," raise and cook them). But what hungry eater pauses to inquire into this?

Nevertheless, a taste or a smell gives us a place to begin. Tastes and smells are a kind of information, telling the body about the food we put in our mouths. Is this safe? Is it nourishing? Will this be good? Our body's needs are simple enough, and easily satisfied, but food and drink can also pique our curiosity. We may pause in the supermarket to look at a fruit we've never seen before (perhaps a dragonfruit); we ask about a surprising shape at the fish counter (maybe it's a monkfish). We wonder who eats it, and how (or if) they cook it. Or we look at something familiar (a bag of granola, say) and realize we know nothing about how it is made. This book is about the questions that food and drink can compel us to ask. It is about the history of food as a presence in the tastes of the present day. It is also about the way culture guides our hands as we take the next strawberry and cut it with a knife, thinking of a pie. This domesticated strawberry is not natural, wild, but already part of the field of practices and beliefs we call culture. Without human intervention, corn on the cob would just be another kind of grass.

This book's title and the opening lines above pay homage to John Berger's 1972 book on art history, *Ways of Seeing,* an adaptation of a television series that introduced many viewers to a new way of thinking about art.[2] Influenced by Marxist cultural criticism, Berger reminded readers that fine art is not simply a heritage of beauty. Everything from the act of painting to hanging paintings in museums tells stories about class, power, and social conflict. Art is a formal exercise in representing and conjuring human experience, but it does not float free of context. Berger sought to unpack the social relations bundled within painting, especially prestigious forms of painting such as modern European portraiture. In a similar way, foods express the ways desire and appetite shape our lives: sometimes dramatically, like gold foil draped over a dish of chicken biryani, or less visibly, as with birds bred over generations to produce more meat faster. The social conflicts and oppressions of the past survive in the cuisine of the present, albeit in greatly transformed ways. So do past patterns of human migration, settlement, trade, war, and travel.

We desire food and drink. It is good to acknowledge this, and to remember that the body's appetites are not to be degraded as somehow "below the neck," an animalistic shame. Our appetites are the heart of our relationship with food, and we can learn much by thinking about them, and even by indulging them. Personal experience is a crucial tool for studying food. But like other human desires, our hunger and thirst can mystify. There are stories in our foods that flavor alone does not tell. Sugar pleases us, but that pleasure says nothing about the history of the colonial plantations where enslaved people once planted and harvested sugar cane. Desire is one of this book's themes—the desire for survival (gruel when the larder is bare), for beloved food (grandmother's noodle soup), for novelties (spices obtained at great risk on the high seas)—but power is another (the power Europeans exerted over colonized natives, for example). So is identity, in the sense that our foods and ways of cooking express our cultural and social roots.

But identities change over time. This pie recipe may have been in our family for generations, but it hasn't been with us forever, and each baker has added or subtracted something. We eat across cultural boundaries, flipping between "family food" and that of others. And no cuisine is permanent or stable. Change has always characterized who we are and what we eat, even if we feel culinary anxiety and cling to dishes we call "traditional" or "authentic." Human communities migrate, or invade each other's lands; new ingredients travel along trade routes. Thus movement is another one of this book's themes. We also attend to the differences between the clean and the dirty, the edible and the inedible, which shape so many of our food practices, from the question of which plants and animals we call food to how we wash our dishes. Tools and techniques are part of culture too, and so are the bodies of food workers. For generations, women ground maize into corn flour to make tortillas on a flat stone mortar called a *metate;* their daily motion, the effects on their knees and shoulders, became part of a way of eating.

This book consists of a series of historical chapters, leading chronologically from the origins of agriculture to the early twenty-first century, interleaved with vignettes drawn from our observations and ethnographic work in different food worlds. In these chapters and vignettes we offer specific cases that raise important questions about food and drink. We survey key ideas from cultural anthropology and history that help to explain human food practices and beliefs, but we do not address ourselves solely or primarily to scholars. Our goal is not to encompass the whole history of human foodways, which a short book (or even a very long one) never could. This book reflects our own past research interests and specialties—even our tastes.

A note of personal introduction, then. We are your authors: Merry ("Corky") I. White is a cultural anthropologist of Japan, and of food and drink in Japan and beyond, who has also worked as a caterer, food journalist, and cookbook writer. Benjamin ("Ben") A. Wurgaft is her son, a writer and historian, who earned a doctorate in European intellectual history while working as a food journalist. Ben has also trained and practiced in the cultural anthropology of science and technology. We both believe that the pleasures of food and drink, and the dynamic challenge of food work itself, add to and don't distract from the intellectual rewards of studying food. These things are all bound up with each other. The chapters and vignettes in this book reflect our diverse interests, but also the decades of good luck that have allowed us to travel, taste, and benefit from hospitality around the world, from growing up eating kosher dills in Minnesota, to cooking with local herbal blends in Tuscany, to sampling croissants in Tokyo. Some of these vignettes reflect shared experiences; others are singly authored.

While the chapters offer a chronological food history that takes us from the origins of agriculture to the present, the vignettes introduce the cultural anthropology of food, which seeks the expressions of meaning in food practice. At the heart of cultural anthropology is observation. The anthropologist brings a trained and purposeful naïveté to fieldwork, open to everything, and to all possible significance. We all bring filters and preconceptions to every observation, but the best way to work with that bias is first to acknowledge it, and then to cast our awareness wide and deep. You never know which details, or senses, are significant: a man carries a grocery bag on the subway, and it threatens to split, carrots sticking out of holes in its side; the sound of church bells draws black-garmented women in for services, while their men sit at an outdoor café, drinking coffee; a bin smells like mellow fermentation or exudes the stench of rotting garbage. Historical research often begins in an archive, and rarely involves fieldwork, but it shares an important feature with cultural anthropology. While historians all have their ideological and methodological biases, we work with evidence, just as anthropologists do, and we have to be open to the possibility that evidence will make us reformulate our views.

In the history and anthropology of food there are different kinds of questions, each answered with their appropriate kinds of methods and evidence. There are empirical questions we hope to answer, and there are theoretical explanations we hope to offer, and part of the art of the practice is becoming clear about which is which. We refine our questions and learn what methods and evidence will help us to answer them.

Anthropology almost always starts with research conducted in the contemporary world, but it often plunges us into the past of a community. Thus a food anthropologist might start by sitting on a stool at a ramen stall in Tokyo, then move on to the origins of the *dashi* that infuses ramen broth, and to Japanese concerns about the future of the waters, the migrations of fish, and the farming of seaweed. History, by contrast, is the study of change over time, and food history often starts with research into the letters, diaries, or physical evidence of past generations of cooks and eaters. Cookbooks and menus are material for the cultural historian of food; shards of pottery serve archaeologists who look at cooking practices. But when we ask how past actors cooked and ate, and made meaning of these acts, we often reach for the tools of cultural anthropologists, for we know that cultural practices infuse and shape everything from tilling a field to setting a table. As we begin, keep these questions in mind: what can we aspire to know about food? What steps should we take to learn it? What can our meals tell us about the structure of our communities? Who are the farmers, who are the cooks, who makes the pots that dinner cooks in? Who makes the wine and who does the dishes?[3]

Duccio's Eden

DOWN AN INTERMINABLE dirt road through the woods, we call "Duccio! Signore Fantani!" and finally hear "*Sì, sì!*" from what looks like a patch of brush. We've been trying to find Duccio for over an hour. We're near Siena, not far from Florence, and we know Duccio Fantani from the farmer's market in the nearby town of Castellina, where he sells herbs. We've been dusting those herbs on pork, into soup, and on roasted potatoes and vegetables for weeks. Now we've come to see where they grow.

We've been searching for Duccio for a long time, long enough that some members of our party have despaired of actually finding him; their hopes have refocused on breaking off for a Campari. But now Duccio insistently beckons us down a hill of scratchy bushes, down the tracks made by his herd of donkeys and into piles of their shit. Some of us, wearing sandals instead of proper shoes, end up with dung caked under our toenails. Duccio keeps waving.

Does Duccio grow the herbs he sells? As he leads us across the hillsides where coriander, rosemary, and fennel grow, we slowly learn that the answer is "yes and no." He's not a forager, if a forager is someone who gathers what grows with no human interference at all. Nor is he a gleaner, gathering the aftermath of formal harvesting. He's more an encourager of his crops, who sometimes propagates herbs from last year's seeds, though most of what he gathers is from volunteer plants. This is not a farm, and although Duccio and his team remain in one place year-round, he isn't an herb farmer. He occasionally builds fences to keep the donkeys away from the best herb beds, but he gives the impression that the fences are a little too infrastructural, by his lights. Slight, with a gray ponytail and piercing eyes, he looks like a wood gnome. He points out clusters of sprouts nestled next to tree stumps, and weedy mixtures of herbs, not in serried rows or homogeneous patches. He calls out *"coriandolo, rosmarino, fienogreco, elicriso!"*—the same list of ingredients featured in his mixed spice jars, which he labels *"aromi da cucina del Chianti,"* the scents of Chianti cooking.

Is this an ungainly garden of Eden, in which nature brings forth its riches *sua sponte?* Again, yes and no. Duccio thinks of himself as the happy bystander of the nearly "spontaneous" growth of juniper, catnip, wild fennel, and helichrysum. But there is some strategy and husbandry involved. He manages water, harboring it through the dry season and doling it out only as necessary. The donkeys that trample and run paths of their own through the property also fertilize the soil. As we carefully step our way across lavender and rosemary, it's possible to imagine that this is a model of the origins of sedentary agriculture. If Duccio built a few more fences and planted a few more seeds, gave in to the impulse to expand his operation, a farm is what he'd have. Despite meeting the criteria, he does not covet the "bio" appellation, the official trademark of organic foods in Italy. He says *"perche troppo costoso"*—it's too pricey to buy one's way into authorized purity by going through the bureaucratic process. His jar labels read *"genuino clandestino,"* advertising his resistance to the stamp of official approval that might eventually boost his revenue, but which offends his countercultural sensibility and politics. His workplace, such as it is, radiates ambivalence about capitalism.

Walking across an overgrown field, we reach a ramshackle wooden structure, late afternoon sunlight streaming through the breaks between planks. Bushels of herbs lie in racks in a drying room; the scent of lavender stops us in our tracks. The next room is like a little alchemist's laboratory, where Duccio's assistants make herbal oils, cordials, and extracts. There is a pre-agricultural, pre-industrial aura about the whole domain, but Duccio understands that it takes artisanal processing to unlock everything herbs offer. It's a reminder that even before agriculture, it took technique and skill to take our sustenance from nature. Not to mention that the oils, cordials, and extracts yield a better margin than the herbs themselves, and in a gentle paradox, provide financial support for Duccio's minimally interventionist, anti-agribusiness project.

CHAPTER I

Nature and Culture in the Origins of Agriculture

WHY DO WE EAT WHAT WE EAT? Charles Darwin, in his 1871 *The Descent of Man,* speculated that agriculture (a hybrid word coming from *agri,* Greek for "field," and *culture,* from the Latin *cultivare,* "to nurture") divides the state of "savagery" from that of civilization.[1] Certainly, the practice of agriculture normally goes hand in hand with many familiar aspects of civilization: a system of property rights, fixed dwelling places, complex forms of social organization beyond the family, and so forth. It may have even helped usher them into being. Darwin imagined a simple "accident" at the root of farming, in which a fruit tree's seeds happen to fall on a "heap of refuse." We can be certain that the real origins of plant and animal domestication and agriculture were more complex, dependent not only on observing happy natural accidents but also on coordinated human action.

This chapter examines the shift from hunting and gathering to agriculture, an unsettled transition over which biologists, paleontologists, archaeologists, and anthropologists still argue. If the human species has existed in its modern form for somewhere between two hundred thousand and four hundred thousand years, depending on what benchmarks for speciation we use, then humans have practiced agriculture for only a small fraction of our history, beginning around the year 11,000 BCE. (Hominid use of controlled fire for cooking seems to have preceded the emergence of our species; thus agriculture came after fire).[2] Agriculture's advent coincided with the end of the Pleistocene (the last Ice Age) and the beginning of the Holocene, the period we still occupy today. In the early twenty-first century many observers of climate change have renamed the Holocene the "Anthropocene," to capture the effects of humans and our technology on the environment. But our effects on the natural world arguably began with agriculture itself, one of the most consequential developments of what is often called the "Neolithic Revolution," in which our species started to make and use tools extensively. In a historical irony, many of the earliest fertile areas that nurtured the transition to agriculture are now degraded. Much of Iraq and Iran, for example, has become unsuitable for farming, and the Sahel, in Africa, is plagued by drought and famine.

Agriculture means tending to, and changing, the plant and animal species that flourish in a given acre of land so that we can eat a higher percentage of the biomass produced on that acre. This definition is capacious enough to include the large-scale industrial farming practices of the early twenty-first century as well as what some anthropologists call "intensification," the simple effort to encourage certain species to prevail in an area, and to discourage others from flourishing. It also includes animal husbandry without sedentary plant agriculture. Whatever its scale, agriculture begins with selecting the plant and animal species most appropriate for our dietary needs. Relatively few of the plant species around us are edible; of the about two hundred thousand wild plant species that were present around 11,000 BCE, we have domesticated only a few hundred. Our primary crop plants are the domesticated descendants of a relative handful of wild ancestors that, because of their nutritional and physical properties, attracted early agriculturalists. Similarly, the animals we eat (or that yield dairy and eggs) descend from wild ancestors that seemed suitable for domestication, often because they were sociable, mild-tempered and lived in a herd or pack structure that made them amenable to human authority. We use (for food, labor or transportation) only a handful of the Earth's some 148 large terrestrial mammal species. While it is true that agriculture was the first step in the human effort to bring nature under control for our benefit, some authors have viewed the process from the reverse angle. If humans benefit from being able to eat a higher percentage of the plants and animals on a given acre of land, so do the species they cultivate, because humans act like bumblebees, aiding their reproduction and spreading them along the paths of human migration.[3] The result is that these species guarantee their survival—becoming domesticated is a successful adaptation, in evolutionary terms.

In the early twenty-first century, a dozen plant species account for 80 percent of the tonnage we grow each year: wheat, corn, rice, barley, sorghum, soybean, potato, manioc, sweet potato, sugarcane, sugar beet, and banana. And some 73 percent of the calories we consume globally come from rice, wheat, corn, and manioc alone. These are the plants humans have come to specialize in eating. Most interestingly, these important crop plants have been with us for a long time on the scale of recorded history. The modern period (approximately the fifteenth century CE to the present) has not seen the domestication of any major new staple crop plants, nor of any new important livestock species. Whether one views the history of agriculture from the perspective of the farmer or the farmed, however, it is important to note the recursive nature of the process: in modifying nature we modify ourselves. While humans are remarkably flexible in their ability to derive nutrition from a limited range of foods—in a famous example, the Inuit living in the Arctic Circle have thrived on whale meat and little else—we have become entirely dependent on the availability of a small set of specific plants and animals for our sustenance. Without our monocultures, we would need to find new subsistence strategies, or return to old ones.

Of course, agriculture is much more than an arrangement between *Homo sapiens* and the plant and animal species that "volunteered" to become part of our biological infrastructure. Agriculture has touched everything from social organization to language to religion. A hundred rituals from cultures around the world—such as sprinkling water from a gourd to encourage rain or sacrificing livestock so that the gods will make plants grow—attest to the importance of the annual cycle of growth, death, and rebirth, and to the centrality of agriculture in human imaginations.[4] Even the more abstract beliefs of historically later monotheistic religions such as Christianity have been traced back to the importance of the agricultural cycle. Agriculture did not simply become a mechanism for human adaptation, subsistence, and flourishing, but a focus for human cultural and social development, just as gathering and hunting had been. Subsistence quickly becomes as much about culture as much as it is about calories.

In his classic book *The Raw and the Cooked,* the anthropologist Claude Lévi-Strauss thought of cooking as a way of mediating between that which humans make or control—the world of culture—and that which we ultimately cannot control, the world of nature.[5] Lévi-Strauss built a system of anthropological thought, called structuralist anthropology, out of such binary distinctions, finding evidence to support his claims in both premodern and modern human cultures. According to structuralism, meaning accrues through oppositions and differences, such as the play of differences between a basket of raw tubers and their counterparts that have baked underneath hot rocks.[6] One of the lessons of structuralism for the anthropology of food has been that the meanings of what we eat are not fixed, and can change as our ability to produce differences changes. Thus new tools and techniques for preparing food have implications for culture, even as culture transforms our tools and techniques in turn. Another lesson is that the structures of meaning that govern our lives are largely impersonal; we may have our personal associations with specific foods, but the meaning of the opposition between the raw and the cooked is larger than our preferences, and carries a meaning we cannot dispute, just as there is something impersonal about the generally agreed-upon meaning of words like "cat" or "night." Foodways become a system of meanings we live in, akin to a language. They respond to the human desire to organize and give meaning to the world as much as they respond to our need for nutrition.

The Neolithic revolution saw an increase in sedentism (settled living), the manufacture of increasingly refined stone tools and pottery, and the adoption of agriculture, the latter being a very gradual, stop-and-start affair ongoing at multiple sites of human settlement. In some cases a given community would take a step towards agriculture and then a step away, only to return to agriculture again. The reasons agriculture began around 11,000 BCE are the subject of much debate, but there is a strong consensus about that time frame itself. As a miniature ice age ended, glaciers retreated, temperatures stabilized at a somewhat warmer point, and more of the earth's land became ecologically inviting. Wild grasses spread across the land, grasses that humans later domesticated as crops.

Many disagreements regarding the origins of agriculture seem to result from the different types of evidence used by investigators: human bones and teeth may tell one story about what was eaten and how it was acquired, whereas stone tools, pottery, and other artifacts suggest others. Seed residue and other preserved plant matter—including phytoliths or "plant stones," crystals formed of calcium oxalate or calcium carbonate within the epidermal cells of plants or between those cells, and then preserved in the soil after a plant decays—tell their own tales. Radiocarbon dating has been one of our best tools for decades, and more recently, genetic sequencing techniques have deepened our understanding of the slow pace at which animal and plant species were domesticated.

But expanding the types of evidence available to us has hardly quelled disagreement and led to a singular consensus about agriculture's emergence. There may in fact be no single explanation of why we slowly ceased to be hunters and gatherers and became farmers and herders, or of how agriculture spread worldwide rather than remaining concentrated in the few geographic centers where it seems to have developed independently: the Near East, certain parts of China (mainly the Yangtze and Yellow River valleys), Mesoamerica, the Peruvian Highlands, and Eastern North America.

When we think of the word "infrastructure," as in the roads, bridges, and waterways we depend upon, we must also think of the biological infrastructure of our fields of crops. All of our accomplishments as a civilization depend on the foundation of this bio-infrastructure. And yet agriculture was not an inevitable answer to the question of how to get food. When viewed from the short-term perspective of most hunter-gatherer communities, agriculture is a surprisingly bad idea. Anthropological research into the lives of the few remaining communities of hunter-gatherers in the modern world has shown that they often work fewer hours per week when compared to their agricultural neighbors, while enjoying at least as many calories for their labors. Bones and teeth recovered from ancient campsites and burial grounds suggest that early hunter-gatherers were better nourished, physically larger, and longer-lived than the first farmers. While an agricultural community may induce a given acre of land to produce more edible biomass per year than does, say, an untamed forest, it requires a massive expenditure of effort (plowing, planting, tending, harvesting) to achieve this result. If abundant sources of food in the form of fruits, nuts, tubers, and animal prey are available, it is "cheaper" from the viewpoint of the individual to simply exploit those resources. The attractions of the hunting and gathering lifestyle may explain why some human communities reverted to these practices after initially adopting agriculture—they may have only adopted it due to shortages within their hunting and foraging territories.

The idea of a sudden and decisive switch from hunting and gathering to farming has been widely disproven. It appears that in many parts of the world there were long periods in which both styles of life were practiced, with the balance slowly tipping in favor of agriculture over many generations. Agriculture was not a choice our distant ancestors made, it seems, but a process they got caught up in.

And yet we became an agricultural species, one that does not simply inhabit ecological niches, but constructs them. Explanations for the early adoption of agriculture have included the simple "inventor" theory—the idea that individuals observed the way plants grew from wild seeds and then replicated the process themselves under controlled conditions. There are also "settlement" theories, according to which the practice of living in permanent settlements, made possible by the slow withdrawal of the last ice age, made agriculture more attractive. Other theories have used "accumulative" personality types, technological innovation, the need to maximize a shrinking resource base under conditions of desertification, the emergence of the idea of property, and even the development of religion, as explanatory mechanisms—and this list merely scratches the surface.

There are also theories that make population pressure the driver for agriculture's development, at least in some parts of the world. Most population pressure models are variations on the following: agriculture may not be better than hunting and gathering when it comes to satisfying the needs of an individual, but it can be superior when viewed from the perspective of a community, and especially so for larger and more settled human communities. Farming can yield greater amounts of food at once and thus allow communities to create food reserves and to feed more individuals; an increase in food supply often leads to an increase in population growth, an observation formalized by the English political economist Thomas Robert

Malthus in the late eighteenth century. According to Malthus, population growth always stays ahead of advances in agricultural yields, and population pressure can, under certain conditions, hold constant even as agriculture intensifies and becomes more productive. It follows that as communities increase in size it becomes increasingly rewarding for them to "invest" time in agriculture. Another feature of many population growth theories is that sedentary agriculture gave rise to an increase in birthrates. Mothers living within settled communities may have been able to have children at closer intervals than their hunter-gatherer counterparts who kept on the move, and who consequently could care for a smaller number of children at a time. Normally, mothers in nomadic communities wait until a child is three or four years old and can walk a long way on its own before having another. But even if the "intensifying" effect of population pressure is relatively uncontroversial, the claim that population pressure *resulted* in the development of agriculture in the first place seems unsubstantiated by the available evidence. Archaeologists have not found evidence that population pressure increased prior to the adoption of agriculture in any given human settlement.

Researchers have found what may be the earliest agricultural site in the world at Abu Hureyra, in modern Syria, where there is evidence of planting as early as 11,500 BCE. Such settlements were established after what is known as the Younger Dryas glaciation event, which began around 12,800 BCE and brought over a thousand years of cold, shattering the ecosystems whose stability enabled human settlement. It seems likely that the Younger Dryas postponed early experiments in agricultural living around the world. The most extensive evidence of uninterrupted early agriculture has been found in three general areas: the Near East, where agriculture took hold by 9,000 BCE; China's Yellow River Valley, with a starting date of around 7,500 BCE; and the Peruvian highlands and Mesoamerica, where the first signs of agriculture date to around 6,500 BCE. It is important to note that the dates trusted by individual archaeologists and anthropologists vary and are likely to change as new discoveries are made.

In considering the sites where agriculture succeeded most visibly, we should bear in mind the remarkable coincidences of factors that helped it to succeed. In the Near East, factors contributing to the success of agriculture included the Mediterranean's climate, with its mild and moist winters and long, hot summers. This produced plants hardy enough to survive the dry season and then grow after the coming of rain but which, because they were "annuals," did not create much indigestible woody mass. Their one-year cycle of life meant that they put more of their caloric energy into producing seeds, which humans could eat.

While our planet features multiple zones of "Mediterranean" climate, including parts of North and South America's West coasts, as well as parts of the Southern coast of Australia, the Near East had both vastly more plants suitable for domestication as well as more large mammals similarly suitable for human use. The major crops in the Fertile Crescent included einkorn and emmer wheat (two very early cultivated wheat varietals) as well as barley, lentils, peas, chickpeas, flax (one of the few early domesticates grown and used for clothing rather than for food), and bitter vetch, whose seeds resemble red lentils but must be purged of their bitterness in baths of water before humans can comfortably consume them. The process of agricultural adoption appears to have been completed by 6000 BCE.

Notably, in the Fertile Crescent animal and plant agriculture had complementary effects. While one reason to engage in animal agriculture is meat, and another is milk (a milk- or egg-producing animal will yield many times as many calories, over its life, than one slaughtered for meat), by domesticating animals we realized another benefit: their labor power, often crucial for agriculture. Notably, in much of Africa herders domesticated animals and practiced nomadic animal agriculture, traveling with their herds, long before anyone domesticated plants.[7]

The most important crops in the Americas were the so-called "three sisters:" maize, beans, and squash, which were grown throughout Mesoamerica by 1,500 BCE, and long before then in many areas. Agriculture appears to have first begun in Mexico and Peru, with one archaeological dig in the Mexican state of Oaxaca indicating that squash may have been domesticated around the same time as crops in the Near East. R. S. MacNeish, one of the most important early figures in the scientific effort to understand the origins of agriculture, found sites in the modern Mexican state of Tamaulipas where chili peppers and gourds, as well as squash and beans, were cultivated between 7000 and 5500 BCE. In Tehuacan, in south-central Mexico, the same crops as in Tamaulipas, plus maize, amaranth, and avocado, could be traced to around 5000–3500 BCE. Dogs and turkeys were both domesticated as food sources. Maize seems to have been first grown in lower and wetter regions, and was gradually adapted to higher and dryer latitudes. In the Peruvian Highlands, beans and chilies have been found and dated to about 6000 BCE. The most important difference between early agriculture in the Americas and in the Near East may have been the absence of animal power in the former: while smaller animals were indeed domesticated at the Mexican and Peruvian sites of early agriculture, they were not the larger, hundred-plus-pound species that proved useful in farming efforts in the Near East.

It seems likely that China's Yangtze River Valley was the first site where rice was domesticated, producing something that began to look like contemporary white rice out of the wild ancestral plant. Evidence suggests that this may have first taken place as early as 11,000 BCE, placing the origins of agriculture in China in the same relation to the Younger Dryas event as the parallel events in the Near East. All of the important crops in China were local domesticates:

foxtail millet, broomcorn millet (the Yangtze River Valley seems to have run on a millet-based subsistence economy at some point between 5000 BCE and 3000 BCE, and millet was used before rice in many areas), soybeans, adzuki beans, mung beans, and rice. A few important animals were also local: pigs, dogs (used for hunting as well as for food), chickens, and buffalo. Other animals (including horses, sheep, and goats) and plants (including barley and wheat) were eventually brought in from other regions.

The most important vectors of agriculture's diffusion led from the Near East to Europe, Northern Africa, Ethiopia, and Egypt, as well as to the Indus Valley, and from China throughout Southeast Asia and across the Western Pacific Rim. Crops also traveled north from Mesoamerica to reach North America. Broadly speaking, plants spread more easily to areas that resemble the ones where they were first adapted. The Mediterranean climate in which many Near Eastern crop plants matured accounts for their success in many parts of Europe, for example. One of the strongest pieces of evidence for such diffusion is language: the worldwide distribution of major language families in Eurasia and Australasia matches up neatly with the archaeological evidence in support of diffusion. The Near East and China, cradles of agriculture, are also the homes of the seven major language families spoken by most modern humans. Agriculture's spread, however, could have taken place two ways: "demic" diffusion, in which agriculturalist populations migrate from one place to another and bring their farming practices and crop plants with them, and "cultural" diffusion, in which the practice of agriculture passes from one group to another through social contact. In the case of Europe, the human genetic record supports both types, likely simultaneous.

As mentioned earlier, Lévi-Strauss argued that for human communities cooking has long served to mediate between the realm of human culture, the realm more under our control, and that of nature, that more frightening and wild space beyond our campfires or city walls. By engaging in both agriculture and cooking, we gather what nature produces and transmute it into useful, recognizable and nourishing elements, and share these around the fire or at the table. Domesticated plants and animals may seem to remain part of the realm of nature—and some could conceivably survive in the wild and produce offspring who would gradually de-domesticate over generations. But others could not. Maize or corn, for example, is descended from a wild, much smaller-seeded ancestral plant called teosinte, a species of grass originally found in Northern Mexico. "Modern" maize, the result of many generations of breeding by humans, can only reproduce through farming. We have selectively bred the plant to produce more of its edible parts, but in the process we eliminated the features that helped teosinte flourish in the wild. Not only is maize effectively a human invention, a rudimentary biotechnology, but it cannot even serve as a central part of our diets without special preparation, due to an interesting nutritional problem. Some of the amino acids and vitamins in maize can only be digested by humans if it is treated with calcium hydroxide, which early farmers probably produced by burning wood to ash, and which can produce an alkaline solution if mixed with water. This process, called nixtamalization, allowed maize to become the dominant staple of the Americas.[8]

One common morphological feature of domesticated grains, including the very important wheat and rice, is that their individual seeds grow from a central shaft called the "rachis," from which they shatter away when the plant is touched by an animal or blown by the wind. This allows plants to distribute their seeds over a wider area. Because the rachis becomes brittle as the seeds ripen, the seeds only disperse once they are ready to establish themselves in soil and, if conditions are favorable, grow into a new plant. Both wheat and rice have been bred so that the rachis remains supple and the seeds stay attached even after ripening, a development which greatly decreases these plants' chances of reproducing successfully in the wild while making them vastly more desirable for human farmers, who can gather all of a plant's edible seeds at once. The so-called "shatter-proof" rachis, and the plant to which it belongs, is one of the earliest successful results of plant breeding, though it is difficult to use plant morphology as definitive evidence of domestication events. Notably there are some crop plants whose domestication remains a mystery. Almonds and cashews, for example, are so toxic to humans in their wild form that it is unclear how it was determined they could eventually be domesticated. Jonathan Swift is widely quoted as having said that it was a brave man who first ate an oyster; the domestication of toxic nuts was a greater challenge still.

Even as agriculture changed crops, it also changed animals. Many domesticated animals have different horns than their wild counterparts—goats being a prime example—and most large domesticated mammals are smaller than their ancestors. Some domesticated animals display lesser intelligence than do their contemporary wild counterparts (intelligence being a survival trait) and many have duller senses, since the survival advantage sharp ears, eyes, and noses afford is less crucial under domestication. The animals we keep for the coats they grow have been bred to maximize hairiness or wooliness.

Farming fundamentally changed us even as it changed our plants and animals. Most importantly, it made us more numerous. Estimates of early human population suggest that around 10,000 BCE there were a mere three million of us in the world. Two thousand years later, in 8,000 BCE, there were 2.3 million more humans, a staggering increase, but nothing compared to modern rates of population growth. Many anthropologists have argued that the advent of agriculture transformed our patterns of social organization, making them more complex. At a very basic level, agriculture means that not every member of a community needs to work in food production. It creates a surplus of human time, enabling some to take on other tasks, from fabricating useful objects to caring for the young or the sick, to acting as priests, to fulfilling administrative functions.

Because it produces material useful for crafts—such as flax, cotton, and wool, as well as oil—agriculture also supported the development not only of craft practices but of the complex set of social practices that depend on crafts, such as patterns of display based on fashion. Most areas of the world developed some form of fiber crop. In the Americas, certain varieties of gourd were grown to produce storage containers rather than for food. Interestingly, the effects of agriculture on population growth and technological change seem to roughly mirror one another, and in a related point, it is likely that population density has effectively increased the rate at which new forms of social organization and technology are developed. Naturally enough, agricultural living and its social formations yielded a proliferation of ways of preparing food, even as migratory agriculturalists dispersed crop plants over more and more of the globe.

Has agriculture had costs deeper and more long-term than the worse personal health of the first generations of agriculturalists? The political scientist James Scott has argued that it has, because growing grain contributed to the formation of states, which collected grain in the form of taxes, and redistributed it to feed their subjects. For Scott, life in those states has advantages but also marked disadvantages.[9] Agrarian life, Scott suggests, eventually facilitated the rise of the political categories of "state" and "subject" in contrast to the egalitarianism of hunter-gather life. Not only that, the redistribution of grain allowed resources to become concentrated in the hands of the few, producing an early form of social inequality. While agriculture preceded the state, early states mobilized the tools of agriculture so that they became technologies not only of sustenance but also of control. The long lag between the rise of agriculture and the appearance of states in the Near East, Scott further argues, suggests that agriculture-based states were simply not the only way of doing business; the so-called "barbarians" lived happily enough in their own way, not eager to settle and adopt the farming lifestyle.

In arguing this way, Scott pushes against one of the dominant popular narratives of world history, that of civilizational progress, where the movement from hunting and gathering to agriculture and from nomadism to settled life, and then the emergence of the state as the dominant political form best suited to manage the needs and resources of a complex society, is a story of improvement. From Scott's perspective, this is the story of the domestication not only of plants and animals but also of human beings, and it had costs, including costs to human freedom. Beyond the walls of cities, nomadic hunter-gatherers persisted, their bands containing the seeds of political forms as yet unrealized, styles of associational life bound up with different ways of getting and sharing food and drink. Eventually staple grains supported not just independent states but empires, as our next chapter shows. Grains, which could be grown, stored, transported, and cooked in predictable ways (even more so than other popular staple crops like lentils), supported armies and bureaucracies that stretched across Eurasia.

One of the useful implications of Scott's argument is that it can shake us free of the assumption that agriculture, and the social structures that took advantage of it, represented simple progress. We do not have to see "Gatherer" and "Farmer" as stages of human development. But the crucial underlying question is this: in human history, have certain ways of growing, processing, cooking, and eating food correlated with certain styles of political life? This question should not lead us to assume that there is "anarchist" food and "totalitarian" food—this is too clumsy and simplistic a way to draw out the point. But some forms of infrastructure, like farming, do seem to encourage a particular style of cooperative work and social life, requiring as they do the labor of many hands. The material affordances of grain, that is, the fact that we can store it, transport it easily, and exchange it for other necessities or prestige goods, eventually aided the rise of the state. Whatever the relative merits of states versus nomadic or "barbarian" communities—and this is a matter of normative moral and political debate—one thing is certain: the states left more enduring records of how they lived.

From the perspective of our species' long history, the transition to sedentary agriculture was rapid, despite its stop-and-start character. The chapters to come will cover shorter and shorter spans of time as this book moves on towards the modern period and the present, but the agricultural transition in our deep past continues to be relevant to the history of modern foodways. Consider an early-twenty-first-century plate of food, the product of relatively recent culinary globalization and experimentation: a taco, a corn tortilla on which a chef has piled beef cooked according to a chili-rich Korean recipe, topped with melted American cheddar. The first thing we notice about this dish is that it mixes multiple cuisines. But if we look more closely, we see that these cuisines are based on ingredients, such as corn, or beef, or milk, that traveled the world well before Europeans began their voyages of exploration and conquest. Our culinary creativity works within raw material constraints and opportunities established long ago.

Akashiyaki at Nishi-Akashi

OCTOPUS BALLS, COMMONLY known as *takoyaki* and actually a kind of griddled dumpling, are omnipresent in Japan, especially at street and shrine festivals. People eat them right in front of the stalls where they're made in cast-iron pans over coals or gas grills, enticing customers with their savory aroma. They are made from chopped *tako,* or octopus, which is battered and then shaped by the dimpled round molds in which it cooks. As the *takoyaki* cook, the maker spins them with a pick, loosening them in the mold even while they brown. They are topped with thick brown Worcestershire-type sauce and sprinkles of *aonori* (dried green seaweed flakes) and *katsuobushi,* translucent curls of shaved dried bonito, which dance in the heat emanating from the balls. There are thin red strips of pickled ginger served on the side, and the balls may get stripes of mayonnaise. These flavors—tangy, sour, sweet, fatty from the mayonnaise, plus the aroma of beached seaweed—are reminiscent of another informal and popular food, *okonomiyaki,* a vegetable-seafood-egg-batter pancake served with very similar toppings.

The opportunity to eat a *takoyaki* variant, *akashiyaki,* presented itself on a stopover along the coast near Kobe, and we sought what was reported to be the best version in the town of Nishi-Akashi. An older lady directed us to a shop, very tiny, maybe five seats around a horseshoe-shaped counter. Always ask an "older lady" in Japan: not only do they know things, they are delighted to be asked, and for you to listen, because their younger kin rarely do. We squeezed in past the magazine rack and coat hooks and found stools. The smell of roasting and baking, smoky and slightly fishy, made it hard to wait for the cook to take our orders. There were only two orders possible: "some" and "more."

Akashiyaki are softer, eggier, more delicate, and less bouncy than *takoyaki*, but they have the same morsel of octopus inside. They are served with a light dashi-based soup for dipping. The soup is sprinkled with chopped scallion and possibly *furikake*, sesame seed, nori, and maybe some dried shrimp or bonito. There are options.

Chefs, historians, and eaters dispute the provenance of Japan's octopus balls, just as all iconic foods get disputed. Was the *akashiyaki* first an Osaka "*nikuyaki*" (grilled meat item) prepared in 1933, which then traveled to the city of Akashi on the coast and became octopus? Or did the dish travel in the opposite direction, going from Akashi to Osaka, where one Endo Tomekichi turned it into *takoyaki* in 1935? Is it possible that the dish we ate in early 2020 in the little coastal town of Nishi-Akashi was, in fact, the ancestor of all the *takoyaki* in all the temple fair stalls and mom and pop shops all over Japan? Behind the uncertainty and the disputes stands an obvious desire to tell a story about a food's origins, to speculate about what the real version might be. There is also the perennial interest in variety, in locality: there is no singular *takoyaki*, just as there is no singular "Japanese cuisine." The real desire may in fact lie in these powerful disputes themselves: a good fight reinforces identity and appetite. It means someone is paying attention.

Local foods are an important element in culinary tourism, which is a significant industry in Japan. But even without travel, the idea that a food has a native locality is often a selling point. Specialty shops serving *akashiyaki* in Tokyo make a virtue of distance by evoking the dish's hometown, just as a shop selling Montreal-style bagels in California might do. Even if you can't be there, you can taste "there."

Eating *akashiyaki* in the tiny, cluttered, rough-and-tumble shop in the village, we felt an instant desire to return before we had even left. Call this "pre-nostalgia," a feeling that set in before we had even finished what was in front of us. We had been "chow-hounds," tracking our food down deliberately until we were experiencing its meltingly soft pillowy texture, the steam coming out from the hole we'd bitten open, the viscous sauce dripping from the ball and then from our chins. Returning to Tokyo, we hunted down an *akashiyaki* pan in the street of kitchen dreams, Kappabashi, where many restaurant supply shops are located. This pan, we vowed, would help us return to that moment. It sits, still in its colorful, encouraging, box, taped shut, awaiting the octopus. Which, unaware of our dreams, floats in its oceanic garden, unmolested.

CHAPTER 2

Staple Empires of the
Ancient World

"EMPIRE" IS A WORD LOADED DOWN WITH GRAIN. The last chapter described the possible origins of agriculture, and the transition from nomadism to sedentary agrarianism. This chapter examines the complex relationship between staple foods, territory, and identity in three ancient empires: Persia, Rome, and China. Each depended on grains that gave a particular structure and coherence to their food, even as territorial expansion and trade made their foodways diverse and complex. An empire (our English word comes from the Latin "imperium") is by definition rule over diverse peoples, either in a large geographically contiguous area or in several widely dispersed ones. "Empire" can imply political and economic control without cultural hegemony, as in the Roman Empire, which allowed conquered peoples to continue their ways of life largely unchanged, but it can also mean the social and cultural hegemony of one group over a collection of very different groups, as in the case of Han Dynasty China. All imperial governments have needed grain to feed their armies and their courts, and to ensure that their subjects do not starve; after all, an empire needs populations from which to extract tribute. This has meant a complex system of administrators to oversee a physical infrastructure of grain-sheds, transport, and milling operations, to process grain and get it ready for cooking.

This chapter deals with Persia from approximately 550 BCE to 330 BCE; the Roman Empire from 175 BCE to about 300 CE; and the Han Dynasty in China between 200 BCE and 200 CE. In Rome, wheat was the sustaining staple; in China it was rice. Wheat enjoyed staple dominance in the Persian Empire, but rice would later become very important both within Persia itself and beyond. We bring the three empires together to observe one rough, but important, point of comparison: staple foods fed large populations with relative efficiency, even as culinary diversity played out in different ways between the center and periphery of each empire, between the seats of imperial power and the far-flung provinces whose residents grew, cooked, and ate food in their own customary ways. Sedentary agriculture made empire possible in a way that nomadic herding, let alone hunting and gathering, did not, and the empires of the ancient world helped to make many peoples into settled agriculturalists, often against their will.

Of course, no staple is enough on its own. Without complementary nutrients, overreliance on a staple can actually cause illness; diseases of nutritional deficiency such as scurvy (caused by a lack of vitamin C) have nothing to do with calories. Most primary staples are cereals (rice, wheat, corn, rye, and barley) and secondary staples include root vegetables such as potatoes, yams, and taro. Pulses, including beans and lentils, as well as chickpeas, cowpeas, pigeon peas, and vetches (a legume often grown as livestock fodder, but edible for humans), are other common secondary staples. Primary and secondary staples work together in what is called the "complementary protein effect." In this phenomenon, the essential amino acid (protein) intake from beans or legumes is greater when combined with a grain such as corn or rice. Nepal's basic diet, *dahl* and *baht*, or lentils and rice, is one excellent contemporary example. Hoppin' John, the dish of beans and rice eaten on New Year's Day in New Orleans, is another, and while modern rice, beans, and lentils have been bred enough that they are unlike their premodern antecedents, the complementary protein effect still applies. As of the early twenty-first century, rice is the most commonly consumed staple in the world, feeding more than half the world's population, with corn and wheat following close behind.

As empires expanded, they moved their staple crops around the world. After all, staples weren't just the basis for sustenance, but the stuff of wealth, too, because they could be stored after the harvest. In some cases this gave a government considerable control over its subjects' rations, and thus over their nutrition and freedom.[1] And grain could be used as a basis for taxation or tribute long before coins came into universal circulation. The harvest was a basis for economic and political power.

And so staple foods often moved from the core of empire to the shifting periphery, always being redefined through trade, conquest, and political deals with local authorities. Although an empire's favorite staple grains might hold constant, ways of cooking those grains would vary across the empire, and so would seasonings, as well as preferred sauces and accompaniments. Peripheral regions affected the centers of population and power, as merchants, soldiers, and messengers traveled. Middle European peasants living under Roman rule might toast their buckwheat groats and eat them dry and salted, while their neighbors only a few miles away might sweeten their groats with sorghum syrup or honey and make them into a pudding. The eastern Mediterranean transformed Roman tastes, even as other conquered lands were made to serve as breadbaskets; this was Egypt's fate under the Persians, and later under the Romans, too.

For some imperial elites, consumption served as a symbolic proxy for political control. The Romans usually saw the foodways of conquered lands as barbaric, but "barbaric" dishes were displayed on banquet tables to demonstrate the reach of the rulers' power. Of course, elites always had a wider range of dietary choices than peasants and could feast together in order to display their affluence and influence. In Persia, elites could command laborers to glean scarce herbs from distant streambeds; in China, as in Rome, enslaved people ran snow down from mountaintops for the iced treats enjoyed by royalty. In Rome, the perks of the ruling classes included peacocks, swans, and spices brought back from the farthest corners of the empire. Sumptuary laws made luxurious foods more exclusive, keeping members of the lower classes from enjoying them even when they could afford them. The same laws kept elite families from excesses of conspicuous consumption, in order to maintain an appearance of relative parity between families. Some aspects of eating that we can recognize today, such as a correlation between cuisine and class, sauces and social stratification, developed very early in the history of food.

Fernand Braudel once noted, "Man is for long centuries the prisoner of climates, of vegetations, of animal populations, of types of crop, of slowly constructed equilibria."[2] In other words, cultural forms began within seemingly permanent geographic constraints. In the ancient world, empire, with its roads, armies, cities, and mercantile activity, was one of the engines by which people linked diverse geographies, vegetations, animal populations, and crops, and learned how each other ate. As empire gradually defied geographic limits, the slowly constructed equilibria of our cultures of field, kitchen, and table began to change dramatically.

Persia

The Greek historian Herodotus, who wrote about a hundred years after the death of Cyrus, the "king of kings" who unified the Persian Empire, observed that "no nation so readily adopts foreign customs as the Persians." Like other historians, Herodotus learned from Greek travelers and from soldiers returning after battles, as well as from his own journeys. While Herodotus's description of Persia has been contested by other historians and in some cases by archaeological evidence, it is nevertheless indispensable, in part because the Persian Empire did not have historians of its own. History writing was not part of the intellectual culture of the Achaemenids (another term for the rulers of the Persian empire, derived from the name of Cyrus's ancestor Achaemenes), and accounts left by the Persian kings themselves often seem suspect and self-aggrandizing.

Herodotus admired the Persian diet and saw it as a "model of civilization"[3] that balanced pleasure and restraint, surprising given the common Greek stereotype of the Persians as voracious in both banqueting and conquest. The Persian imperial diet has a special place in culinary history as the first "refined" high cuisine in Eurasia, just as the Persian Empire was the first of its magnitude and grandeur in its part of the globe, and Herodotus's strong response was not unique; the very idea of a refined, as opposed to a common cuisine, was a novelty, and readily associated with the power of the Persian Empire itself. Herodotus noted that from a Persian perspective, the Greeks were immoderate eaters, going beyond what hunger demanded, even as Persians were shocked to see Greeks consume no sweet dishes. For Persians, the absence of sweet dishes was nearly unthinkable.

The Persians must have represented a culinary puzzle to the Greeks, since they had alien customs, yet did not fit comfortably into the category of "barbarian." Herodotus's account of the difference between Persian and Greek eating habits, the former showing restraint and the latter gorging themselves, may simply have come from a misunderstanding that arose when Greeks, unused to elaborate meals, ate at the tables of wealthy Persian hosts. The Greeks would have eaten as much as they could of the first dishes served, unaccustomed to meals being doled out in courses. Their Persian hosts would, by contrast, have eaten sparingly of each dish, anticipating the next to come.

Before they established an empire, the Persians were tributaries of Babylonia and Assyria. They lived to the east of Mesopotamia, on the other side of the Zagros mountain range. Descended from nomadic tribes, their early cuisine seems to have included a gruel made from barley, as well as lentils and vetch. They ate dairy in the form of yogurt or cheese made from ewes' milk, and meat in the form of roast or boiled beef, lamb, or goat. The Persians also enjoyed nuts, including almonds, dried fruit such as dates and apricots, and various herbs. Cyrus established himself as the central political authority in the Persian Empire in approximately 550 BCE, conquering Mesopotamia. As he expanded his empire he joined the Persians with the sedentary agriculturalists they conquered, from the shores of the Aegean Sea in the West, all the way to the Indus River in the East. Wheat quickly became their principal crop. The empire eventually encompassed Mesopotamia, Syria, Egypt, and parts of Turkey, India, and Afghanistan, and it flourished during the so-called "Age of Pericles," often taken to be a high-water mark of Athenian Greek civilization. The Empire was eventually ruled from four capital cities—Pasargadae, Babylon, Susa, and Ecbatana—with another palace-city, Persepolis, at their center. The Persian Empire encompassed the Fertile Crescent. Watered by the Tigris and the Euphrates, this was one of the first places where wheat and barley were domesticated, and an early site of animal domestication as well. The empire's geographic reach provided excellent conditions, both cultural and ecological, for a diverse, rich, and balanced cuisine.

Herodotus chronicled the succession of the three first "great kings" of the Persian Empire in the following way: Cyrus the Father was the patriarch who gave unity and life to the empire, followed by his son, Cambyses the Tyrant, a harsher ruler, and soon Darius the Shopkeeper, so-called because his administrative reforms shaped the economic structure of the empire for generations. Under Darius's rule and after, the Persians managed their territories (some twenty to thirty states depending on the phase of the Empire) through satraps, representatives of Persian imperial interests who held authority over local governors. As Pierre Briant has pointed out, the Persian strategic approach to conquered states emphasized continuity, not the displacement or general reorganization of local populations.[4] Rather than replace local systems of administration wholesale, the Persians tended to keep governments in place when officials were willing to give them allegiance, homage, and taxes. Only in particularly rebellious regions, or where a powerful local ruler threatened trouble, did they take more dramatic action.

Nor did they have much interest in cultural or religious hegemony, though Darius established an official religion with the god Ahura-Mazda (a principal deity of the Zoroastrian pantheon) at its head. Given the multilingual world the empire spanned, official documents were written in a combination of languages, including Elamite, Persian, and Akkadian, rather than the Persian emperors imposing their own language on all. Tributes to the emperors flowed in, often in the form of foodstuffs: bread, wine, salt, and other items that traveled well. The Apadana Reliefs in Persepolis, the imperial city which Darius began building and which his son Xerxes eventually finished, show processions of people bringing gifts of food and wine in various vessels. The Greek historian and philosopher Plutarch remarked that Xerxes would not eat a fig if he had not first conquered the region that produced it.

As the Persians built their empire, they absorbed farming techniques from the peoples they overwhelmed, beginning with the more technologically sophisticated Elamites, wheat-growers whose kingdom was south and east of Assyria and Babylonia. Wheat, mostly eaten in the form of bread, would quickly displace barley in the Persian diet. For Herodotus, who measured the world by his own parameters of civilization, agriculturalists were on a higher plane than herders, and thus from his standpoint, the Persians had accomplished a great civilizing leap forward by moving from ancestral no-madism to farming. While enslaved people performed some of the agricultural labor, free laborers did the majority of it. As Herodotus reported, rich Persians ate especially well, roasting ox, camel, and ass and washing it all down with copious amounts of wine drunk from *rhyta,* drinking horns made in the shape of an animal head and used by peoples across the eastern Mediterranean. (Herodotus was part of a long and contested tradition of imagining Persians as drunks.) They also gorged themselves on desserts. The Persian sweet tooth was famous, but dessert wasn't just tasty; like the entire meal, it could be a means of social display. Much as a host could demon-strate his wealth by serving large amounts of meat, he might serve a dessert featuring abundant sugar, honey, or spices.

In Egypt the Nile watered substantial farmland, good for growing wheat, and the country became the breadbasket of the Persian Em-pire; later it would serve Rome in the same way. The old Persian words for bread seem to indicate that they baked it two ways: as an "uncovered" or "naked" bread, baked in some type of oven, and one "covered" in ashes. Many archeologists have surmised that ash bak-ing, feasible without an oven, was one of the earliest methods of making bread. As János Harmatta noted in an important article on bread in Persian lands, improving the way we bake bread usually in-volves taking one of two routes: improving the techniques by which we bake dough (an oven, or a better oven; a pan or dish to put the dough in), or improving the dough itself by introducing a leavening agent that sours the bread slightly while making it rise and helping to preserve its freshness.[5] In many cases, early bakers pursued both routes at once. Evidence suggests that the Persians learned the use of the oven, possibly through an intermediate stage involving the use of a clay baking vessel, and then it gradually spread throughout their empire. It appears that they followed the path of improving baking technique—but not necessarily that of improving the dough itself with leaven, though some of the lands encompassed by the Persian Empire, such as Mesopotamia, had long known the techniques of leavening. There is evidence that Persian material culture, including cooking techniques, traveled beyond the Empire itself, into parts of Eastern Europe and South Asia. One of the many Persian words for bread, *naan*, has traveled far and wide, and is very similar to the common modern words for bread in Bengali, Hindi, Punjabi, and Pashto.

In the Greek soldier-philosopher Xenophon's description of Cyrus's formal dinners, we learn about a canny ruler who used everything from seating arrangements to the distribution of dishes to communicate to his court and officers just whom he favored most.[6] Gifts could be coercive. Every little gift reminded the receiver of his obligations to his ruler. Yet Persian formal dining patterns (royal or otherwise) weren't simply about power, wealth, or the social hierarchy. Meals were also full of symbolic religious resonance in a world that could scarcely be called secular. Persian cosmology understood the mortal world to be "fallen" but redeemable if humans performed the correct actions, restoring righteousness. The line between raw and cooked food was the line between a spiritually fallen order and an improved one. To cook food (*pac* in Persian) and thereby make it edible was, symbolically, to redeem fallen matter; such was fire's power. Milk was thought to "cook" in the mother's body. And foods had symbolic meanings of their own. Eggs recalled the cosmic sphere. Because roosters crowed at dawn, chicken was associated with light. The Persians tended to look down on raw foods, and also— whatever the Greeks said—on eating to excess. And yet, serving large amounts of food meant power. One Greek, Polyaenus, described a lavish dinner for Cyrus that included a variety of types of wheat and barley flours, animal protein including cows, horses, rams, and various birds, as well as dairy foods and dried fruits and nuts made into cakes. The imperial kitchens were evidently large and staffed by many cooks. But many diners shared those lavish dinners, and lavishness served as much of a social or political function as it did a gustatory one.

According to a set of administrative documents found in Persepolis, known as the *Persepolis Fortification Tablets,* the Persian Empire employed a rationing system in which the royal granaries and storehouses would distribute food and other goods to the population in proportion to their rank, from members of the court all the way down to craftspeople, farmers, and other manual laborers. And just as the lavish displays at banquets symbolically represented the generosity of the King of Kings, so did the rationing system. In such a fully organized economy, in which food was often controlled directly by the state, the Empire's power was an intimate part of daily life. Throughout the Empire, and beginning with Darius's reign, the Persians worked to improve their supply of plant foods, creating gardens that were both practical and symbolic, representing visions of Paradise. Fed by complex irrigation systems, the gardens often featured Mesopotamian and Persian plants, including grapes, which the Persians planted wherever they went. Persians' techniques for preparing rice and their growing sense of its importance as an additional staple along with wheat came from India; only in the late medieval period would rice outstrip wheat's popularity in Persia, after which it would become indispensable. Also from India came a few sweets, such the deep-fried, syrup-soaked *jalebi,* which became *zulbia* in Persia, the ancestor of what Syrians, Armenians, and others call *zalabiam.* The modern European distinction between sweet and savory foods, and the practice of relegating sweets to the end of the meal and only in certain dishes, was not salient in Persia, and Persian cooks often sweetened savory dishes with sugar, honey, or fruit.

The Persians also created *halva,* a food now associated with the entire Middle East, usually made of sesame seed paste, honey, and pistachios. Persian *halva* might also contain dates, walnuts, rosewater, and saffron. Persian *sharbats* (from which modern sherbet and

sorbet is derived) were purees of fresh fruit or flower petals sometimes watered or iced to be served as a drink, or served with cream or
yoghurt as a spoon sweet. *Sekanjebin,* a thick syrup made from vinegar, mint, and sugar or honey and mixed with water, seems to have
been a court favorite among the emperors, a cooling afternoon drink
to sip in the decorative "paradise" gardens. This drink finds an echo
in Arab-influenced dishes that later became popular in the Roman
Empire and, much later, a modern echo in sweet-sour Sicilian, Sar-
dinian, and southern Spanish cuisines. Later Arab scholars often referred to Persian antecedents for their own dishes, such as *zirbaj,* a
dish of meat and vegetables prepared with vinegar and sugar, as well
as mastic, coriander, cinnamon, ginger, pepper, and mint.[7] They also
drew on Persian ideas about how food functioned as medicine, and
these ideas became sources for their own "physik," which placed
food and medicine on a continuum, organized on principles of "hot"
and "cold" substances, having nothing to do with temperature but
rather with their effect on the body. A sweet-and-savory dish like *fes-
enjan,* for example, a chicken dish containing walnuts ("hot") and
pomegranate seeds ("cold"), would be balanced and would help to
maintain the body's balance. Some of these dishes, and principles,
would eventually appear in Roman foodways as well.

The Persian Empire was carved up into kingdoms after it fell to
Alexander the Great—who, some historians believe, inherited
the empire to the point where he should be called "Last of the
Achaemenids"[8]—but its culinary effects were felt for generations.
One example is the sauce often called *karyke,* based on honey and
must or vinegar, thickened with breadcrumbs and flavored with
herbs, which was enjoyed throughout the ancient Mediterranean
world. But even as Greeks ate *karyke,* many inveighed against what
they perceived as the excesses of Persian eating, making Persian
high cuisine a kind of foil for their own preferred ascetic dining practices. Persian appetites at banquets were, in this Greek view, like Per-

sian appetites for conquest, whereas the Greeks themselves were moderate eaters (note the reversal of Herodotus's view, here) and territorially self-contained.[9] Not all the Greeks agreed, and some of the more prosperous emulated Persian high cuisine, while some—the Spartans, famously—rejected the idea of luxury at the table, as did Plato, in the *Republic* (circa 370 BCE), which contains a criticism of rich dining whose unnamed target must be the Persians.[10] Ironically, after the Persian Empire fell to Alexander the Great, wealthier Greek states such as Athens began to create elevated cuisines of their own, often building from Persian foundations when it came to sauces. The Greek response to the Persians began a tradition in Western thinking about food: the love of eating well, and the belief that one should not eat too well, often travel together.

Rome

The year was 50 BCE. Gaul had been entirely conquered by the Romans, including a small Gaulish village in what is now southern France, whose inhabitants ate a simpler diet than their conquerors, though this would slowly change.[11] As the Greek Posidonius observed of the Gauls, "Their food consists of a small number of loaves of bread together with a large amount of meat, either boiled or roasted on charcoal or on spits. . . . Those who live beside the rivers or near the Mediterranean or Atlantic eat fish in addition, baked fish, that is, with the addition of salt, vinegar, and cumin."[12] He noted that they did not consume much olive oil, unlike the Greeks or Romans. They boiled much of their grain into porridge, as the early Romans and the Greeks had done, but they also used bell-shaped ovens to bake simple flatbreads, not so different from those baked in Roman Italy. Gaulish households baked their own loaves as a rule, but eventually independent bakeries began to appear, following a Roman pattern: most Romans did not bake their own bread. By 25 CE, the Roman state regulated commercial mills and bakeries, which tended to be integrated with one another, and there were some three hundred of them in the city of Rome itself, each of which baked enough bread each day to feed three thousand people. Grain or bread became a central part of the work of the *annona,* the administrative system that distributed food to Roman citizens, something done not simply to ensure that everyone had food, but because an inadequate food supply would have dire political consequences.[13] Many professional bakers were freed slaves, and their social status was low, though they made the staff of life. Rome was repeatedly rocked by shortages and famines throughout its history, and grain was crucial.

Roman rule reached all the way West to the British Isles and to Spain. To the East, the Roman Empire encompassed Armenia and Mesopotamia. Towards the South, Roman rule stretched to the Sahara, and towards the North, it reached Scotland, as well as the Rhine-Danube Germanic frontier. The Romans tolerated cultural diversity throughout their empire—naturally, as one traveled north in Roman Europe, one encountered more milk, butter, and meat, not to mention beer. But Roman culture became a pervasive influence the empire in several ways: linguistically; through customs such as the institution of the civic sacrifice; and through cooking. In addition to their bread-making, and their famous road-building, the Romans brought olives and grapes everywhere, and planted them wherever they would grow. In North Africa, Egypt served as a breadbasket, especially after the Romans exhausted most of Italy's soil, and spread their ways of baking staple grains all over Europe.

But the Romans did not begin as bread-bakers. The small farmers who lived in what would become Roman Italy grew barley, which thrived in Italian soil, and cooked it into *puls,* much as the Greeks had done; barley grew well throughout much of Greece, too. This early Roman porridge may have resembled contemporary polenta, though polenta is typically made of corn, a grain that would not reach Europe until the Columbian Exchange, which began in the fifteenth century. Like the Greeks, who divided grains (their staple, or *stipos*) from "additions" (*opson*) like vegetables, fish, cheese, or olives, early Romans might have added something to their porridge. Cato the Elder, writing in about 160 BCE, described a dish of *puls* made with cheese, honey, and eggs. One theory of the origins of Roman bread-baking begins with *far*, or emmer wheat, which early Roman farmers might have used for their porridge, and which, when baked, might have become something like contemporary focaccia, a flat but spongy bread, good for dipping in sauce or oil. Neither emmer wheat nor barley are good for baking raised breads, since they lack the right kind of gluten-forming proteins. Eventually the Romans began to work with a new kind of wheat, *triticum aestivum*, whose gluten proteins did a better job of forming strands and trapping gases, allowing bread to rise.

At the height of the Roman Empire, many types of bread, made from many kinds of dough, graced Roman tables. There were types for specific applications, such as long-lasting bread for soldiers on the march or sailors on a voyage. There were fancier breads, made for the rich out of laboriously refined white flour, or including honey, milk, or wine, or even candied fruit, cheese, or the very valuable pepper, the preeminent spice of the Roman kitchen and table, imported from India. In rural areas, poor people would bake bread out of whole grains, incorporating ground-up peas, beans, chestnuts, or acorns. The most common bread shape was a round loaf, fairly flat, slashed into four quadrants before baking to make the resulting bread easier to divide. Well-preserved examples of this bread have been found in the bakeries of Pompeii, among the ruins and volcanic ash. A great deal of bread was made using a *patina*, a flat pan that could be placed on a fire or in an oven.

By contrast with their rural Gaulish counterparts, in more Romanized parts of Gaul Roman colonists and Romanizing Gauls ate in ways that reflected the common patterns of Roman culture, such as the use of cooking and eating to communicate differences of class, social influence, and power. More than quantity divided the food of rich Romans from that of the poor. In fact, the rich essentially ate an entirely different cuisine, and throughout the Empire, locals who Romanized began to display typically Roman patterns of social differentiation through food. The rural Gaulish villages never displayed the classical Roman split between "high" and "low" ways of eating. They did adopt Roman sauces, such as *garum,* made from fermented fish, and they began using olive oil as well. Testifying to these changes are the shards of *amphorae,* which Romans used to transport these valuable liquids across their empire, found by archaeologists throughout the region. Again, our picture of how Romans transformed food practices throughout the Empire suggests slow change through contact, as the Romans brought new ways of growing, cooking, and eating, and provided for their colonies in a distinctly Roman fashion.

If wheat was the most important Roman staple, olive oil and wine were close behind, and ubiquitous in the diets of rich and poor alike—as were fermented fish products, most famously *garum* but also including *liquamen, muria,* and *alec.* In a world without refrigeration, products like oil, wine, and *garum* were especially precious. In a world largely reliant on bread, olives and fish provided necessary nutrients. There is a general consensus that *garum* closely resembled modern Southeast Asian fish sauces such as Thai *nam pla* and Vietnamese *nuoc-mam.* The technical term for the process by which these sauces are made is controlled enzymatic autolysis. Fish of many types can be layered in a container with salt, and enzymes in the fish start a process of self-digestion so that they break down, becoming mostly liquid, without the mass spoiling.[14] Constant high heat and a great deal of salt is necessary to keep the mass in biochemical balance, and so *garum* and other fish sauces were usually made at factories along the coasts of hot countries around the Mediterranean; Pompeii produced *garum,* as did sites in what is now Morocco, Libya, and Spain. A constant traffic of ships carried amphorae across the Mediterranean. Notably, the *garum* and olive oil factories weren't carrying "local" delicacies to Roman consumers, so much as Roman delicacies that happened to be produced in the diverse territories Rome controlled. By enriching Roman trading stations and ports along the Mediterranean, *garum* (ubiquitous on the Roman table, but sometimes quite expensive) arguably encouraged the spread of Roman imperial power—a case of food providing economic incentives for colonization.

The Romans consumed *garum* as a table sauce, adding it to their foods, and they also added it to their other sauces (for example, *garum* mixed with wine made *oenogarum*), which were often more complex than the ones the Persians had made. Possible ingredients included the ubiquitous pepper, as well as dry spices like anise, celery seed, coriander, and cumin, but also nuts and dried fruits, as well as fresh herbs, pre-made sauces like *garum,* olive oil or honey, eggs or wheat flour.[15] If there was a dominant flavor profile in Roman cooking, it might be described as sweet-and-sour, and in general what we know of Roman cooking suggests a cuisine of contrasts, particularly at the tables of the wealthy. They had no sugar and relied on honey and fruit for sweetness.

In addition to bringing baking techniques, grapes, and olives wherever they went, the Romans brought almond, apricots, cherry, peach, and quince and medlar trees to northern Europe. They had broad beans and lentils (when the Romans acquired the Egyptian obelisk that now stands in St. Peter's Square in the Vatican, it came by ship, along with 120,000 units of lentils), beets, cabbages, collard greens, kale, radishes, and turnips. They grew endives, escarole, and shallots. The Romans' favorite meat came from the pig, of which Pliny the Elder wrote, "there is no animal that provides more variety to the tongue: its meat provides nearly fifty flavors, while other animals only one."[16] But they also ate cattle, sheep, and goats, as well as smaller mammals, such as dormice (raised in special vessels built for the purpose) and rabbits. Of sea animals they ate many kinds, from fish to squid to shellfish.[17]

We are fortunate that so many Romans wrote extensively about their food, but one source has become inescapable: this is *De Re Coquenaria*, generally attributed to Marcus Gavius Apicius, though it is unclear if Apicius was a historical person or a mythical figure to whom many culinary feats and indulgences could be attributed.[18] Apicius was reportedly a very wealthy man, so dedicated to living and eating well that he committed suicide rather than moderate his indulgences after his fortunes declined, or so the story goes. But the actual recipes in *De Re Coquenaria* are written in simple Latin, such as a cook with minimal education might have used. Not only that, they are written in multiple styles of simple Latin, suggesting multiple authors, and further suggesting that "Apicius" was simply a name given to a collection of recipes composed by different hands. The rhetorician Cicero listed "cook" among those "trades and occupations" which he found "disgraceful," because they are "the servants of physical pleasure: fishmongers, butchers, cooks, poultrymen, fishermen. . . ."[19]

In elite Roman households, enslaved people from all over the Roman empire did much of the cooking, but preparing dinners (the only serious meal of the Roman day, called the *convivium*, which also means "living together") in high Roman style demanded more than knowledge of ingredients, tools, and recipes. It also required sensitivity to the complexities of Roman taste, one signature element of which was ambivalence about luxury and simplicity. Throughout much of Roman food history, frugality and luxury stood in opposition, as did the familiar and the exotic, the domestic and the foreign. These oppositions aligned with one another, as Romans simultaneously celebrated foods associated with the early days of Rome, and foods associated with Roman power and the expansiveness of their empire.

Romans, especially the elite Romans whose gastronomic lives we know best (as usual, they left more written records than the poor) ate in ways shaped by opposing tendencies towards simplicity and complexity, and they tended to moralize about their choices, as indeed they tended to moralize about many aspects of culture and social life. Some Roman writers attributed to their ancestors a certain salutary simplicity of diet, and saw contemporary dining habits as corrupted by foreign influence—even when foreign influence was the direct result of Roman imperial expansion, as Romans brought the dishes of conquered peoples home. The historian Suetonius praised the simplicity of Emperor Augustus's diet in this spirit: "he preferred the food of the common people, especially the coarser sort of bread, whitebait, fresh hand-pressed cheese. . . ."[20] Wealthy Romans displayed their social status at mealtimes by having elaborate dishes prepared, often incorporating exotic ingredients, but at the same time—and sometimes at the very same meal—they displayed their admiration for the old imagined frugality. In the writings of Pliny the Elder we learn of a large dinner at which the wealthy host served himself and a few friends luxurious dishes, while his other guests ate simply. Apparently this was an effort, however confused it may seem, to have the best of both worlds at one meal. Juvenal took what we might now call a "farm to table" approach, having fresh meat and vegetables brought to Rome from his farm in Tivoli. This gave him the moral credibility of a yeoman farmer and the sophistication of a host offering excellent food. It was as if he responded to an imperative: do not forget Rome's agricultural past, or the land itself. Notably, while exotic foods from the outskirts of the empire might appear on the banquet tables of the wealthy, these dishes did not much change the central parts of the imperial Roman diet. They appeared on elite dinner tables for the same reasons an emperor might have warriors in his retinue from all parts of his empire, to demonstrate what he had conquered and who owed him fealty. There is a historical echo here: some say Rome itself began with salt, as merchant caravans halted on the banks of the Tiber at the stopover village that later became the Eternal City. Rome began with imported flavors.

You could call the central tension in Roman foodways "diacritical taste," the practice of shuffling between the foods of multiple social classes as we eat. Diacritical taste is a way of communicating to one another about our differences, including our relative status in a social hierarchy. This is what Romanizing Gauls were moving towards, as they acquired not just Roman crops and Roman bread ovens, but also Roman ideas about what food meant. Similar transformations were taking place throughout the expanse of the empire, changing what food meant across Europe, the entire Mediterranean world, and beyond. Persian high cuisine may have been the world's first, chronologically speaking, but under Roman rule the idea of high cuisine, as opposed to low, became a food language that everyone, wealthy and poor, could recognize. Roman social classes were relatively fixed, so that one's birth determined one's place in the social order, but it was hard to control how people ate; wealthy commoners, such as parvenu merchants, could emulate their social "betters" by eating as they did. Sumptuary laws were common, a sign of official anxiety about class boundaries. These laws theoretically limited commoners' ability to dine as elites did, but they were often observed in the breach.

Roman banquets became the stuff of legend. A typical one included many courses, for prestige was measured in the length of an event as much as in the sumptuousness or rarity of its dishes. Banquets had a kind of architecture, including several levels or stages: they began with the *gustatio* course, consisting of small simple appetizers, which might include shellfish, salads, marinated vegetables, and especially salted foods such as bacon and salted fish, to whet the appetite and also to encourage drinking. Olives and bread were almost inevitable starters. *Gustatio* dishes, and the drinking that accompanied them, were meant to prepare the body for what came next.

The main course was the *mensa prima* (first table), consisting of several complicated dishes intended to impress, and often meant to evoke the broad reach of the Roman Empire. Some of these were stir-fried dishes, similar to but probably not derived from those of China; others might include such expensive indulgences as parrot brains or a giraffe roast, reflecting the host's wealth. (Romans ate parrots when they could, as a foreign delicacy. Native to most continents but not to Europe, the parrot seems to have first come to Europe with Alexander the Great's forces, who found them in India in 327 BCE.)[21] One climactic presentation would invariably be intended to receive applause. Originality and the element of surprise were important here; the whole banquet was a theatrical experience. Slaves might sing as they carried dishes around. Food engineers and artists might construct a stream through which cooked fishes appeared to swim. A modest serving vessel might open to reveal a surprisingly complex or luxurious dish. One ate with one's eyes and ears as well as with one's mouth, and the Roman banquet was more than nurturance, it was entertainment.

The next course, which also contained several dishes, was the *mensa secunda,* or "second table," usually sweet in flavor. Romans, like Persians, did not relegate sweet dishes to the end of the meal. The *mensa secunda* was meant to show the skill of pastry chefs and artists. The table would be covered with sweetmeats and fruits, nuts, dates, cakes, marzipan, honey buns, and pastries with crushed nuts and honey, resembling baklava. At the right times of year, a wealthy host might send slaves to the mountains to bring back ice for a version of ice cream, sorbet, or shaved ice with syrups and fruits. At one banquet described in the courtier Gaius Petronius's *Satyricon,* the host presented a statue of Priapus, god of the phallus, his sexual organs made of sweetmeats and bread for the guests to devour. Such meals were accompanied by a series of perfumes wafted through the air from braziers burning herbs, spices, and dried flowers. Some of these were meant to create a mood, some to help digestion, and connoisseurs would enjoy the game of untangling the skeins of scent in a mixed bouquet. Knowing what they were smelling, sipping, and eating gave elite Romans an edge over ordinary citizens; the art of the banquet was an art of developing taste and cultural capital.

Notably, banquets had nothing to do with the tradition of the orgy. Orgies centered around ecstatic ritual dances, rather than gustatory or sexual excess, and they focused on union with the gods, not with humans. Indeed, even at a lavish banquet, the Romans valued a certain reserve, which was a personal virtue, but also a political one: implicitly the restraint of empire, a subtle demonstration of power and wealth.

Han China

To write about ancient Chinese foodways means navigating a set of received modern ideas. China, writers and scholars often say, is the place where everyone cares about food, the place where hungry mouths, famine, and the constant specter of population growth have required a gastronomic total mobilization of plant and animal species. The Chinese delight in crab, but they eat tree bark too, as the Western-educated twentieth-century philologist, philosopher, and writer Lin Yutang put it.[22] As Lin Yutang also observed, in the Anglophone world most self-appointed serious intellectuals would never write on food, but in China they have written about food for millennia. There, scholars, poets, and thinkers have always been allowed, even encouraged, to take meals seriously. For example, in the third century CE, Shu Hsi wrote an entire rhapsody in praise of noodles and dumplings, each type of which had to be eaten in its proper season.[23] China, the story goes, boasts our world's longest-enduring civilization, and its food traditions are often thought to have primordial origins. Thus the archaeologist K.C. Chang suggested, "Few other cultures are as food oriented as the Chinese, and this orientation appears to be as ancient as Chinese culture itself."[24]

But we need to take such received ideas with a grain of salt. Food's prominence in Chinese culture is indeed real and ancient, but Chinese history is marked by cultural and political discontinuity, and by the diversity of this huge contiguous region, a diversity that stems partly from China's geography. Under the Han Dynasty, imperial China unified distinctly different food cultures without homogenizing them. If we wish to speak of "Chinese" food culture, we must deal with the play of unity and diversity, just as in the Persian and Roman cases. Nor is there anything eternal about familiar Chinese mainstays like tea, soy sauce, or tofu; all these elements took time to develop, although now many forms of Chinese cuisine are unimaginable without them.

Han Chinese cuisine contained contradictions. Just as in Rome, luxury, and the use of exotic, expensive, hard-won foods demonstrated power, but official philosophy and morality demanded a certain display of pastoral simplicity and frugality. The heights of luxury existed alongside gestures towards an idealized rustic life that elites, including poets and philosophers, might conjure by consuming simpler foods. Ostentation and elaboration were immoral, said the sages, who decried complication in foods and abhorred the use of ingredients obtained at a distance. But sometimes rusticity itself became a kind of theater, resulting in ostentatious performance.

The Han Dynasty succeeded the short-lived Qin (221–207 BCE), which had itself ultimately succeeded the Zhou after the tumult of the Warring States period. The name "China" derives from the Qin Dynasty, who gave their name to the region they ruled. The Han in turn gave their name to the ethnic Chinese, who became the Han people, in contrast to the other ethnic minorities of China, which include the Hui, Tibetans, Uyghur, and many others. During the Han Dynasty, which lasted over four hundred years, from about 206 BCE to 220 CE, a full half of humanity lived under either Han or Roman rule.[25] If a quarter of humanity, living around the Mediterranean, ate wheat or barley as their main staple, another quarter enjoyed millet or rice, though many Chinese ate wheat too, ground into flour and usually prepared as noodles or buns.[26] The Chinese have long divided *fan*, which means a staple starch like rice, noodles, or bread, from *t'sai*, the smaller quantity of cooked and seasoned vegetables or meat eaten with them. Food served without *fan* was not considered a meal, although it might be a snack, something that is still true in China today. At a banquet, *fan* would come at the end of a meal, and if guests then gorged themselves on rice, noodles, or bread, it would shame the host, who must not have provided enough *t'sai*.

The Roman and Chinese Empires both fell within Eurasia's temperate band and benefited from its flora and fauna. But whereas the Mediterranean facilitated travel, intermingling, and integration between political and cultural groups—often through conquest—China's river valleys and mountain ranges kept its regions apart. The climates of Northern and Southern China differ considerably, the north being cooler and dryer and the south hotter and wetter, and crops could not thrive across regions.[27] Part of the Chinese imperial project was to unify those regional communities whose names still bespeak culinary diversity: Cantonese, Sichuan, Hunan, and Shandong are just four of the cuisines most familiar to Westerners. Both Rome and Han China established themselves on the basis of antecedent states. Both were monarchies with considerable aristocracies that participated in the government, and both had robust bureaucracies both central and distributed, so that they could govern many regional administrative units. And there was contact between the two, with culinary consequences—the Chinese got grapes from the Romans, either directly or secondhand. This happened legendarily (but probably not factually) through the work of Emperor Wu (140–87 BCE)'s envoy Chang Ch'ien, the most famous traveler of the Han period.

China boasts impressive floral and animal biodiversity, as well as a broad range of geographies and climatic conditions; the only climatic type it lacks is Mediterranean. Because China lies between impressively bio-diverse Southeast Asia and the Near East, where so much early agricultural development took place, it has always been well situated for culinary borrowing. Like the Romans, the Chinese differentiated themselves from "uncivilized" outsiders by reference to their foods; the Mongols, for example, were milk-consuming nomadic herders, and seemed inherently unsettled. Some culinary differences could be tolerated within the bounds of empire, and others marked an unacceptable, threatening otherness. The culturally distinct regions that came under Han control might influence the home cuisine of the Han, but only if they were considered sufficiently exotic.

As in the cases of Persia and Rome, we know more about the diets of Han Chinese elites than we do about commoners' daily meals. Grave goods buried in the tombs of elites often include foodstuffs, conveying useful information about the foods, beverages, and preparations that high-status Han Chinese valued. In one noblewoman's tomb, small slips of bamboo were inscribed with descriptions of how to cook and season the foodstuffs also stored there. Methods including roasting, scalding, frying (the wok appears to have been developed during the Han Dynasty), and pickling or otherwise preserving ingredients; seasonings included soy sauce (fermenting soy beans was a technique perfected during the Han period), salt, sugar (made from cane), and honey.[28] Paintings in the tombs of nobles have even detailed the sequence of dishes served at banquets, which always began with wine, often followed by a meat stew or thickened soup called *geng*. Then grain dishes (for nobles, rice rather than the cheaper millet) appeared, with a dessert finishing the meal. These paintings depict exotic meats, probably served for prestige: fatted dog, bear paw, panther breast, suckling pig, and deer, as well as lamb and beef. As with Persian and Roman feasts, hosts could signal their status with the number of dishes they served. By contrast, most Han Chinese ate meat only a few times a year, usually following the annual slaughter of a pig. Details of feasts, and of the imperial kitchens themselves, are easier to come by than stories about the daily meals of peasants, who ate a nearly vegetarian diet by necessity rather than by choice. But the Chinese imperial interest in agriculture, and the number of preserved written records, has taught us much about how the Han government provisioned for its people. No other civilization, until the rise of industrial agriculture in modernity, reached the same heights of agricultural productivity; only Egypt came close.

"Few people have transformed their countries' landscapes more thoroughly than the Chinese," writes E. N. Anderson.[29] In pursuit of greater agricultural yields and natural resources, the Chinese have long engaged in deforestation, in building dikes and redirecting water to irrigate farmland, in creating terraces in order to grow crops. Geography has not determined human fate in China, so much as human choice and enterprise has shaped geography. Irrigation and public works projects such as the Min River irrigation system, also known as the Dujiangyan, were important even before the Han Dynasty. The Han, however, took greater pains than their predecessors to acquire knowledge about China's population and their needs, and to determine how to provide for them. In the year 2 CE, they conducted what may have been the world's first census, learning that their population consisted of some sixty million people. Long before that, the Han government supported agricultural research, as well as the publication and distribution of agricultural almanacs and guides, which its officials spread far and wide. Governmental involvement in publishing this literature, and in public works projects such as irrigation, were two pillars of Han agricultural policy. Others included low or moderate land taxes, maintaining a class of small farmers who either owned their land or rented it (small independent farms, the bureaucrats observed, were more productive than big ones), and providing food in times of famine.[30] The Han period also saw the world's first standardized system of weights and measures used in agriculture, and the first act of a government to support farm prices, not to mention a sophisticated bureaucracy to oversee all this. Han agricultural experts learned to adapt crops from outside China to suit their local climates.

Surviving fragments of Fan Sheng-Chih's first-century BCE farming manual tell us a great deal about Han agriculture. The Han planted staple grains multiple times throughout the year, which in the north meant growing wheat in the winter and millet in the summer. Farmers pretreated their seed, often using a fertilizer made from manure, cooked bones, and silkworm debris. They irrigated their rice paddies so that the water would be warm in the springtime but not too hot during the summertime. Farmers attended to how their soil received moisture, which in the dry north meant pulverizing their soil so that the resulting surface could capture more water. In the winter they covered the soil with snow so that the wind wouldn't blow it away. Farmers grew gourds, and sometimes grain, in pits to trap moisture. Every scrap of organic matter that contained nitrogen was saved for use as fertilizer, and the farmers seem to have had a profound knowledge of soil types. Iron tools were common. Despite the government's involvement with agriculture, rural peasants lived under considerable pressure to maintain the productivity of their farms, in part because their taxes were often levied in the form of crops and other agricultural products. Notably, Fan Sheng-Chih's favored methods of farming were labor-intensive, and in the view of some scholars this emphasis on labor shaped Chinese agriculture's future in a fateful way, emphasizing not technical innovation, but rather human biological energy, as the means to make the land more productive. This would later inhibit China's agricultural productivity, creating a kind of "high-energy equilibrium trap" into which the Chinese poured labor in order to maintain yields, even as the population, and thus the drain on those yields, increased.

Fan Sheng-Chih described "Nine Staples:" "wheat, barley, millet, glutinous millet, spiked millet, soybeans, rice, hemp, small beans," adding four items to a common list discussed in Han food writing, "The Five Staples," which usually included two species of millet plus wheat, barley, and rice. The rotary grindstone seems to have reached China from the West by the third century BCE, facilitating the transformation of grain into flour for making noodle or bun dough, called *bing*, a common staple especially in the wheat-eating north. The Chinese also turned grains into beer, wine, and liquor. But soybeans, often cooked into a bean stew, were the relevant staple for millions of poorer Chinese during the Han period. Soybeans, introduced to China by about 1000 BCE, grew even during bad years, and became a bulwark against starvation. Other prominent plants in the Chinese diet were adzuki or red beans, bamboo, Chinese cabbages, gourds, melons, mulberries, scallions, taro, and the leaves of elm trees; green onions, leeks, mallow, mustard greens, and water peppers were also common, as were magnolias and peonies.

Many of Han China's fruits and vegetables were native, but others came from foreign lands. These include coriander, cucumbers, onions, peas, pomegranates, and sesame, many of which came from the Fertile Crescent, from India, or from North Africa. The melon, which seems to have originated in Africa, and the bitter orange, which came from Southeast Asia via the Indus valley, both reached China very early, probably by 2000 BCE. Other fruits included apricots, jujubes, lotus, longans and litchis, oranges, peaches, plums, and the aforementioned grapes. Seasonings and spices included Szechuan pepper, brown pepper, galangal, ginger, and sugarcane honey. The *Book of Songs* (also called *The Classic of Poetry*), a compilation of poetic works dating from the eleventh to the seventh century BCE, lists at least forty-five edible plants (by contrast, the Hebrew Bible mentions twenty-nine).[31] Notably, the Han had no tofu, something only developed hundreds of years later, probably during the late T'ang (618–906 CE) or early Song Dynasty (960–1279 CE). Tea, eventually brought to China from the border areas between China and India, was not commonly drunk and cultivated until the T'ang.

Although most Chinese could only eat it once or twice a year, pork was by far the most popular meat, preferred over the somewhat more readily available chicken. The Han Chinese, who could never afford to eat much beef, began to shy away from it even more under the influence of Buddhism, which reached China during the Han Dynasty, but outright vegetarianism was always rare, and usually driven by meat's expense rather than by religion. Affluent Chinese might eat ducks, geese, pheasants, pigeons, and other wild birds; they might also eat horses, sheep, and deer, and many types of fish and other seafood, including pond-raised carp. For the Han Chinese, meat meant wealth and power. So it may be unsurprising that figures with nearly superhuman skill at butchery appeared again and again in early Chinese writings. We find one version in the poem "Carving Up An Ox," attributed to Zhuangzi Zhou (fourth century BCE):

A cook was butchering an ox for Duke Wen Hui.
The places his hand touched,
His shoulder leaned against,
His foot stepped on,
His knee pressed upon,
Came apart with a sound.
He moved the blade, making a noise
That never fell out of rhythm.
It harmonized with the Mulberry Woods Dance,
Like music from ancient times.

Duke Wen Hui exclaimed: 'Ah! Excellent!
Your skill has advanced to this level?'
The cook puts down the knife and answered:
'What I follow is Tao,
Which is beyond all skills.
When I started butchering,
What I saw was nothing but the whole ox.
After three years,
I no longer saw the whole ox.
Nowadays, I meet it with my mind
Rather than see it with my eyes.
My sensory organs are inactive
While I direct the mind's movement.
It goes according to natural laws,
Striking apart large gaps,
Moving toward large openings,
Following its natural structure.
Even places where tendons attach to bones
Give no resistance,
Never mind the larger bones!
A good cook goes through a knife in a year,
Because he cuts.
An average cook goes through a knife in a month,
Because he hacks.
I have used this knife for nineteen years.
It has butchered thousands of oxen,
But the blade is still like it's newly sharpened.
The joints have openings,
And the knife's blade has no thickness.
Apply this lack of thickness into the openings,
And the moving blade swishes through,
With room to spare!
That's why after nineteen years,

The blade is still like it's newly sharpened.

Nevertheless, every time I come across joints,

I see its tricky parts,

I pay attention and use caution,

My vision concentrates,

My movement slows down.

I move the knife very slightly,

Whump! It has already separated.

The ox doesn't even know it's dead,

and falls to the ground like mud.

I stand holding the knife,

And look all around it.

The work gives me much satisfaction.

I clean the knife and put it away.'

Duke Wen Hui said: 'Excellent!

I listen to your words

And learn a principle of life.'[32]

The cook in the poem identifies himself as a Taoist, a follower of a religion which gained strength in China during the Confucian Han Dynasty, and greatly influenced its food culture through its emphasis on balance. The poem's beneficiary is Duke Wen Hui, and the lesson he learns, "a principle of life," is also a principle of governance; many scholars have observed that all early Chinese philosophy is at least in part political philosophy. Showing up again and again in early Chinese literary works, the cook's lesson is an allegory about leadership, suggesting a way of governing by adapting to, rather than fighting, one's circumstances or environment, "inserting oneself" into opportunities as the butcher's knife finds a joint.[33] Conservation of natural resources is a common theme in Confucian writings both before and during the Han period, as is the idea of a ruler leading his people through exemplary behavior, including the benevolent management of agricultural resources.

The poem's image of the skillful cook teaches us that food was a rich source of instructions for living. Another literary genre, the rhapsodic poems called *fu,* shows the centrality of food in daily life. Two known *fu* from the Han period, "Summoning the Soul" and "The Great Summons," make food and cooking part of a ritual appeal to the soul of a deceased relative. The speaker asks their departed loved one to return, to taste what they used to enjoy in life. Indeed, food offerings have long been a central element of ancestral veneration and worship in China, continuing through the present day.[34] In some cases, frugal and sensible Han Chinese families have incorporated "used" meat offerings into their own cooking. Thus do the living and the dead feed each other.

Since at least the Han Dynasty, the line between cooking and medicine in China has been very thin, just as it was in Rome after the rise of Galenic medicine (developed from the work of Galen, a Greek physician born at the end of the second century CE, who practiced medicine in Rome). Plant- and animal-derived substances have served as medicines and then made their way into the regular diets of those who consume them, and foods are thought to influence health, according to a medical system that emphasizes the maintenance of health and the prevention of illness, rather than treating specific ailments in isolation. The values and principles of Chinese cuisine were, and still are, organized around a theory of the body that stresses balance. At its basis lies the idea of *qi,* often translated as "breath" or "energy" but understood quite materially in much Chinese thought: everything has *qi,* not metaphysically but in its substance. And the *qi* of something—including of a food—might be "*yang*" or "*yin,*" thought to have a masculine, hot character or a feminine, cool character. As the *I Ching* or "Book of Changes" put it, both *yang* and *yin* are aspects of the cosmos itself, but had more prosaic meanings too: *yang* meant the sunny southward slope of a hill, and *yin,* the north face in shade. Ancient Chinese culinary manuals instructed physician-chefs to treat bodily ailments by adjusting a patient's diet or by prescribing herbal and fungal potions.

One of the important questions in Chinese food history has been what drives the sheer range of Chinese eating, the enthusiastically omnivorous character of Chinese cuisine. For China is, in fact, a place of constant culinary invention, where nearly every available resource has been used to its maximum potential. Another similar question is about how the Chinese came to make their farmland so productive. Some scholars have argued that population pressure has been the engine of invention in China, creating a need not only to maximize agricultural yields, but to eat as many kinds of plants and animals as possible.[35] The developments of the Han period suggest that, at least in ancient China, population growth and dietary exploration were not necessarily linked in a tight causal relationship. While the Han period saw the population rise and fall, it did not see the massive population boom of the later Song Dynasty (960–1279 CE) when the population doubled from about sixty million (the average population during the Han period) to about 120 million. E. N. Anderson has argued that agricultural experimentation and intensification became an established tradition in China long before the Song Dynasty population explosion. "We know," Anderson wrote, "from modern experience that people living on the margin of real want do not experiment: they cannot afford to."[36] But the Chinese have enjoyed periods of less want, when it was not a dangerous gamble to try new plant and animal species or new methods of planting and harvesting, giving Chinese cuisines their remarkable reach. One technological legacy of the Han Dynasty now hangs from hooks in millions of households, an efficient means for transforming all manner of things into meals: the wok, in which small portions of vegetables and animal protein can be stir-fried, cooking quickly and demanding a minimum of fuel.

Coffee and Pepper

WHITE FLOWERS WITH A STRONG gardenia-like scent flutter on the branches of small coffee trees on a hill near Oh Sieh Lair in Ratanakiri Province in the northeast corner of Cambodia, bordering on Laos and Vietnam. Nearby, next to a large shed, millions of small dark brown dots are spread over a cement platform: tellicherry peppercorns drying in the hot sun, their aroma mingling in the air with the coffee blossoms. I have an interest in agricultural development and I'm learning with my nose. I pick up a handful of peppercorns, half-dried, and rub them between my fingers. I get a whiff of floral perfume with notes of earth.

But I didn't come because of agriculture, or to sample these scents. I came to learn what is needed in this very poor corner of Cambodia, and to help build elementary schools for the children of local farmers, as well as for the children of the "mountain people," an ethnic minority group originally from Vietnam and often treated as outcasts. Though families value schooling, sometimes education has to give way to the need for children's labor. Teachers rarely have more than high school educations—and for that, parents have to send their children to the capital, Phnom Penh. Poverty is deep, here. Life expectancy at birth is thirty-nine for men, forty-three for women. The farmers here live on the margin, growing and sensing the coffee and pepper, and they have experienced much political and military turmoil. Some were co-opted by the Khmer Rouge in the 1970s or run over by incursions from neighboring Vietnam. French colonials planted the first coffee trees here in the late nineteenth century, and the Vietnamese planted those trees' descendants and treated them with pesticides and chemical fertilizers.

Although I came with an interest in schools, my own research in coffee drew me to the trees and their promise for local development. Recently, the Cambodian coffee industry has received material support from foreign investors, along with an influx of foreigners, like myself, who have an interest in seeing Cambodia's coffee industry develop. But coffee plants mature slowly, and the industry rewards patience; some have turned to peppercorns as a faster option. Tellicherry pepper, arriving originally from India's Malabar coast, grows in many parts of Cambodia, not only in Ratanakiri but in Mundulkiri and elsewhere. And a peppercorn from Cambodia's southwest, *kampot,* is now making its way onto the world's gourmet stage. *Kampot* is reddish and has a distinctive heat and aroma. For the merchants who market it, Cambodian regional identity is part of the attraction.

On my first visit here, I asked about the coffee trees, seemingly ignored for the most part, and my question led to efforts to develop the coffee crop and raise more money to build schools. I'm well aware of the historical echoes in this development project. After all, this land has grown coffee and peppercorns at the behest of foreign powers. Each in their turn, coffee and pepper have represented a kind of colonial dependency on far-away masters. Nevertheless, the current Cambodian government hopes that these crops can be sustainable enough that the locals don't turn to growing opium poppies, somewhat easier to grow and extremely profitable. Cambodian coffee has started to find an audience, both in the capital, where visiting tourists buy it, and overseas. In both cases it enjoys some cachet as a "heritage" crop, though its reputation is still growing; "heritage" takes time to mature just as coffee plants do. Coffee and peppercorns are desirable because they stimulate the senses, and they can tie poverty-stricken areas like this one to foreign markets and appetites.

Smell, like taste, is an intimate sense, more intimate even than touch. Smell and taste both work by bringing something into the body. When we smell, little molecules of a substance enter our noses, without our having any say in the matter. The process is fairly simple: volatile materials, having an unstable structure, "off-gas" molecules of themselves. These travel through the air, enter our noses, and hit receptor neurons that send signals to the brain. Organic matter tends to be more volatile than inorganic; the scent of moss is stronger than the scent of the rockface on which it grows. Smell offers a valuable interface between a witness and the world around her. Smell reminds us of our vulnerability; many smells, like rottenness or smoke, can signal danger. In the mid-eighteenth century, Frederick the Great of Prussia used *kaffeeschnufflers* (coffee sniffers), people with sensitive noses, to discover illegal coffeehouses, banned for fear of seditious activity: the nose is a spy.

And of course, smell contributes to the multisensory experience of eating, which involves many individual parts, ranging from the movement of the jaw as we chew, to the flavor carried in the fat of an animal's meat. Taste is not only on the tongue. Sense researchers disagree about how much our sense of smell contributes to our experience of the taste of food, but they tend to agree that olfaction (sensing with the nose) is a major contributor, despite the fact that smell may be our least powerful sense, less developed in humans than in many mammals. Our sense of smell may be comparatively weak, but for some, smell has nevertheless stood as an ignoble reminder of our animal natures; this is how the philosopher Immanuel Kant regarded smell, ranking it far lower than our most powerful sense, vision. When we gaze out on the world, we direct our vision with some sense of control. By contrast, when we smell, something enters our body, and the only way to stop it is to pinch our nostrils shut and breathe through our mouth.

But sensory anthropology means opening those nostrils, as well as our eyes, ears, and taste buds, to things that we might not otherwise notice. Observation through all the senses may offer surprising benefits; the sidewalk smells a certain way after rain if it's made from concrete, another way if it is brick, and noticing this may open up deeper perceptions of the urban scene. Every smell has its situational—and cultural—context. For example, as we get used to the smell of pot in our neighborhood where cannabis is now legally sold and smoked, it becomes ordinary and not redolent of illicit indulgence. The smell of burning leaves in a rural area may simply signal autumn. Walking through the Nishiki Market in Kyoto, you can catch the scent of a dozen different pickle brines, each telling a different story about fermentation.

For Europeans, spices like pepper once embodied longing and avarice. They are now so common that their former rarity is hard to imagine, as are the dangerous journeys made in order to find them. For hundreds of years Europeans associated the smell of spices with luxury. Spices signaled wealth to the nose and mouth. After all, spices could only be present in Europe if someone, or more likely a chain of adventurous merchants, had undertaken a dangerous journey. Vast amounts of money could be made from one shipload of nutmeg. And some decided to let others make the risky journey for them. Pirates waited for the "spicers" returning from the distant Moluccas, and English tax-collecting vessels could effectively act as pirate ships, boarding the long-haul boats and seizing cargo beyond what taxation demanded.

But here in Cambodia, in the twenty-first century, pepper has a modestly profitable, much less colorful presence. It is valuable, but not the object of perilous voyages and violent seizure. In Ratanakiri, I have heard, a new crop, easier to grow at larger volumes, will soon replace both pepper and coffee: cashew nuts. Native to Brazil, these nuts represent something special to the Cambodian government, a resource of Cambodia's own choosing. For the deputy chair of the Cambodian Cashew Nut Policy Joint Working Group, Reach Ra, the goal is "to turn Cambodia into a major producer and supplier of cashew nuts . . . to serve the local, regional and global markets."[1] In choosing these nuts, the policymakers turn from the storied and aromatic coffee and pepper crops to a much less romantic commodity, an easy decision to make in the interests of farmers' survival and national economic sovereignty.

CHAPTER 3

Medieval Tastes

A Cook they hadde with hem for the nones,
To boille the chicknes with the mary-bones,
And poudre-marchant tart, and galingale.
Wel coude he knowe a draughte of London ale.
He coulde roste, and sethe, and broille, and frye
Maken mortreux, and wel bake a pye.
GEOFFREY CHAUCER, Prologue to *The Canterbury Tales*, 1392.

ONE OF GEOFFREY CHAUCER'S PILGRIMS was a cook. *The Canterbury Tales* describes a person well versed in all forms of cookery prominent in late medieval England. This urbane cook had meat dishes in his repertoire, knew the use of spices, and probably cooked for elites; spices, after all, were luxuries. This cook loved pleasure and ale. That he went on the road as a hired cook implies that he was something of an adventurer. Pilgrims from all walks of life were vectors of culinary change, influencing the places they visited and the homes to which they returned. Travel was the road to culinary novelty, and it is not for nothing that Chaucer's epic collection begins with a meal, and unfolds as a storytelling contest whose prize is another meal at journey's end.[1] This chapter is about the foodways of medieval Europeans and the forces that changed them: travel, shifting patterns of land use, the changing dynamics of rural and urban living, and developments in agricultural techniques and tools. And medieval Europe was scarcely isolated from non-European food cultures. Spices reached Europe by land and sea routes, presenting a powerful incentive to voyage out in search of more. As John Keay puts it, the supply of spices "seemed as providential and precarious as the weather," and eventually the appetite for spice, the desire to enjoy it more regularly and more securely, would change everything.[2]

A note on the origin and use of the term "medieval" is helpful. First, the use of (originally Latin) terms meaning "middle age" or "middle ages" began in sixteenth century Europe, in what historians generally regard as the early modern period. It was a way to label an era that European scholars believed themselves, and their civilization, to have left behind. During the Renaissance, it became common to think of civilization's history as a sequence beginning with antiquity, followed by a "middle ages" or "medieval period," then opening onto modernity through a rebirth of learning.[3] Such a chronology was self-congratulatory. The Renaissance humanists who established this way of viewing things effectively inherited the religious metaphor of a movement from darkness to light, a metaphor alive and well in medieval Christianity.

Furthermore, "medieval" and "middle ages" are European terms, and we should be cautious when using them to describe non-European places and times. While historians will sometimes speak of non-European sites with this terminology—"China in the middle ages," for example—it is crucial to drop the European connotations. The Khans dominated the "Asian middle ages," their rule extending across mainland Asia. The great temple complexes of Angkor Wat, still visible in present-day Cambodia, were built in this period, and gunpowder was invented in China by the eleventh century. And even when we consider Europe, we should be careful not to let "medieval" or "the middle ages" seem too familiar, as if we know exactly what they describe. The names of some medieval foods, like roast meats or baked bread, are still in use, but the medieval versions differed from the foods we know; the animals were of different breeds, not conditioned for industrial production, and slaughtered at older ages, often after doing farm work. Medieval grain was usually more coarsely ground into rougher flour, and much of it was not made of wheat. Medieval dishes would have tasted different, even if called by familiar names, like "pie."

Chaucer's pilgrims did not travel as culinary novices. They took a keen interest in food even before they left London, bound towards Canterbury via Watling Street, an ancient Roman way running between Canterbury and St. Albans. Their counterparts in continental Europe might have tasted foods transformed by the Arab presence on the Iberian Peninsula. The Moors—Muslims of Arab descent—controlled up to 70 percent of Spain for over seven hundred years, starting in 711 CE and ending with the final fall of Granada in 1492 (through the Moors had previously been expelled from most of Spain). The Romans had grown citrons, but the Moors were the first to grow other more familiar citrus fruits, like oranges, on European soil. Many Spanish foods have Arabic origins, the trace of which lingers in names that begin with "a," like *arroz*, rice, or "al," like *albondigas*, meatballs, or the Mexican "al pastor." The sturdy cakes that pilgrims carried were sweetened and preserved with honey (especially important in the centuries before sugar reached Europe), and flavored with flower-waters, like orange and rose, both markers of Arab influence. Christian pilgrims, like other medieval Europeans, pickled their fish in vinegar, preserving them for storage or travel.

The pilgrims who traveled to Santiago de Compostela—the name suggests *composium*, "burial ground," or *campus stellae*, "starry field," in Latin—in Galicia in northwestern Spain, where the apostle St. James is said to be buried, ate special almond cakes, a version of which is still baked today: the *Tarta de Santiago*, a celebratory cake for those who complete the pilgrimage. This is a dense, sugary almond cake with the sword of St. James inscribed in the frosting; ironically for these quasi-sacramental Christian cakes, sugar first entered Europe through the agency of Muslim physicians and cooks. The pilgrimage dates from the ninth century, when Compostela, already a sacred place for Christians, acquired an additional political significance because northern Spain was a Christian refuge while the southern Iberian Peninsula was under Moorish control. Kings and high officials were baptized and eventually buried at Compostela, their religious piety validating their political power.

Paths from many points in Europe converge on the pilgrim's road to Compostela (other roads led to the other two major Christian pilgrimage sites, Rome and Jerusalem). For more than a millennium, pilgrims traveling to Compostela have shared stories and food from around Europe and beyond. Tales and dishes from many countries mixed on the road, but the foods that came to typify this particular pilgrimage were Galician specialties, particularly local scallops and other seafood. Fish held a special attraction because pilgrims usually practiced austerity, which for many Christians means choosing fish over terrestrial meat, as they did during fast periods; the tradition finds its contemporary echo in the Christian practice of eating fish, not meat, on Fridays, the day Christ is said to have died. In theory, gastronomic austerity leveled differences of class and wealth during the pilgrimage, but in practice wealthy pilgrims still ate better than poor ones.[4] The bread of peasants, made of rough grain like rye or millet, and so dry it had to be soaked in wine or water before eating, was not the bread of the wealthy, made of finer wheat flour. As the pilgrimage gained popularity, the scallop shell of St. James became an emblem that pilgrims wore around their necks. Some say the pilgrims used them to eat the food offerings they received, scooping up just a single shell's worth of porridge. Whatever the truth of this story, many pilgrims brought shells back as souvenirs.

Pilgrimage had its paradoxes when it came to food and the body, and so did the Christian theological context through which pilgrims moved. Eating had religious connotations for medieval Christians, most basically because since the start of Christianity, Christians had distinguished themselves from Jews by avoiding Jewish dietary practices. Where Jews rejected certain animals as un-kosher, kept meat and milk dishes apart, and observed careful methods of slaughtering the animals they did eat, Christians held that spiritual life was not dependent on such ritual concerns. Paul (born Saul of Tarsus, a Jew) inveighed against the laws of *kashrut,* among other Jewish strictures.[5] And yet the body and its appetites mattered to Christianity. Food and sex could be distractions from a pious life, and fasting was often seen as a way to curb both appetites. As Caroline Walker Bynum puts it, fasting—especially for women—was thought to "force the body towards virtue."[6]

The medieval Christian calendar was full of fasting days, usually not days of complete abstention but of limited sustenance. However, some foods—bread and wine—were critical to a major Christian sacrament, a ritual meant to enable contact with the divine. The faithful consumed the blood (notably, blood was a forbidden food for Jews) and flesh of their redeemer through the miracle of transubstantiation. In eliminating Jewish dietary law from their lives, Christians nevertheless kept eating and food central to their spiritual lives. Bread was an ever-present if ambivalent symbol. In a fourth-century CE sermon, St. Augustine had compared a Christian's spiritual progress to making leavened bread out of the "grain" of the aspiring Christian: "When you received exorcism, you were 'ground.' When you were baptized, you were 'leavened.' When you received the fire of the Holy Spirit, you were 'baked.'"[7] Just as individual grains become one in a loaf of bread, so were Christians unified in the body of Christ—the same bread they would themselves consume.

Christian pilgrims often began their holy journeys with a fast (contra Chaucer, whose pilgrims start their journey with a meal), and committed themselves to asceticism and the mortification of the flesh. Strangely, asceticism did not always mean denying themselves good eating along the way. It may seem ironic that the famous French dish *coquilles St-Jacques* (French for St. James) is made with a cream and wine sauce, the scallops sautéed in butter and finished with the cream sauce in the shell in which they are served, but pilgrims sometimes ate well. Inns served them simple food: cold cuts and cheese, bread (peasant bread or better), stew, or even the medieval counterpart of modern *minestrone,* made of vegetables and beans. Some pilgrims ate *empanadas,* a turnover or hand pie filled with meat, fish, or vegetables. These were the ancestors of our modern empanadas, cheap and easy to eat while traveling. Pilgrims found beer, at the time the very symbol of welcome and health, in every inn. Other possible drinks included wine (omnipresent across Europe) as well as regional specialties including perry (fermented pear juice), mead, or in France, *piquette,* a kind of sour wine.[8] Pilgrims might find beer in monasteries, too, if they sought the hospitality of a religious order along the way.

Beer is a drink with many independent origins. It has developed almost spontaneously around the world, from sub-Saharan Africa to Iceland. Some archaeologists even suggest that beer preceded bread and was in fact the origin of leavened bread (as opposed to unleavened breads such as *lavash, chapatti,* and *matzoh*) because natural yeasts in the air created fermentation in damp flour or in liquids. The resulting beer could then "start" bread by acting as a leavening agent. Evidence of beer-like drinks, and the pottery in which they were made and served, has been found at Mesopotamian and pre-Dynastic Egyptian archaeological sites. There are also ancient Egyptian statues of women kneading barley for beer making, and there is evidence that honey was used to sweeten and preserve beer. In Egypt, sub-Saharan Africa, Latin America, and many other parts of the premodern world, women have long been the ones who made beer (or similar drinks) by chewing grain, spitting into a common receptacle, and letting the saliva-fermented liquid develop for a few days, after which it is strained and served.

Benedictine monks may have been the first to add hops to beer, creating the distinctive flavors we associate with the beverage.[9] In any case the Benedictines have a long association with beer. In France, Saint Arnold of Soissons (about 1040–87 CE), a Benedictine abbot and bishop, was made the patron saint of beer makers. He is usually depicted with a bishop's mitre and a mash rake, used to stir the mash as beer ferments. In life, Saint Arnold observed that those who drank ale heavily were less likely to succumb to disease than those who did not. According to one tale, he enjoined his congregation to drink beer instead of water, saving them from the plague. Whether beer was actually healthier than water in all cases is, however, a subject of historical debate.

Beer was not associated with rowdy levels of drunkenness. Much of it was brewed to have a low alcohol content (this was often called "small beer"), allowing people to drink without becoming incapacitated. In medieval Europe, women usually were in charge of their families' health, and they were wise to give their children this "small beer." Notably, beer was not an industrial or craft product produced by professionals outside of the home. Making beer was part of ordinary housekeeping, or in other words, women's work.

Beer and ale can be made from almost any grain, but barley (whose virtues included being a hardier crop than wheat) has long been the grain of choice for most European beers. The other common main ingredients are hops and yeast. Barley is first "malted," or dampened and allowed to sprout roots, at which stage it grows rich in starches. It is then heated to stop the growth, and to allow its enzymes to produce sugar. Malted barley can be roasted to heighten its taste and darken its color. Hops, a flowering vine, are added as a preservative and to provide a bitterness that balances the sweetness of malting. Yeast converts the sugar to alcohol, which acts as a preservative and, to some degree, a purifier.

The women known in England as "ale-wives," who made beer in their households and shared it with neighbors and kin, were put out of a job when the Catholic Church instituted a new regime of beer production. With the cooperation of monarchs in France and what is now Germany, the Church issued permits for beer-making (in fact, for the use of *gruit*, the herbal ingredients such as yarrow that gave beer flavor; hops were seen as an alternative to *gruit*), and charged a fee, effectively a beer-making tax. Meanwhile, the Church's monks could help to pay for their own monasteries by brewing beer with *gruit*. What was bad for households, where the cost of the license would be prohibitive, was indirectly good for beer itself: the monks had the time and resources to experiment, producing substantial improvements in the quality of ale and beer, and making products generally superior to those made at home. Later, during the Protestant Reformation, Martin Luther himself encouraged fellow Protestants to resist the Church's monopoly on *gruit* by simply using hops instead. Luther even suggested that the herbs in *gruit* had hallucinatory effects, implying that the Church's beer had incapacitated Europe.[10]

Road travel created the need for refreshment at inns, taverns, and alehouses, usually involving simple meals, as well as wine and beer.[11] As they developed reputations for good food and service, inns and taverns competed to make the best "table d'hote" or "host's table," a fixed meal. Only later did *a la carte* menus appear, and only in cities, for medieval hospitality did not mean giving guests a choice. The earliest urban eating-houses were only allowed, at first, to serve a "restorative"—a broth—to visitors, thus the eventual name "restaurant." However, taverns meant more than food, drink, and a chance to rest. They were also places to hear news from afar at a time when the lines of locality were closely drawn, and the terms "foreigner" or "stranger" might apply to someone from another town or village, much less from another country. Anticipating the seventeenth-century coffeehouses of England and America, medieval inns and taverns catered to a wide variety of customers, including travelers far from their homes.

Given the ubiquity and normalcy of restaurant meals in the modern world, it is worth mentioning how unusual eating outside of the home was for people of most social classes in medieval Europe. Eating with one's family was practically a secular sacrament in many communities, and for husbands and wives to eat together was often taken as a sign of a marriage's health.[12] In the City of London itself, there were no restaurants resembling the modern sit-down kind before the fifteenth century, although there were "cookshops" where people (primarily the poor and working-class) could buy pre-cooked food.[13] Those without an oven at home could prepare dishes of food and bring them to professional kitchens that offered the use of their ovens. Taverns and inns were complex social institutions indeed, because they made typically domestic resources (a place at the table for dinner, a bed for the night) available for hire outside the home. These were places where ideas about publicness, privacy, and sharing space with people of different social backgrounds could change.[14]

The largest European "pilgrimage" of all was the Crusades, a movement not so much to convert, as to conquer and exterminate, the Moors (sometimes called the "Saracens" until the sixteenth century, when the word "Muslim" came into common European usage.) A long-running series of campaigns initiated by the newly militant Church, the most important of the Crusades took place between the eleventh and thirteenth centuries, beginning with Pope Urban II's 1095 call for an armed expedition to the Holy Land to retake Jerusalem from Islam and followed quickly by a "People's Crusade," not directly sanctioned by the Church, in which Christian peasants made their way towards the Holy Land, often slaughtering Jews (proximate targets of hate, as opposed to the distant Moors) as they found them. This was a time of new boldness for Christian Europe, based partly on the fact that Christianity had finally spread not only throughout the Mediterranean, but also through previously pagan lands in the British Isles and Scandinavia. The word "Crusade" was itself only coined in the late sixteenth century, derived from the French "croisade," meaning "bearing [or being marked by] the Cross."

While conquering the Holy Land for Christ may have been their official mission, the young crusaders brought back local foods, and sometimes, as captives, the women who made them. However, most of the officially sanctioned crusaders were very poor, young, provincial men for whom any food away from their family's hearth would have been exotic, yet not in a tantalizing way. For them, the foods of the Holy Lands were as "heathen" as the people they met there. Only the spices were of lasting interest, and these for their monetary rather than their gastronomic value. Militant Christianity effectively employed young men from all over Western Europe, who in peacetime had formed roving gangs, unruly threats to the social order. Armed with papal indulgences that promised them direct access to heaven if they were killed in Christ's service, these men found a new calling in fighting the putative enemies of the Church in the East, such as the Seljuq Turks who had defeated the Christian Byzantine Empire in 1071. By sending them off to fight elsewhere, their home communities could be rid of these pugnacious youths. Looting along the way was another perk, and spice was prominent among the spoils brought back home. Spices had previously only trickled into Europe via important trading routes, especially the Silk Road.

But so far we have only described roads and certain foods enjoyed along them. Eating itself was an uncertain affair in medieval Europe. Grain supplies depended on the harvests, and the harvests depended on the weather. Too little rain was disastrous; too much rain could rot stored grain. Historians' views vary, however, regarding whether unpredictable harvests were the most important factor in food security, or whether the management techniques of feudal Europe, or myriad other social factors—from export bans, to government price controls, hoarding, frequent military engagements, and so forth—played a more important role. During the military conflicts between the rival Tuscan city states of Florence and Siena, for example, the Florentines did all they could to disrupt Siena's grain supply.[15]

Whatever the cause of uncertainty, storing and preserving grain against future need was important, but also laborious and expensive. The poor went hungry far more often than the rich, something that can never be blamed on the weather. Malnutrition and starvation are usually manmade phenomena and reflect social inequalities. Frequently hungry, European peasants ate a great deal when they could, to support their demanding work. Their diets, consisting mostly of grain, protein in the form of legumes (peas, vetches, and beans, for the most part, in England), and scant amounts of meat, could provide 3500 to 4000 calories per day. Only the most prosperous English peasants would eat eight ounces of pork, or other meat (the most common meat animals were cows, goats, sheep, and pigs), per week. Many things took food from peasants' plates, including the tax collector, who often took payment in grain and other transportable foods such as eggs and cheese. Taxation regularly exposed peasants to malnourishment. A huge part of a person's day went into planting, harvesting, tending, or processing and cooking, food; the amount of labor and time involved beggars the understanding of most modern people. And the crops and animals of medieval Europe were generally smaller, yielded less food, and required more processing (more work in the kitchen) than their twenty-first-century descendants.

Want gave rise to fantasies only a starving peasant could imagine. French peasants spoke of "Cockaigne," and their counterparts in the Low Countries referred to "Luilekkerland," both of them variations on a theme: a Paradise on Earth that you could reach if you knew where to look, a walled garden of sorts and an echo of Eden.[16] But these walls were made of porridge, and you could eat your way through. In Cockaigne meat was not just plentiful; animals actually wanted to be eaten. Birds flew into peoples' mouths already cooked, and pigs walked around with forks sticking out of roasted and sliced backs. The streams ran with wine, beer, or anything else you desired. Needless to say, no one had to work to enjoy this, and the other chief pleasure of the body, sex, was readily available too. The order of virtue and vice, in Cockaigne, was the opposite of the order of Christian Europe: sloth, gluttony, and lust all became virtues, or at least encouraged paths to pleasure.

Back in the mundane world, social class largely determined what medieval people ate. Unfortunately, as for other periods before the development of widespread literacy and recordkeeping, we know more about the daily lives and meals of elites than we do about those of peasants. We must reconstruct the latter from a combination of archaeological evidence, chronicles, histories, legal documents, and the surviving inventories of the estates where peasants farmed.[17] And we know about aristocrats' banquets most of all. The banquets recorded in the court of Henry IV were stupendous concentrations of wealth. At his wedding to Joan of Navarre, in 1403, there were three "introductory" courses of meats of all kinds: poultry, including rabbits (then and sometimes today included in this category), capons, woodcocks, squabs, swans, geese; red meats from venison to mutton, pig to beef; and three courses of fish, each including five or six different dishes.

Each course also contained a sweet, mixed in with the savories since sweets had not yet been relegated to a final course called "pudding" or "dessert," and the savory dishes themselves contained sweet ingredients, as well as spices a modern western eater might associate with savory flavors.[18] Each course had its "salads" and "jellies," one shaped like a crowned panther, another, a crowned eagle. At similar banquets it was not uncommon to see a castle on a table, perhaps made of ground meat. Or one animal might be sculpted out of the flesh of another. The conceit of masquerade was present at every feast, a development that attracted Chaucer's attention. The Parson, a character in *The Canterbury Tales*, inveighed against such theatrical banquets, viewing them as expressions of the sin of pride.[19] We seldom see, in the surviving menus of the period, any reference to greens or other vegetables, but this is probably because they were too commonplace to mention.

Historians have explored the successes, failures, and overall political economy of medieval European agriculture in great depth.[20] If the Roman world was characterized by the widespread cultivation of farmland, the centuries after the Empire's fall (which was also the fall of Roman high cuisine) saw the reforestation of much of Europe, as both farming and populations declined. Generations of peasants ate very simple diets, depending mostly on the grains that grew in their local climate, supplemented by other vegetables and an occasional bit of animal protein. When Charlemagne's Frankish armies marched in the later eighth century, he had to order the farmers in his empire (which united much of central Europe) to plant specific crops to ensure that his armies would have enough to eat. One surviving document, the *Capitulare de Vilis,* which describes the organization of the estates of the Carolingian royals who followed Charlemagne, gives us a sense of the crops grown and the foods eaten by the Frankish nobility; their range was extensive, including root vegetables like burdock and carrots, cabbage, and leafy greens that tolerated colder temperatures, such as lettuce and arugula. The Franks had onions, shallots and garlic, and various gourds, including squash. The *Capitulare* lists radishes and fennel, as well as fruits including apples, figs, quinces, cherries, plums, pears, peaches, and medlars. Certainly, it seems unlikely that a given noble household would see all these items in a single year. Before sugar began to reach European elites in the eleventh century, honey was the only sweetener most people knew.

From about the eleventh century to the mid-fourteenth-century arrival of the Black Death, Europe slowly grew more prosperous.

Farmers benefited from what is often called the "medieval climatic optimum," warmer and drier conditions that lasted from about 700 to about 1200 CE. This allowed crops to be grown higher on hillsides, made more arable land available, and led to larger harvests. None of this meant that farming was easy or reliable. Farmers in the high middle ages faced the challenge of increasing productivity to keep up with population growth without exhausting the soil itself. But fallowing was an uneven practice, and in some places the soil was used continuously, depleting its nutrients. Like agriculture everywhere in Europe, English agriculture was susceptible to crisis, and was managed under feudal arrangements that denied peasants the resources they might have used to change their farming practices. Given these circumstances, decisions about what to plant each season were gambles, often gambles on survival.

And yet there were new tools. River-driven mills and windmills transformed the way the English processed grain, just as they changed grain processing across Europe. This was very significant, because from the early to late medieval period, Europeans depended more and more on grain as their primary source of calories. The Cistercian order of monks contributed to the spread of milling, since they made widespread use of mills near their monasteries. According to one count, by 1086 CE in England, 5624 water mills were operating, some even mounted on barges.

Early agricultural tools such as hoes were supplemented by two new forms of plough, the knife plough and the mold board, which were great improvements over the "scratch" plough, driven by human labor since antiquity. The mold board, attached to another innovation, the horse yoke or collar, was heavier and able to plow deep into clay-rich or water-logged fields, creating longer furrows that were more efficient to hoe, water, weed, and harvest. Horses were more efficiently harnessed with non-choking collars and other tack, and horseshoes gave horses better traction in mud. This was also a time of felling trees. Forested land became agricultural land from England to Central Europe. Those areas that could support livestock farming were often more economically dynamic than those that could not, in part because it was easier and cheaper to bring animal products to markets far from the farms; cows could be walked, and dairy products, especially cheese, packed a great deal of value into a small package.

While increased agricultural yields did contribute to widespread population growth, populations declined sharply after 1348 due to the Black Death. This bubonic plague began in Asia, killed millions in China by 1331, and then wiped out a huge portion of Europe's population (varying from a third to two-thirds, depending on the region), hitting the poor especially hard. European elites had a sufficiency of food, better sanitation, and a supply of servants who helped insulate them from the pestilences and miseries of the poor. The Black Death also drew governments' attention to the safety of food and drink sold in marketplaces, and many cities passed ordinances requiring meat and fish vendors to retire spoiled goods, which in summer meant anything that did not sell the first day it was brought to market.

The plague generated fresh interest in health regimens, and food was usually considered "the first instrument of medicine."[21] Although medieval doctors, tending to the needs of elites, drew from the teachings of the Greek physician Galen, with his holistic view that health derived from moderation and the observance of a regimen of proper exercise and diet, commoners in the late middle ages also benefited from vernacular guides to healthy living. The pharmacopoeia of the day were usually guides to herbs and plants, and while commoners would not have read these works themselves (indeed, literacy levels were low across Europe) there was an explosion of literature written in Middle English that included plague tracts such as Johannes de Burgundia's *Tractatus de morbo epidemi* of 1365, which gave advice about avoiding the plague itself, and dietary guides. This literature grew with the advent of printing in the fifteenth century, as did a burgeoning new genre, the cookbook, though early cookbooks were not written for the general public, but by professional cooks for other professional cooks. The most famous early cookbook was Taillevent's late thirteenth or early fourteenth century *Le Viandier*, which reflected the dining strategies of the royal household for whom the author cooked. The Cook in Chaucer's *Canterbury Tales* would have known something about medicine, since he practiced a form of it. Capons were thought to be good for the sick, and someone had to cook them. Nor was it coincidental that spices both flavored foods and served as pharmaceuticals, because the medieval logic of dietetics observed no division between the medical and the nutritional. Spices came from the East, and the idea that they might come from an earthly Paradise was common.[22]

The period following the Black Death saw a rising trend of urbanization, as peasants whose farms were no longer able to support them sought areas of concentrated resources. Despite its massive cost in lives, the Black Death only temporarily slowed an ongoing set of changes. By the mid-twelfth century in Europe, urban living had started to seem less remarkable, less an exception in a primarily rural society. Urban hubs were linked by the spokes of old roads originally made by the Romans. Information and goods moved along ancient paths of empire. Slowly, rare luxuries such as spices made their way from the roads into society at large, influencing tastes. Arab traders moved prestige goods like silk to castles and palaces, along with spices that elites could afford. Merchants praised the curative powers of turmeric or ginger, and implicitly celebrated the social status that turquoise and amber, coral and ambergris conveyed to the buyer. Culinary novelties came to the wealthy first. One such food was the Middle Eastern innovation fruit "leather," which reached France and Italy before making its way to the rest of Europe. This substance, a dried and flattened slab of fruit such as apricots, was created to preserve fruit out of season, and for travel. A strip of dried fruit could be eaten by hand or cut into small squares and dissolved in a cup of hot water, creating a nutritious and tasty beverage. New tastes tended to "trickle down" from truly wealthy elites, who developed those tastes first, to the less wealthy, who emulated the tastes of their social superiors.

The Silk Road, as it is commonly called, was established during China's Han Dynasty, and for centuries it was a major force in connecting and developing Eurasia, linking China, the Indian subcontinent, Persia and Arabia, and Europe. During the Byzantine era (fourth through eighth centuries CE), the Silk Road continued to facilitate long-distance journeys and the exchange of goods. Later, during Europe's middle ages, Islamic influences and the hegemonic power of the Mongols left their marks on the goods and travelers along the several different routes that made up the Silk Road. Silk may have given the route its name, but spices, ingredients, and recipes traveled along it too.

Indeed, many have credited the Silk Road for bringing noodles to Europe. This is not quite true; there is no single birthplace for noodles, pasta, or dumplings, all of which seem to have developed multiple times in multiple places. The story that the legendary voyager Marco Polo, who traveled the Silk Route between 1279 and 1295, brought pasta to Italy from China (or as some Italian sources prefer, from Italy to China) is almost certainly apocryphal. There is evidence that the noodle antedated his voyages in both Europe and China. Noodles and dumplings are both forms of dough made from grain flour that has been cooked in boiling water (or in the case of some dumplings, steam). A noodle can simply be pinched or hand-rolled bits or skeins of flour and water, boiled in water, and thus noodles were likely "invented" many times, and in many places, wherever flour was milled. The word "pasta" in Italian translates directly and simply into English as "paste." The same flour and water paste could become flatbread, and if airborne yeast produced fermentation, a crude loaf of bread might result. In Roman Italy, in the first century BCE, sheets of dough were used in lasagna-like dishes. Arabs had noodles, called *ittriyya,* dried, string-like shapes of semolina dough. Semolina, the endosperm of durum wheat, was used in puddings, breads, couscous, and pasta in Arab North Africa, and is still common in the region; it had reached Norman Sicily by the 1120s. In 2002, an excavation along China's Yellow River found a preserved four-thousand-year-old noodle, which had been made by pulling and stretching dough by hand. Such hand-pulled noodles, served with spicy lamb, are still popular in Xinjiang and other parts of western China, an important feature of local culinary identity.

From China through Central Asia and Russia to Europe, and from the Han Dynasty to the present, culinary traditions have always been strikingly continuous along the Silk Road. In addition to sharing the noodle, most cuisines on the Road involve some sort of staple flatbread, from the pancakes served with lamb or duck in China to the *chapattis* of India, the *lapyoshka* of Russia, and the *lavash* of Armenia. Communities isolated by mountain ranges in Central Asia also have versions of these breads, their recipes transmitted by the traders' caravanserais. Such breads bake quickly on bricks, flat stones, or even the backs of shovels. The communities along the route also share a fondness for lamb and dried fruit.

During the medieval period the most common spices along the Silk Road were cumin, coriander, and cloves, the latter almost as pricey as nutmeg (a product, along with mace,[23] of the tree *Myristica fragrans*), which became the world's most expensive spice, and even ended up in *The Canterbury Tales,* where it was "notemugge to putte in ale."[24] Arab traders brought other spices to Europe, including ginger and cinnamon, and Chinese merchants carried anise, sesame seeds, cumin, and coriander in their kits. But Europeans grew tired of middlemen, whether they were Arabs, Chinese, or the Venetians who often dealt with the former groups. The European powers eventually went to seek out spices where they grew. At first European ships followed known routes, and then gradually tried to improve upon them, seeking easier access to rare and costly ingredients like cinnamon, nutmeg, and peppercorns. The early spice missions were gambles with long odds: for every three ships that sailed east, only one returned. Not only that, sometimes a returning ship was not one of the original "spicers," but a pirate ship completing the mission of their victims, carrying stolen spice. Of course, spices—nothing more than dried aromatic seeds, roots, bark, fruit, bulbs, or tubers—were incredibly profitable. For those willing to take risks in the interest of wealth, there was ample incentive to attempt the journey to India (for pepper and other spices) or to the islands of Indonesia (for mace and nutmeg and cloves).

Despite the importance of the Spice Islands in the Indonesian Archipelago, India has long been the most important high-volume source for most spices. As of this writing India is still the world's largest spice producer, growing and harvesting 86 percent of the world's spices per annum. Stories of Indian spices had intrigued the ancient Greeks, though only the most elite had any chance of tasting them. Romans, whose empire reached further to the east, enjoyed more access and developed a special taste for peppercorns. The records of Roman expeditionary forces show that even ordinary soldiers bought pepper in India. Malabar, the southwestern part of India, became a destination for Roman spice traders. There they could also find cardamom, pepper, and cinnamon, this last item possibly having grown further to the east, in Indochina. Frankincense and myrrh, familiar from Jewish, Roman, and Christian rituals, were used as incense and to scent or preserve food. Such spices appear in the Bible, and had a long presence in Mediterranean Europe, showing up in the famous first century CE Roman cookbook attributed to Apicius, and even in Tamil writings that describe Greeks journeying to South Asia and paying a great deal for pepper.[25]

The European search for seaborne routes to the "Spice Islands"—the Moluccas, including the Banda Islands, in what is now the Indonesian Archipelago—began fitfully. The Moluccas presented a difficult target, for Arab traders had kept the islands' location a secret, ensuring their control over the nutmeg and mace trade.[26] But the Portuguese found the Moluccas and seized control of them in 1511. The Moluccas would remain under Portugal's control until the seventeenth century, when the Dutch displaced the Portuguese. As different European powers seized islands, they fought with both arms and diplomacy to determine who would control each part of the region. To secure their hold on nutmeg, the Dutch would trade a North American island called Manhattan—the historical land of the Lenape People—to the British, getting in exchange a tiny island called Run, where nutmeg grew. "In the 1667 Treaty of Breda," the Dutch acquired a piece of land far more valuable than the future financial capital of the world. The Dutch then built their power in the Moluccas, forbidding export of seeds or plants from the Spice Islands, and effectively controlled the export of nutmeg, mace, and cloves.[27] Until the eighteenth century, these islands were the only source of nutmeg for Europeans, but in 1769 a Frenchman, Pierre Poivre (his surname means "pepper"), smuggled nutmeg to the French-held island of Mauritius, in the southwest Indian Ocean, where the tree flourished.

Pirates and privateers became at least as common as the spice traders themselves. Their typical strategy was to lie in wait for returning ships laden with hard-obtained cloves, cinnamon, and nutmeg, and seize them. And pirates were not the only danger returning ships faced. National navies might raid ships flying foreign flags; the English Navy, for example, effectively acted as a privateer fleet. In 1665 the diarist Samuel Pepys, who was serving as surveyor to the British Navy, witnessed a British raid of Dutch ships. He reported that "the greatest wealth lie in confusion that a man can see in the world—pepper scatter[ed] through every chink, you trod on it; and in cloves and nutmegs, I walked above the knees—whole rooms full . . . as noble a sight as ever I saw in my life."[28] Naturally, spice ships expected to defend themselves, and sailed well-armed. Military escorts became *de rigeur* for spice carriers.

The spice conflicts would eventually fade in the eighteenth and early nineteenth centuries, largely because by then, spice production was no longer limited to India and a few islands in Southeast Asia. The French and British brought seeds and plants from Indonesia to their colonies in the Caribbean and off the coast of Africa, and found that they grew well there. But even as spices became more widely available, and thus cheaper, they retained an exotic aura, linked to Pacific or Caribbean islands in the imaginations of many Europeans. They could fantasize that these islands were places where an Edenic nature gave forth its wealth *sua sponte,* something easier to imagine if you have no direct experience of tropical heat and disease.

But before spices became more commonplace, the spice trade enriched and transformed certain European ports. Consider Venice, "La Serenissima," at the north of the Adriatic, with an enviable harbor. Venice had been the center of the Roman spice trade until the fifth century CE, prior to its rise as a city-state in the tenth century. Throughout the middle ages it was the most important conduit between Western Europe and the Arab world. Venetians came to dominate most East-West trade, including the slave trade, between the thirteenth and fifteenth centuries. Certain foods were introduced to Europe here; sugar cane came to Venice from India, brought by Arab traders, and the Venetians processed it into "cakes" or "loaves" or made it into small candies or candied fruits. (The word "candy" comes from the Arabic word for sugar, *kand.*) Spices now associated with sweet dishes in Western Europe, such as cinnamon, were freely used in meat and vegetable dishes. In the early sixteenth century, coffee reached Europeans through Venice, and was initially received as a "heathen, Turkish drink."[29]

In fact, to other Europeans Venetians began to seem exotic themselves, and suspiciously so. They seemed insufficiently European and Christian, and too preoccupied by Mammon to pay much attention to God. By the fifteenth century, before the European powers began their territorial games in pursuit of spices and wealth, Venice essentially controlled the flow of spices into Europe, much of it arriving through trade with Egypt. At the time of Christopher Columbus's 1492 voyage, about 1.5 million pounds of black pepper came through the city-state each year. Venetian buildings were often decorated with Oriental motifs, domed or arched like Islamic or Buddhist structures to the east.[30]

Some historians have argued that the spice trade led to such a concentration of wealth in Europe that it was a factor in the rise of early capitalism itself.[31] Wolfgang Schivelbusch, in his *Tastes of Paradise,* makes an even more sweeping argument: spices, he suggests, were a culinary catalyst in the transformation of the European world from medieval to modern, incentivizing trade, exploration, and economic development (not to mention slavery and conquest) all at once.[32] But part of the allure of spices fell away even as they helped to make the modern European world. Eventually spices lost their old medieval associations with faraway, possibly Edenic, places off to the east. Cut off from Paradise by their widespread availability, spices were secularized, even as they gained new associations with colonialism and the struggle for international power, a contest largely between European rivals. Whether or not we embrace ambitious historical claims made on their behalf, spices, and the spice trade, helped to transform the world in many ways. The search for spices helped to catalyze the most significant shift in global foodways since the advent of agriculture itself: this was the exchange of biological organisms (plant, animal, microbe) between Eurasia and the continents that would be called the Americas. It began with Christopher Columbus's effort to reach the Spice Islands by way of the Atlantic, and for that reason we now call it the Columbian Exchange.

Before Kimchi

IN 2003, I FLEW TO SEOUL FROM KYOTO, where I was living, to eat Korean food with friends. Soon I would see my error in thinking of "Korean food" as a unity, a singular national cuisine; it's easy to make a comprehensive statement about a cuisine when you aren't in its home places. Living in Japan, for example, turned "Japanese" food into a complex set of cuisines, not a single thing at all.

At a restaurant in Seoul called Jihwaja, I ate a meal of dishes from the late fourteenth to early fifteenth century, emulating the court food of the early Choson Dynasty. This meant a meal made without ingredients introduced from the West, like chili peppers, which didn't arrive in Korea until the sixteenth century. This was thus an un-Korean meal, as modern Koreans understand their food. Korean dishes are iconically red and spicy, deriving heat and color from chili peppers that grow in Korea but that are not native to the Korean peninsula. The delicacies I ate that day were not spicy and were much paler and more delicate than the foods we take for Korean today.

Around that time, a Korean television series had become a hit: *Daejanggum*, a melodrama about early modern Korean court cooking and medicine, which conjured a more isolated version of Korea. The show, which followed the adventures of a young woman protagonist, offered viewers a welcome escape from the Asian financial crisis of the late 1990s. It allowed them to romanticize the past by looking at images of pre-globalization banquets. *Daejanggum* was part of a cultural retreat from globalization and foreign influence, a celebration of Korean indigeneity. So was my meal at Jihwaja, which had opened in 1991.

Jihwaja's menu required so much explanation from the waitstaff that it practically had footnotes. There were several soups, spotted throughout service: one flavored with miso paste and shredded vegetables; a cold seaweed soup; and a clear beef soup. There were dumplings (*mandu*) and noodles, oyster stew with salted shrimp, tofu dishes, many side dishes made with eggs and radish and cabbage and seafood—and much more that escapes memory. But there was also a more modern surprise: an apologetic server produced kimchi, made with *gochujang*, the post-Columbian, and ubiquitous, red chili condiment. As if not even this pre-Columbian Korean meal could do without this particular version of kimchi.

With that kimchi, Jihwaja bowed to the simple truth that there is no such thing as a pure version of any national cuisine, if that would mean a style of cooking untouched by other places and traditions. But even without the chilis in the supplementary *gochujang*, the meal was not indigenous. Chinese influences were everywhere, for it was from China that soybeans (and thus miso, and soy sauce) came to Korea, as well as rice and chopsticks.

We can try to peel away the layers of "foreign" foods and remove them from our cuisines, but there is no center to reach, no absolutely Korean food, no "natural" state of any national cuisine. Such a thing simply does not exist. But there may be something distinctly modern about the effort to make one by reaching into the past. You could call the gesture an expression of "modern archaism," whose real meanings have to do with vexation at the contemporary world, a strongly felt need to escape the present. Thus do people reach for "authentic" foods, and attempt to codify culture and identity in dishes somehow validated as forever reliable and true. And thus do people seek the "original," the first iteration of a dish. In a turbulent world, why not dream of a less difficult past, one in which a single, undiluted culture settled every issue of meaning, every question of flavor, creating a sort of mental pilgrimage to a source, an origin? Myth has its temptations. There are controversies surrounding the origin of kimchi itself. Some archaeological evidence speaks to ancient origins for this dish (which after all, does not require the post-Columbian chilis that go into *gochujang*); ceramic fermentation vessels suggest that *kimjang*, the practice of making kimchi, is thousands of years old. Yet other scholars have argued that kimchi is less ancient, and postdates Chinese and Japanese influence in the Korean peninsula, leading to controversy and debate. If "authentic" national cuisines are myths, the interesting thing is that people keep looking for them.

The day after my meal at Jihwaja, I still felt overwhelmed, and could barely look at food. I glanced wanly at my Korean breakfast, which smelled delicious despite my condition: a bowl of *jook* (rice gruel) topped with kimchi. If there is no kimchi, are you really eating?

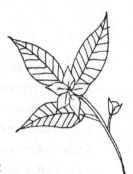

CHAPTER 4

The Columbian Exchange

Or, the World Remade

THE "COLUMBIAN EXCHANGE" refers to the movements of plants and animals between Eurasia and the Americas beginning in 1492. This chapter describes how two continentally delineated pantries became one, with effects so broad that Alfred Crosby, in his classic study *The Columbian Exchange*, invoked the idea of a sudden and decisive tectonic shift, as if the global redistribution of the potato were the sudden up-thrusting of a volcanic island chain.[1] He was not being melodramatic. Think of pizza, which features a base of crusty flatbread with an ancient history in Europe, topped with new-world plants like the tomato, and you might nod in agreement.

In the early modern period Crosby's biological tectonic shift reshaped agriculture and foodways around the world. It began when Europeans reached what they eventually called the Americas, "discovering" lands already well-known to the people living there. They introduced strange new animal and plant species like the pig, the cow, and the horse (itself a terrifying weapon of war); they introduced deadly diseases against which the natives of the Americas had no biological defense. And they traveled back to their own continent bringing staple crops and other food plants that would transform the tables of commoners and elites from the British Isles to East Asia and beyond. Chinese regional cuisines received the chili, which had first appeared in what is now Ecuador, and the peanut, originally domes-

[92]

ticated in what is now Paraguay or Bolivia. Soon Chinese aristocrats demonstrated their wealth by offering their guests exotic ingredients brought from distant places, as ancient imperial elites had once done. And the European colonization of the Americas would reshape foodways on the continents of the "New World" both for natives and for settlers and their descendants, as it reshaped everything else.

Culinary cultures worldwide changed beyond the recognition of earlier generations. Consider more menu items typical in Italy today: a plate of antipasto, including roasted peppers and zucchini, or a pasta or polenta course with fresh tomato sauce. Italians had pasta before 1492 (indeed, before 1295, when Marco Polo returned from China) but they had none of the other items. Korean food contained no chili. The familiar heat we associate with Korean dishes was a sixteenth-century latecomer. And the iconic potatoes of Ireland hadn't made it there yet. Some of the foods that traveled to the Old World, like corn and manioc, were un-nutritious or even poisonous without the processing techniques developed by New World natives.

No one sailed across the Atlantic for exploration alone, for the risks of high seas voyages in the fifteenth century were far too great. When Europeans sailed west to reach the Spice Islands, they sought wealth. They hoped that these new routes would be safer, shorter, and less pirate-infested than the familiar easterly routes. The first adventurers were Spanish and Portuguese: Christopher Columbus, Vasco da Gama, and Ferdinand Magellan are familiar names from the first generations of voyagers who sailed in the late fifteenth and early sixteenth centuries. Improvements in shipbuilding facilitated their expeditions. The shipyards of Genoa and Portugal developed a boat called a "carrack" or "nau," a square-rigged, six-sailed larger ship well suited to ocean sailing; more fragile medieval boats had rarely ventured beyond the Mediterranean. At the start of the sixteenth century the Portuguese sailed carracks on long expeditions east, and by 1515, Portuguese traders were trading silver for spices in

Goa, already (as of 1510) a Portuguese possession. These ships displaced over a thousand tons of water, and soon made it to China and Japan, opening up East Asian trade routes. As is well known, Columbus mistook the islands of the Caribbean for an extension of the Spice Islands of Southeast Asia. His journals often refer to his proximity to "Cipangu," his name for Japan, the same name Marco Polo had used. But the plants, animals, terrain, and human populations that Columbus and his crew encountered were new, unfamiliar to anyone who had visited the real Spice Islands.

As Charles C. Mann points out in his *1491*, a study of pre-Columbian civilization in the Americas, much of the accumulated writing on Native Americans has been characterized by the erroneous belief that they did not modify their environments.[2] In fact, natives in the Americas were as diverse as peoples elsewhere in the world, and so were their relationships with nature. The Americas had their own "Neolithic Revolution," and their own emergence of agriculture. Native Americans farmed throughout what would be called South, Central, and North America, in many cases transforming the environment to do so, though some groups did live more or less as hunters and gatherers, subsisting in environmental niches they modified less intensely.[3] In North America, East Coast tribes burned the forest along the shore to a considerable depth as they made fires to smoke fish; from the Great Plains to the Atlantic, Native Americans used fire to groom and thin the forests, creating artificial plains in which they cultivated herds of bison as a food source. Fire was also a ubiquitous tool for hunting.

By the time Columbus arrived, many cities had flourished in South America, such as those of the rival cultures Tiwanaku and Wari (forerunners of the Inca); some Mayan cities had populations in the millions, all fed by farming, with maize prominent in their diet. In fact, one explanation for the sudden collapse of Mayan civilization is that as their population grew they developed too much of their land for farming, and soil erosion destroyed their agriculture when they needed it most. While many native communities in North America, particularly on the Great Plains, lived technologically less sophisticated lives, they nevertheless traveled, traded, and communicated across great distances; there were trade networks a thousand years old at the time of Columbus. In the year 1491 there was no empire on Earth larger, in terms of territory, than that of the Inca, though it would collapse not long after the Spanish arrived.

As late as 1834, a historian like George Bancroft could still argue that pre-Columbian North America had been "an unproductive waste," meaning that it had not been developed for agriculture. But as many scholars have since shown, the combination of disease and European conquistadors destroyed not just humans, but the civilizations they built throughout the Americas. Indeed, the illusion that Europeans arrived in a landscape as untrammeled as Paradise was false: the diseases Europeans brought with them as they infiltrated and conquered the continent killed so many natives that signs of civilization, such as the native modification of the natural environment to secure food sources, began to vanish. The forests filled in the gaps where fire had trimmed them, the terraced hillsides became overgrown once more, and the herds of food animals dispersed.

Christopher Columbus (born Cristoforo Colombo in Genoa, 1451, died in Valladolid, Spain, 1506) set out to find a shorter route to the Spice Islands than the well-charted but perilous eastern one. He had the financial backing of his royal Spanish masters, King Ferdinand and Queen Isabella. The usual routes from Europe were long. Merchants went through the Mediterranean, across land to the Red Sea, through the Arabian Ocean to the Bay of Bengal and on to the Moluccas. By then everyone knew that the earth was round: contrary to legend, Columbus was not setting out to prove a global theory. Instead Columbus, extrapolating from the idea of the world as a globe, figured that the Spice Islands could be reached by going west over the sea, and surmised that this would be a shorter journey. He hoped for clear sailing and open waters, free from the pirates who haunted the Indian Ocean. When he reached the Americas, located inconveniently in the way, he persisted in believing them to be the sources of spices, though the landscape, natives, flora and fauna were completely different from those described or brought back by returning spice traders from the Moluccas. In search of cloves, nutmeg, and pepper, Columbus instead found "*aji,*" the local word for chili peppers. He landed at what he called Hispaniola (the island is now the Dominican Republic and Haiti) and at other Caribbean islands, but displayed a curious resistance to the reality of what he had done. He kept insisting that he had made the trip almost to the Moluccas. Columbus sniffed and scraped at local trees, seeds, and roots, swearing they could be cinnamon, cloves, or ginger, explaining that they didn't taste just right because they were "out of season." And to the end of his life, Columbus believed he had been only a day's sailing, a hair's-breadth away, from the Moluccas themselves.

Though he returned to Europe without eastern spices, Columbus's voyage encouraged many to follow. The Portuguese sailor Fernao de Maghalaes, later known as Magellan, embarked on his own famous voyages in 1519. Magellan had the benefit of Columbus's findings. He knew beforehand that America was between the Iberian Peninsula and the riches of spice. But he did not know how much of America one had to literally encompass by sailing around it. Much of his voyage around South America and across the Pacific consisted of desperate days at sea without fresh food or water. After Magellan's death at the hands of a chieftain in what are now called the Philippines, his remaining sailors finally found the Moluccas and the prized cloves. In the end, only four of the almost three hundred sailors who had left Spain with Magellan returned home, and with hardly any reward to show for their deadly journey.

Later, legends of the gold of El Dorado ("the gilded one")—a land of gold-cobbled streets and precious stones embedded in marble palaces—tempted many European ships to the New World, and many did not return. In fact, more ships increased the risk of ocean travel as pirates learned the most heavily trafficked trade routes and preyed on outbound and inbound travelers. None of the adventurers operated independently. Rather, they were representatives of European states and their nobility, who served as financial sponsors. From the fifteenth to the seventeenth century travelers explored new routes to known targets such as the Moluccas, or launched even riskier voyages of discovery, seeking new lands and new sources of profit. The Europeans found human populations, crops, and animals of kinds they had never seen before.

Portuguese and Spanish visitors to the southern portions of the New World found that they needed to adjust their own diets, in part because of tropical climates utterly unsuited for propagating some European crops, especially fruit trees or grains like wheat, which required more temperate climes. The tropical humidity affected prepared foods as well. One missionary said that the wheaten wafers used for Communion would "bend like to wet paper, by reason of the extreme humidity and heat." Local starches such as manioc could be used to make a bread-like substance, but the European appetite for wheat bread could not be satisfied in Brazil. And European prejudices were a powerful force. Many explorers and settlers did not consider what the local "Indians" ate to be civilized or even properly human food. The local populations were no doubt surprised by the visitors' foods and doubted their humanity as well.

At first the Spaniards and Portuguese tried to propagate European nut trees, such as walnuts or hazelnuts, but they planted them in areas too warm for these species to thrive; in any case, the sailors were not expert farmers to begin with. Corn and manioc made acceptable substitutes for some familiar foods, but the Europeans found the potato (originally from Peru) less palatable. On Columbus's second visit to "Hispaniola," in 1493, he brought seeds and cuttings of some European plants, and found that they sprouted, took root, and grew quickly and effectively. Perhaps the most important was sugarcane, originally from the Indian subcontinent. It would become one of the most economically significant crops in the New World. Grapes, from which the Europeans hoped to make wine, did not fare well. Coffee and tobacco did better. Europeans also brought domesticated animals (the largest domesticated animal in the New World, before contact, was the llama), such as horses and cows for transport and to yield meat and dairy products. Some fruit-bearing trees thrived, such as peaches, which were native to China but, because they had been transported to Europe through Persia, were sometimes called "Persian Apple." The banana tree, brought from the Canary Islands by the Europeans, grew quickly in some areas. So did figs, pomegranates, oranges, and lemons, although the latter, like most citrus, needed cool nights, and failed in excessively warm and moist climates.

The Aztecs who dominated Mexico and Central America (north of the Maya and far north of the Inca) were exemplary agricultural engineers.[4] Through conquest and administration they created a sophisticated agricultural society based on corn, which they irrigated using ditches called *chinampas*. The Aztec Empire is sometimes also called the Triple Alliance, as it was made up of three distinct Nahuatl-speaking city-states, Mexico-Tenochtitlan, Tetzcoco, and Tlacopan. The dominant Mexico-Tenochtitlan controlled the Central Mexican territory from the fourteenth century until the Spanish conquest; the Spanish would make Tenochtitlan their stronghold. Now Mexico City sprawls across the site of former Aztec rule.

Many northern Native Americans relied on "the three sisters"—corn, beans and squash—as their agricultural staples. As mentioned in chapter 1, corn is a cereal, a grass, whose ancestor is *teosinte*, a wild grass of Mexico and Central America, though there is some dispute over its history. Charles Mann writes that the creation of modern, domesticated corn from this plant was "a feat so improbable that archeologists and biologists have argued for decades over how it was achieved."[5] Modern corn is fairly hardy, can grow in warmer and cooler climates, and can adjust to longer and shorter growing seasons. Its kernels store well when dried. The Aztecs grew many kinds of corn, including yellow, black, blue, and white varieties. They also produced a corn-based beer, called *chicha*. To make this beer women would chew sprouted corn or other grains, spit it out, mix it with water, and allow it to ferment before boiling and straining it. A contemporary version of *chicha* is now produced by industrial means; in place of saliva (a good fermentation agent) yeast is added. Contemporary Tibetan and Ladakhi women, however, still make barley or millet beer, *chhaang,* in a similar fashion.

Corn may be a bountiful crop, but it is rather low in some nutrients, such as calcium. A diet high in corn needs more supplements than diets based on other staples. However, when prepared through nixtamalization to enhance its nutritional value, corn can be a satisfying staple, a good material out of which to make cakes, mush, bread, or flatbread. Nixtamalization is not an obvious processing technique: treating corn with ash might have occurred accidentally at first in the pre-Hispanic Americas. The conquistadors and later European visitors to Latin America had little interest in native preparation techniques, however (how could "uncivilized" people have any knowledge worth acquiring?), and so they ignored nixtamalization. This had dire consequences for populations in Europe who would grow dependent on corn without learning how to process it correctly. Many were stricken with pellagra and other vitamin deficiency diseases, which were often fatal.

In fact, at first Europeans saw corn as fit only for livestock and denigrated its use as human food; as one sixteenth-century Englishman, John Gerard, noted, "Wee have as yet no certaine proofe or experience concerning the vertues of this kinde of Corne; although the barbarous Indians, which know no better, are constrained to make a vertue of necessitie, and thinke it a good food: whereas we may easily judge, that it nourisheth but little, and is of hard and evill digestion, a more convenient food for swine than for man."[6] But corn became especially influential in Central and Southeastern Europe. By the late nineteenth century, more corn was grown and eaten in Romania than wheat, which was primarily grown for export. The "national dish" of Romanian peasants was *mamaliga,* a kind of corn porridge rather like Italian polenta, washed down with corn liquor.

There are other New World foods that require processing to make them palatable and safe for human consumption. Manioc (also known as yuca or cassava), for example, contains dangerous amounts of cyanide. Manioc was a staple food in the New World, growing where almost nothing else could, and yielded more reasonably nutritious calories per acre than any other New World crop. It is now tropical Africa's most important crop, feeding most of sub-Saharan Africa as a staple food. Nigeria is the largest producer of manioc but it is eaten everywhere, often as a starchy pudding-like food (a "swallow") with small amounts of vegetable, fish, or meat as condiments. Although it demands processing to remove the toxins, once processed manioc stores well for long periods of time. There are two types of manioc, "sweet" and "bitter." Ingesting the latter can be fatal if the cyanide is not processed out of it. The Tupi-Guarani Indians of central and coastal Brazil knew how to do this, as one fifteenth-century European traveler described. He reported that the Guarani people took the manioc root and "rubbe it on a stone and so it turneth to curdes, which thei take and put in a long, narowe bagge made of ryndes of trees [bark] and press out the liquor and gather it in a vessel, and when the iuce is out ther resteth in the bagge the floure as fine and white as the snowe, whereof thei make cakys and bake them upon the fier in a panne." Other techniques included pressing, boiling, soaking, and burying, the latter allowing the manioc to ferment.

It was highly unusual for a European traveler to take note of such practices, or to appreciate their value.

Potatoes and sweet potatoes, which became nutritional mainstays in many countries, first came to Europe as mere curiosities.[7] At first encounter the Europeans shunned potatoes, at least as human food, but potatoes had obvious advantages, for they grew easily, displaying good cold tolerance, and in large numbers. Still, their adoption as a food for humans took time. As late as Diderot and D'Alembert's 1751 *Encyclopedie,* the potato gets disdain: "This root is insipid and mealy. It cannot be classed among the agreeable foodstuffs, but it furnishes abundant and rather wholesome nutrition to men who are content to be nourished. The potato is justly regarded as flatulent, but what are winds to the vigorous organs of peasants and laborers?"[8] Elites despised foods they thought of as "windy," nor were they merely "content to be nourished." They required foods that lent them a certain prestige. Few foods from the New World fit the bill, at least at first. Elites would discover the potato's culinary possibilities only later, when the French court finally received the potato, delicately sliced and properly fitted out in truffles, cream, and butter. In generations to come the potato would be set out in casseroles with garlic and cream for the *bourgeoisie.* Notably, potatoes would eventually offer a kind of strategic advantage to the peasant farmers who grew them. While tax collectors or thieves could find grain stored after the harvest, a crop of potatoes was protected, hidden by the earth in which it grew.[9]

Other trade routes influenced the world's foodways from the fifteenth through seventeenth centuries. In some of the most difficult sailing conditions in the world, boatmen carried foodstuffs throughout Oceania, especially among the Micronesian and Polynesian islands. In Latin America archaeologists have found stone adzes from Hawai'i, which arrived as long ago as the fourteenth century. Such evidence attests to one of the longest uninterrupted premodern sea voyages, over 2500 miles of open water. Polynesian trade circuits crisscrossed the Pacific Ocean, carrying coconuts, other fruits, and pigs. Oral histories in the South Pacific tell of boats navigating by the stars to distant islands, carrying men and women selected to create new colonies. Polynesians traded foods between islands, carrying the means for planting and propagation from place to place. Fish and sea plants of many kinds were readily available. Staple starches included cassava and corms (the underground bulb of many different plants, including flowering ones), as well as other roots and tubers such as taro. Breadfruit was plentiful and was preserved and fermented in deep pits. Coconuts provided food and drink and the shell became a vessel for eating and drinking, as well as a source of fiber for weaving and construction. Most of these foods grew of their own accord and needed little tending or cultivation until the human population depending on them grew too large; here, too, we can observe the way human societies sometimes tip towards settled agriculture, as opposed to gathering, as their numbers increase.

Just as the Columbian Exchange moved people, plants and animals across the Atlantic, so the later movements of people and plants from Africa changed the menu of the Americas, though African food traditions often get neglected in our accounts of how the Americas changed. One of the most significant of the crops brought from Africa is rice, a staple food whose history links Africa and America and contains an irony: the food culture of an enslaved people would influence the foodways of their enslavers.

Stories of rice's origins and movements abound, and sometimes conflict with one another. The standing assumption is that rice originated in the Indus Valley, and that migratory groups brought it to East Asia, where it was domesticated in what is now China.[10] While it is often thought that Portuguese explorers and traders subsequently brought rice to Africa, in fact an independent indigenous African rice, *oryza glaberrima,* has been cultivated in West Africa for at least 3500 years. A whole cultural system, including planting techniques, gendered divisions of labor, and ideas about spirits who can make the earth productive, grew up around it.[11] African rice came to possess what Joanna Davidson calls a "core cultural logic," involving rituals, spirit-propitiating music, and dances at planting and harvest times. Rice became essential to a community's sense of identity. Rice rituals celebrated the staple, honoring it as it sustained a village. Rice, Davidson writes, "has been . . . perhaps *the* central feature that has textured land and livelihoods, persons and population flows, desires and dreams and disappointments." She quotes one person in Guinea-Bissau, her field site in West Africa: "Who are we without our rice?"[12] This rhetorical question might be asked in many rice-growing regions, such as Japan and parts of China, where a meal isn't a meal without rice, and the most substantial portion of people's daily caloric intake comes from this grass.

Enslaved African people established their preferred staple in the New World, and they brought their knowledge—rice values, rice rituals, and rice practices—too.[13] They brought their cultural expectations for how rice is to be prepared, distributed, and communally consumed. Their rice culture has exerted a strong and enduring influence in the Americas, particularly, but not exclusively, among those whose ancestors carried it across the Atlantic. Michael Twitty, reflecting on his African roots in Sierra Leone's rice culture, says that his relatives would say, "if you haven't eaten rice, you haven't eaten that day."[14] His Sierra Leone jollof rice, the "red rice" dish of memory and identity, connects him trans-Atlantically to his family's homeland. Jollof rice, cooked with tomatoes, onions, bell peppers, and spices, is so basic to his family that there is no recipe for it. A child learns about this rice by sitting in his grandmother's kitchen, alert to the pinch of this, and the handful of that, that makes the dish her own. Jollof rice was only one part of what Jessica Harris calls Africa's "extensive rice kitchen," which also includes the cracked rice of

Senegal, said to absorb sauces better than whole rice grains.[15] Enslaved Africans also brought hot sauces, "a connector of people throughout the African Atlantic world," as are the dried smoked shrimp of the Caribbean, used in Creole and Cajun foods as well as in Jamaican recipes.[16]

The Geechee-Gullah of Georgia and South Carolina retained many West and Central African foodways, using local "low country" ingredients to make dishes that were clear descendants of their ancestors' foods in Africa. Some of their ingredients had African roots, including rice and okra (the Gullah word for okra is "gumbo"), benne seeds (sesame seeds), and groundnuts (peanuts, themselves originally a New World crop). But some of their techniques, including their use of large pots for stewing large vegetables, their pilaf-like preparation of rice, and their use of "red" rice and long-grain Carolina rice, set Geechee-Gullah cooking apart, making it very different from other Africa-derived foodways in the Americas. This is an economical and practical cuisine. One-pot cooking saves fuel and doesn't require many vessels. In hard times, yams could cook in the ashes by the fire, while meat (if any) might hang above the cooking pot, smoking.

Peanuts returned to the Americas with enslaved peoples after having set down new roots in West Africa. The former British colony The Gambia, a small nation in the middle of Senegal along the Gambia River, has a large-scale production landscape of peanuts, the country's major export. One of your authors, on a visit to The Gambia, was served *domoda*, the "national dish" featuring vegetables, including yams and chicken in a rich groundnut sauce. This was both hospitality and a proud demonstration of locality. Peanuts feature in many West African sauces and stews, and in their North American descendants.

While African American cooking, often categorized as one foodway simply called "soul food" despite its great diversity, is well known, the souls who shaped it are usually not. The most famous African American agricultural scientist, George Washington Carver (1864–1943), many of whose contributions involved the peanut, was born to enslaved parents. His early work was on plant diseases, and his many innovations included using crop rotation and peanut-growing (since peanuts are a crop that "fixes" nitrogen in soil) to revitalize land depleted by cotton production. He invented more than three hundred peanut-based products, including oils, soaps, paper, and peanut-based medicines. Enlisting the support of the House of Representatives to get tariff protection for peanuts, he got a standing ovation as he cited their benefits and uses. In recent decades African American food historians, such as Harris and Twitty, have worked to bring the stories of African and African American foods to public light.

The Columbian Exchange was the most dramatic modern "biological event" affecting world food systems, but it was hardly the only one. The slave trade was another, as were myriad forms of colonialism and imperialism. Humans, plants, and animals have been redistributed around the world. Gradually, the exotic has grown familiar. The simple fact of biological reshuffling has become easy to ignore. Take the pineapple, a New World fruit that probably originated along the Paraguay River, and which Brazilian natives carried and planted as far as the Caribbean; Columbus found it in Guadeloupe in 1493. Pineapple is a bromeliad, which can be cultivated through cuttings taken from the crown of the fruit. The trees produce fruit within three years of planting. The fruit looks rather like a pinecone, hence the Spanish *pina* (Columbus called it *"pina des Indes."*) It is also called *anana*, or *ananas*, by the Tupi-Guarani peoples of Brazil. When pineapples reached England, they immediately became news. The English diarist John Evelyn wrote in 1661 that he saw the famous "Queen Pine" that had been brought from Barbados and given to the King; the first pineapple in England had arrived only four years earlier. By 1719 pineapples grew in European hothouses, and the fruit had become a symbol of wealth and hospitality. On older British doors, New England fenceposts, and French colonial mansions, you may see a carved wooden pineapple, signifying "welcome: here you will receive the best we have to offer." Europeans introduced the pineapple to Asia. Missionaries and traders (including, perhaps most famously, the Jesuits) brought pineapple cuttings with them, among other plants, and though they learned about native crops in the course of their travels, they also distributed new species. It is thought that a Spanish ship first introduced the pineapple to Hawai'i in the 1500s. However, pineapples would only gain their close association with the Hawai'ian Islands after 1813, when a horticulturalist reintroduced them there.

The foods we eat are not only an index of cultural change but result from the modern redistribution of plants and animals across the planet, a set of shifts that began with a European quest for wealth, and then ran wild in the centuries after Columbus. Setting the stage for that redistribution was a form of biological warfare: the attack by European microorganisms, which devastated the native population of the Americas and meant that, generations later, few of their descendants would taste the fruits of the Columbian Exchange.

The Spirit Safe

WE'RE TOURING A WHISKY DISTILLERY. High up on a metal platform near the stills, our guide shows us a rectangular box where several pipes, snaking out from the large tanks of the stills, converge. Tapcocks release small amounts of amber liquid, the developing whisky, into tasting cups. (Whiskey is spelled with the "e" in the United States and Ireland. It is generally spelled whisky without the "e" in Scotland, Canada, and Japan.) The door to this box is open. There's a slot for a padlock, but it's empty. This box is the "spirit safe," a device first used in Scotland and seen on many stills around the world, but never used for its original purpose here in Japan.

We're in Saitama Prefecture, north of Tokyo, at the prizewinning Chichibu Distillery. The owner, Akuto Ichiro (Japanese surnames precede given names), whose ancestors include several sake makers, founded his distillery in a town known for the quality of its water, a town where several beer breweries and sake distilleries already stand. Corky's research has brought us here. She is conducting an ethnographic study of the whisky industry in Japan. Part of the study is observing the work of distillation and the ways workers find value in what they do. Ethnography is about observation, rather than testing hypotheses that we bring to the field, but an observer always travels with baggage and expectations. For example, we expect Japanese whisky making to differ from its antecedent in Scotland, and we are looking around for the signs.

In Scotland, our Chichibu guide tells us, the spirit safes are locked because of a lack of trust. The workers might taste the product too often; they might steal. Management doesn't trust labor. Here in Japan things are different. Management not only trusts labor, it values labor's contribution to flavor. At Chichibu, whisky is made to very high standards, and involves not only the master but everyone on the floor as well. Everyone in the distillery, from the master to the women bottle-labelers on the floor, tastes the product. And everyone has a role to play in ensuring the high quality of the whisky. The larger narrative of Chichibu, we learn, is about teamwork and shared accountability, which translate into a better-quality whisky. Shared responsibility flows through the unlocked spirit safe.

This may be a true story about Chichibu, but it is only partially true about the spirit safe. There's a discrepancy between Chichibu's story of the spirit safe and the history of the device in Scotland and beyond. Scottish distillers didn't develop the spirit safe to keep their staff from tasting or stealing, but to comply with new taxes the state levied on them beginning in 1823. The spirit safe allows someone to sample whisky as it comes out of a still's condenser without opening the condenser or interfering with production. A hydrometer in the safe would also allow an operator to assess alcohol content from the outside. Tax bureau agents, rather than the distillers, held the keys. The agents visited distillers and opened their spirit safes to measure alcohol content, which had to be standardized across casks. Working without a spirit safe, as many American craft whiskey producers prefer to do (and which US law allows), means making "cuts" (switching containers that catch distillate) by taste and smell, rather than by measurement; one master distiller tells us that working with a spirit safe in the original way would be like making spirits via paint-by-numbers, rather than letting experience, intuition, and his senses guide him.

There is a lesson to learn from the discrepancy between Chichibu's story about the spirit safe and the history of that device, but it is not that the history is right and the Japanese distillers are wrong. The point of the clash is that the tales we tell about food and drink, and their origins, can circulate and remix. They readily depart from the original facts and take on new, vernacular meanings. Those vernacular meanings, and the way they express culture, interest us in the midst of fieldwork (not that we ignore the facts). After all, it suits Chichibu's purposes to tell a story about how Japanese distilleries emphasize teamwork, and, implicitly, are more "trusting" places. Spirit safes mean one thing at Chichibu, and another in mid-nineteenth-century Scotland, and another to contemporary American craft distillers; some artifacts are good to tell stories with. And anthropologists are storytellers too. We can quickly become enmeshed in the stories we pick up in the field, and we need to repeatedly check them against alternative stories, because we are interested both in factual accuracy, and in the way facts can look different depending on the purpose of the story at hand. Eventually, we do get our wee drams of Chichibu's whisky. It is beautifully made. It has bright notes, and depths, and it tastes—so we are told—of the local water.

CHAPTER 5

Social Beverages and Modernity

IN NEPAL IN THE 1970S, hotel workers made coffee with care, demonstrating their skill. They spooned Nescafe powder into a cup, followed by a spoonful of sugar. They brought out a heavy, silver-plated teapot with a narrow spout, steaming. A "coffee wallah" would drizzle the hot water over the sugary instant coffee, vigorously stir-ring with the other hand—or there might be two people working the cup, one whisking with the spoon very rapidly while the other poured the water, a little at a time. A high crown of beige foam appeared, cousin to what Italians call the "crema." The performance turned an industrial coffee product into a treat appropriate for an elite guest. And similar feats took place not only in Nepal, but also throughout the postcolonial world in the later twentieth century, wherever Nes-cafe traveled.

Food unites people who break bread together at the table, but cof-fee and tea—and the often-forgotten third member of the trio, chocolate—unite people in other ways at bars, counters, sidewalk ca-fes, and other social spaces, much as alcohol does. These three bev-erages, made from plants grown far beyond Europe, became part of Europe's colonial expansion throughout the world. All three were darkened by labor exploitation even as they gained status, first as lux-ury goods, then as objects of mass desire, and finally as ubiquitous features of daily life for Europeans. Coffee, tea, and chocolate are nutritionally inessential, but they function as stimulants, mood-changers, and social lubricants.

Of the three non-alcoholic social beverages, chocolate was the first one Europeans embraced, though coffee and tea eventually succeeded and superseded it. Of the three, only tea is now regularly drunk in the regions where it grows. Coffee, like chocolate, mostly gets consumed far from its roots. Why these three beverages, in particular? All have pharmacological, mind-changing qualities. They provide energy for socializing or a sense of private comfort. The current universality of these public drinks—perhaps especially coffee—suggests stories of movement just as salt, wheat, and sugar have their histories of trade and conquest. While alcoholic and caffeinated drinks have similar social functions, their histories are very different, and so are their usual connotations—the style of socializing we expect to do with them. The rabbi, the minister, and the priest walk into a bar for alcohol, but they have a very different kind of conversation over afternoon tea or coffee.

Tea

Tea is not only *camellia sinensis*, the originally Chinese tea plant; the word also means other botanical infusions, whether stimulating or calming. In the Arab world, for example, the category of tea might include hibiscus (Egypt) or black tea with cardamom (Persia) or mint (Morocco). During Japanese heat waves, *mugi-cha*, or barley tea, is the crucial beverage, brewed and drunk cold to deal with the humid heat of summer. Infusions of all kinds have served as *materia medica* and sources of pleasure and sociability. *Camellia sinensis* was the object of both high connoisseurship and mass consumption in China long before the English turned it into a colonial crop. Chinese tea originated in Southwest China and Tibet, and legends of its origins abound. In one story, an emperor was drinking a bowl of hot water in a garden. Leaves from a tea plant fell into it accidentally, yielding a pleasantly tannic flavor. Whatever its origin, tea was definitely popular in China, both as medicine and as social beverage, by the sixth century CE, and was sometimes used as money. Tea came to Japan in the bags of Buddhist priests, traveling along with Buddhism itself. Philosophers and poets expostulated about tea's flavors and pharmacological powers. The poet Lu Tong (790–835 CE) noted tea's physiological-poetic effects on the mind:

> The first bowl sleekly moistened throat and lips. The second banished all my loneliness. The third expelled the dullness from my mind, sharpening inspiration gained from all the books I've read. The fourth brought forth light perspiration, dispersing a lifetime's troubles through my pores. The fifth bowl cleansed every atom of my being. The sixth has made me kin to the Immortals. The seventh . . . I can take no more.

Lu Tong's readers would have understood that tea made him emotionally volatile, and they would also have understood the importance of brewing tea leaves several times in order to reach Lu Tong's heights of experience. For many tea drinkers, though, multiple steepings aren't just a way of getting new flavors from the same bag of leaves, but also a way of economizing. By the time Spanish and Portuguese missionaries reached East Asia, in the sixteenth century, *cha* or tea still seemed both medicinal and social—and while tea's associations with medicine would gradually drop away once it reached Britain, Lu Tong's sense of its function as an "upper" remained relevant.

Later European poets and writers, aware of writers like Lu Tong, would invoke Eastern tea appreciation in an orientalist fashion, exalting it sometimes to the point of parody, which spilled over to discussions of coffee. Alexander Pope's satiric verse "The Rape of the Lock" (published in 1712, during the first coffee boom in England) invokes tea to elaborate on the dangerous intoxication caused by coffee, which leads to a great crime, the snipping of a damsel's lock of hair:

> For lo! The board with cups and spoons is crowned,
> The berries crackle, and the mill turns round;
> On shining Altars of Japan they raise
> The silver lamp; the fiery spirits blaze:
> From silver spouts the grateful liquors glide,
> While China's earth receives the smoking tide. . . .

"Berries crackling" describes coffee roasting; the mill turns round to grind the beans. "Altars of Japan" means lacquer trays; "China's earth" means ceramic cups, used for coffee and tea alike.

Thomas Webster's 1862 painting *A Tea Party* shows an afternoon tea service in a working-class English household. The service includes tea, milk and cakes, a sugar bowl, and bread and butter. The painting's charm lies in its depiction of children, who serve each other tea to emulate adult behavior. They sit on the floor, near a woman who might be their grandmother, and are absorbed in their own meticulous replication of the "party" many adults would have enjoyed. One holds a doll, as if she were educating a new generation in the finer points of tea etiquette. Few images could be more emblematic of a particular kind of mid-nineteenth-century Englishness, and two elements in Webster's painting are products of Great Britain's colonial expansion. There is the tea itself, which the British first obtained through trade with China, and then produced on massive plantations in British India. Then there is sugar, produced by British colonies in the Caribbean, whose transformative effects on British diet and social life would rival those of tea.

Tea was quite well known in England by the mid-nineteenth century, and had been for generations, but Webster's scene reflected the mass market that the British East India Company had created by growing tea in Darjeeling, in the Himalayan foothills. The story of British tea in India begins with a Scottish botanist named Robert Fortune, who disguised himself as a Chinese nobleman and entered the Wu Si Shan hill region on a mission for the East India Company. Fortune stole seeds and plants, but just as importantly he was able to visit Chinese tea-processing workshops and learn the methods by which leaves were sorted, dried, fired, and rolled. He learned that green and black teas actually come from the same plant, though they are processed quite differently. His hosts taught him how to make tea multiple times from the same leaves. They told him that the third cup would be the best, whereas the very first infusion was "for your enemies," describing its bitterness more bluntly than Lu Tong. The seeds and plants that Fortune smuggled out became nursery stock in India, where *camellia sinensis* already grew in the region called Assam, though the Assamese took their tea primarily as medicine for headaches and gastro-intestinal distress.

By the mid-nineteenth century, Darjeeling and Assam were household words in Britain. The British also grew tea in Ceylon (now Sri Lanka). Growing, harvesting, and processing tea is labor-intensive, and throughout the British Empire, workers migrated to sites of tea production. For the East India Company Indian tea had many benefits, perhaps the most important being that the Company could transport it without paying the high excise taxes leveled on Chinese tea. Tea came to organize economic life in many parts of the British Raj, just as it began to organize social life back in England. The ease and lower cost of growing tea in British India allowed India-grown tea to supplant Chinese tea on the home market; it became one of the most profitable imports of the British East India Company. Tea became cheap enough for most to afford, and cheaper even than beer for poor laborers with unreliable incomes. Tea's promoters touted it as an alternative to gin, often thought of as a cause of public drunkenness and ruined lives. A hundred years earlier, William Hogarth had made this case in his famous pair of engravings "Gin Lane" and "Beer Street," which depicted depravity, abuse, poverty, and disorder on one road, and health, prosperity, and social order on the other. And tea was naturally much more "sober" than beer. In addition to convincing people to refrain from alcohol, the campaigning teetotalers of the 1830s had another priority: to unite families around their own private hearths, over tea. Beer had become suspect, not only because of its alcohol content, but because it seemed to keep men away from their homes, as they primarily drank beer in taverns, which were usually all-male social spaces.

British society was changing thanks to industrialization, which refigured lives around productivity and established new ways of dividing the day, particularly but not exclusively for factory workers. Homes became spaces of solace and support, away from the dirt and danger of industry, and tea (more than coffee, more than beer) was the beverage of domesticity. In the factories, managers increasingly measured workers' productivity, and tea and the sugar that sweetened it were ideal sources of energy. Gradually, even the poorest members of British society began to consume a product imported from the other side of the world. As economies of scale and colonial regimes of production reduced tea's costs, tea boosted workers' productivity in British factories. In 1700 some twenty thousand pounds of tea were imported; only ten years later this had increased to sixty thousand pounds, and by 1800 the imported tea amounted to twenty million pounds.[1] Tea was thoroughly English by the mid-nineteenth century and became a normal part of each day for most Britons. Its associations with the East and with colonial power were still there, sometimes conveyed by orientalist cartoons of tea-drinking mandarins printed on tea packaging.

One minor mystery is why tea beat coffee in the British Isles. Coffee arrived first, in the early seventeenth century, and quickly gained a considerable foothold. There was nothing like it; weak, low-alcohol or "small" beer was the everyday social beverage of choice at the time. There was no precedent for a beverage that was hot and bitter and caffeinated rather than cold and alcoholic. Coffee arguably created an entirely new category of drink. Tea's victory over coffee may be explained by the fact that tea worked better as a mass-produced cheap beverage; many British consumers preferred low-quality tea to low-quality coffee, especially when they doctored the former with milk and sugar. The reason was that bad coffee's heavy, bitter taste often prevails over such additions. Another explanation, just as important and more explicitly political, was that coffee was not a British colonial crop. And in fact, tea only dominated coffee after the British East India Company established its plantations in Assam, Bengal, Darjeeling, and elsewhere.

As Webster's painting shows, making tea can be a social act. Brewing is often ritualized, even made ceremonial. Tea is a convener, a social stimulant leading to conversation and shared time. In Morocco, tea preparation is a chance to train the young, and boys learn to pour boiling hot water from a distance of two or even three feet over the pot. Elders watch, comment, criticize, and instruct. Why that height? It is not just a coming-of-age test of muscular control. The elders explain that making tea this way aerates the water, enhances flavor, and creates froth, which is a sign of good hospitality. Making tea well is a way of demonstrating adulthood, at least in one small area of life—much as the children in Webster's painting emulate adults in preparation for the teatimes of their grownup years.

The mid-nineteenth century English home set its schedule around tea. Teatime came at the end of the workday, providing rest from productive work done outside the home, as well as from the labor done inside. In many homes, "tea" was also a light meal, and for children it might be the last meal before bedtime. This tea would most likely include sweet dishes, cakes and puddings, reflecting the ubiquitous presence of sugar in everyone's diet. Sugar had become an ingredient and not just a condiment.

Tea (in many forms) now has sway over much of the world, especially in East Asia and extending through Central Asia to the Middle East. Tea is part of daily socializing in China and India and has been thoroughly assimilated in former British colonies. The beautiful tea service and its gear in Turkey, the elegantly served fruit teas of Korea, and the meditative tea ceremony of Japan reflect local tastes and traditional versions of sociality; tea often serves as a vehicle for expressing hospitality or kindness. And yet we can also sip tea at a sidewalk café, free of any assumption of formality.

Sugar

Thomas Bertram, a character in Jane Austen's novel *Mansfield Park,* owned a sugar plantation in Antigua, one of many British Caribbean holdings worked by enslaved people.[2] Sugar grew best on Caribbean islands that had fresh water, but Antigua had little, making its plantations more vulnerable to drought. During times when England and France were at peace, Bertram and other Antiguan plantation owners could get water from nearby French-held islands, but war made this impossible. At one point in *Mansfield Park,* Bertram leaves England to travel for two years (likely 1810–12) to tend to his plantation, which may have suffered from drought or from the mismanagements of an unscrupulous overseer. There is much conjecture in the Austen critical corpus about the decline in the family's fortunes. It was common knowledge in England that sugar could make or break a family. Like its companion, tea, sugar had become a dietary necessity across the class spectrum by the mid-nineteenth century in Britain. Productivity was all, and sugar's capacity to provide energy for work, both industrial and white-collar, was as important as its sweetness.

Beginning in ancient Greece and then running through the late medieval era in Europe, sugar (sucrose) was usually seen as medicine. In the Arab pharmacopoeia, sugar was used in decoctions, infusions, and other kinds of medicinal treatments, and it traveled across Europe with Arab traders, as well as with Spanish and Persian merchants. Galenic medicine was based on the theory of the humors and sought balance in the body. Galenic physicians identified sugar as a "hot" substance, effective in balancing "cold" substances or conditions. It was not, for example, for treating young men, who were seen as hot by nature. But for the right patients, sugar could heal a wide variety of ills. It could break fevers, cure a stomachache, halt lung disease, and clear skin eruptions. Its role in creating tooth decay was recognized, but oddly, it was also used as a dentifrice.

Gradually, sugar began to be used as a spice, as a condiment, and as a flavoring ingredient. Among European elites it became a way to demonstrate wealth, and decorative desserts made of shaped sugar served as banquet centerpieces. In wealthier Sicilian households, a decorated solid sugar lamb was placed on the Easter table year after year, a kind of family heirloom and a mark of the family's good fortune. As Sidney Mintz put it in his *Sweetness and Power: The Place of Sugar in Modern History*, eating sugar "dramatized privilege," much like eating crushed pearls.[3] As sugar became more available in Britain, it began to be used as an ingredient in cooking and baking, and rested in sugar bowls on almost everyone's table. It was also used as a preservative: fruits might be crystallized or candied in sugar for out-of-season use.

The concept of dessert emerged relatively recently in European history. It was more common to end a meal with nuts and fruit until the late seventeenth century when "sweetmeats" were added to the menu. Only in the early nineteenth century did the "pudding" course, in England, become an ordinary and expected part of a meal. But, by the 1890s, the average Briton consumed about ninety pounds of sugar per year, much of it with tea and coffee. That figure does not include the sugar in industrially processed foods, which were gaining popularity. The British rationed sugar during World War II, and afterwards consumption skyrocketed, with effects visible in the teeth of people who were children then, who were suddenly and generously given candy treats.

Sugar only provided calories, not nutrients, and it was used as a caloric supplement by a working society whose diet was often monotonous and nutritionally inadequate. Sugar's great importance in British life only increased as it became cheaper and more plentiful. As Mintz argued, it gradually went from being a luxury of the very wealthy that carried a great "display value," to a necessity for workers and their families. Sugar could make life sweet in the small bits of time that industrial living left for pleasure. Sugar could help make a busy and difficult life seem better than it was, both by its calories and by its symbolism, for even after it had become a normal part of a working-class existence, sugar, like tea, carried a trace of its old association with the rich. Mintz has shown that sugar was part of a set of "aspirational" consumer goods, allowing consumers to feel that they might "*become* different by *consuming* differently."[4] In a status-conscious society, sugar offered an illusion of elevation.

Viewed from the perspective of world-spanning networks of production, sugar was a basis for the growth of an economic and political system, a system reliant on the possibility of "scaling up" dependency on sugar. Practically speaking, the British government, and businessmen like Austen's fictional Bertram, continued to expand their colonial holdings and worked to increase demand for sugar at home. Adding colonial sugar to colonial tea guaranteed both habituation and profits. Sugar thus simultaneously enriched the powerful while providing millions with a tangible sense of upward mobility, though this was usually a sweet fantasy. From a Marxist perspective, refined sugar was indeed an "opiate of the masses," and "its consumption was a symbolic demonstration that the system that produced it was successful."[5]

Chocolate

"Chocolate . . . a journey to distant lands to help the best cocoa varieties grow and thrive. Forming relationships of friendship, respect and partnership with the people who live where cocoa grows, keepers of ancient knowledge. An encounter with the past and a link to the future." Thus reads the label on a bar of chocolate, 70 percent dark, from a single origin source in Venezuela, made by a chocolate-maker named Amedei, in Tuscany, Italy. This is strange language, and not only because it is the language of marketing, which tends towards hyperbole. This product copy seems to unwittingly evoke chocolate's bitter history of colonialism and exploited labor, even as it spins a romanticizing contemporary dream about chocolate's roots and workers. Like tea, like coffee, chocolate can have drug-like effects—creating, some say, a satisfying palliative for life's cares. Chocolate, like tea and coffee, was, for the longest part of its history, a beverage, and pre-eminently a social beverage.

Like coffee, chocolate's main markets are far from the lands where it is grown. Cacao thrives in humid, tropical conditions, and seems to have emerged first in what is now Mexico. The Olmec people were first to turn the cacao plant's large beans into a beverage, and much later, the Maya—as far back as 1000 CE—consumed chocolate as a ritual drink, frothed with a carved wooden spinning "whisk" called now in Mexico a *molinillo*, a mill. Their word for the beverage, made from powdered cacao, was *xocolatl*, "bitter water"—from which our "chocolate" comes. Cacao, whole or powdered, was used at Mayan wedding ceremonies, or as offerings to the gods, or as tribute to rulers. A luxury item, it was also used as money, as were peppercorns and nutmeg in Europe. Warriors drank *xocolatl* for energy before going into battle. The homelands of the Aztecs were too cool and dry for growing cacao, but as the Aztec Empire grew, they acquired new farmlands, and the trade in cacao built the fortunes of Aztec merchants.

Spanish conquistadors brought cacao back to Europe in the sixteenth century, after they conquered Mexico. As Europeans colonized warmer countries, they spread cacao production around the world, and it grew sharply by the early 1700s, about the same time as sugar plantations began to spread. Chocolate houses sprang up in England, the first one opening in 1657, not many years after the first coffee houses. Indeed, in many establishments chocolate and coffee were both served, as men gathered to socialize, exchange information, and talk politics, though coffee eventually eclipsed chocolate as a beverage of choice.

In the eighteenth century new technologies enabled more efficient grinding of cacao seeds into paste. In the nineteenth century, new techniques developed in France and Holland allowed chocolate makers to separate cocoa butter from chocolate, yielding cocoa powder, and making it possible for chocolate makers in those countries— which had established colonies in Africa and other warmer areas, where they could grow their own cacao—to produce solid chocolate. Other leaders in the creation of chocolate candies, bars, and "eating chocolate" (as opposed to "drinking chocolate") were certain influential Quaker families of England: the Frys, Rowntrees, and Cadburys. The industrial history of Quaker chocolate is also one of innovation in the treatment of labor. Although earlier Quakers made fortunes in the slave trade, by the nineteenth century most were abolitionists, avoiding slave labor in the fields and also establishing better living conditions for industrial workers in Britain. They built housing tracts and saw their workers as members of the "corporate family" of the firm. Not all chocolate production had this benevolent scaffolding.

Chocolate, like coffee, tea, and sugar, became an "affordable luxury" for the middle classes. Unlike coffee and tea, chocolate gained an additional association with celebration. In 1861 Richard Cadbury linked chocolate and romance by putting chocolates in a red heart-shaped cardboard box, an innovation that reached the American market at the end of the nineteenth century. Chocolate signaled both decadence and sexual seduction and appeared alongside hearts-and-flowers imagery each and every February 14, St. Valentine's Day. By the early post-World War II years in Japan, chocolate and Valentine's Day had become synonymous, as the confectionary industry promoted the sale of chocolate. But while American women could expect chocolates from their love interests, Japanese women had to purchase chocolates for the men in their lives, including men to whom their obligations were non-romantic: *giri choko* or "obligation chocolate" was given to colleagues and bosses as well as to romantic partners. The confection industry noted that the Japanese tradition of "return gifting" could be exploited and established a second holiday on which chocolate reciprocity was required: "White Day," March 14, a month after Valentine's Day, when the male recipients of the previous month's chocolates would give white chocolates to the women who had given them brown.

Less ritually or romantically, the US military included chocolate bars in the ration packets given to soldiers in the Second World War, following an earlier example set by the British. In 1937, the US government had asked the Hershey Company to create a chocolate bar for military emergency use. They wanted a four-ounce bar with a high caloric value and a high melting temperature. They wanted it to be tasteless; they did not want it eaten for pleasure. The resulting "D ration bar" of chocolate, sugar, skim milk, and oat flour was exactly what was ordered. As you might imagine, the D ration bar never became an object of post-war nostalgia for the troops, but it helped propel Hershey towards dominance in the American market. Across the Atlantic, the counterpart British bar, Bendick's Sporting and Military Chocolate, now discontinued, gave chocolate a muscular, masculine quality that no heart-shaped Valentine box could convey. On their expedition to the peak of Mount Everest in 1953, Sir Edmund Hillary and Tenzing Norgay famously depended on Kendal Mint Cakes (a Lake District sweet) because chocolate was still under wartime rationing in England, but all Everest expeditions since have carried chocolate. One of us, trekking up the Kali Gandaki river between Dhaulagiri and Annapurna, had her chocolate rations eaten by her guide, who disappeared while she slept, and she soldiered on sola, unfortified by what was and is a source of energy and solace.

Chocolate is now primarily a sweet worldwide, enjoyed in company with sugar, but chocolate is also an ingredient in savory foods, most notably in *moles,* the preparation used in Oaxacan and other Mexican cuisines, close to cacao's geographic origin. A *mole* is a refined, layered thing. Often about thirty different ingredients go into the sauce and there are regional and family variants that create and demand connoisseurship across, and beyond, Mexico. And a *mole* calls for specific kinds of cacao, rather than for chocolate in general.

Chocolate marketing campaigns can make a troubled history of exploitation seem almost romantic, but many in the industry now pay close attention to labor conditions. Much Latin American chocolate now comes from Brazil, Peru, Ecuador, and the Dominican Republic. Comparatively little is produced in Mexico, though in 2019 a campaign to reconstruct the ancient Mexican cacao industry began to take shape. Many consumers have become concerned about the near-slavery conditions of cacao labor in sub-Saharan Africa (no longer colonial, but still exploitative). Some manufacturers, in turn, have started to change their ways. Agencies such as Fairtrade and Equal Exchange have begun to certify chocolate operations as environmentally sound, and sound in their treatment of workers; the same is true of tea and coffee production.

Coffee

Coffee is ubiquitous, at least in countries that import coffee beans. Few people in coffee-producing countries drink it. Huge economic disparities divide the lives of most coffee drinkers from the lives of most coffee producers; only in Brazil do people who produce coffee also drink it regularly. But in the coffee-drinking world, the beverage is everywhere, consumed across all social categories except age; like tea, coffee is usually thought of as a beverage for adults. As with tea and chocolate, environment is crucial in coffee production. Coffee grows best in tropical and semi-tropical regions twenty-five degrees north and south of the equator. Altitude and moisture contribute to quality: the best beans (by the standards of experts) grow on slopes between three and six thousand feet above sea level, and the premium varietal is Arabica. However, the varietal Robusta (heavily grown in Vietnam and Brazil) is a close second, valued for making espresso and iced coffee. Robusta is also hardier than Arabica—the name literally means "robust"—and can grow at lower altitudes. Robusta is more resistant to pests and coffee diseases, such as coffee rust, which creates characteristic rust-like marks on the leaves of coffee plants and threatens crops in many coffee-producing countries.

Coffee first grew in Yemen and Ethiopia where, according to legend, a goatherd named Kaldi noticed that his goats were especially frisky after eating certain red "cherries" from a bush. Investigating, he picked the berries and took them to his imam to inquire about their properties. The imam tried some and found himself invigorated. After many experiments, the community developed a technique for drying the cherries of the coffee plant, then grinding them up and boiling them in water to produce an infusion. The imam and his fellow priests found that, after drinking it, they could stay awake to pray late into the night. The legend of Kaldi is probably just that, but it suggests that coffee's power as a drug stood out to its earliest users.

From northeast Africa, where it was cultivated by the sixth century CE if not before, coffee came to Europe in the bags of Arab traders who brought it to Malta and the Iberian Peninsula in the early 1500s. Later, coffee moved further north and west through the travels of a handful of Europeans. It made its way to Sicily by ship and reached Venice by the 1530s. Not long after, in the mid-1500s, Portuguese missionaries and traders took it as far east as Japan, where the Japanese understood it as medicine, specifically a cure for insomnia.

In the early 1600s, a young student from Crete named Nathaniel Canopius brought coffee to Oxford and served it in his college rooms. Eventually a coffee shop opened in Oxford and in the same year, 1652, Pasqua Rosee, a Greek or Armenian (his origins remain mysterious), established London's first coffee house in the area now called the City, and the beverage caught the attention of merchants and bankers. Coffee took hold on the continent a few decades later, in Vienna, in another development whose details remain murky. The facts have been covered over by the following story, which may be a myth: the Ottoman army was defeated at the Battle of Vienna in 1683, and they left behind their camels, laden with saddlebags. Some of those bags contained a strange bean that the Austrians could not identify. A Pole, Georg Franz Kolchitzsky, who worked for the Austrians as a translator, had enough experience with the Ottomans that he recognized the beans for what they were: coffee. He took the bags back to Vienna and started what is said to be the first continental coffee house, the Blue Bottle (Hof zur Blauen Flasche), in 1686. Novelties often encounter resistance; an early-seventeenth-century Pope, Clement VIII, was asked to ban coffee as an Islamic and thus anti-Christian influence, but tasting it, he said, "this Satan's drink is delicious. . . . We shall fool Satan by baptizing it and making it a truly Christian beverage."[6]

Soon, the cocoa houses of London became coffee houses and coffee held sway there until tea supplanted it. The British did not grow coffee in their colonies. By the mid-seventeenth century, the Dutch had begun to develop coffee in Sri Lanka (then Ceylon) and from there they grew coffee in Java and throughout the East Indies. Dutch Java would eventually displace Yemeni Mocha, called after the Yemeni port city of that name, in international trade, and the name Java would become synonymous with coffee around the world. Coffee dominated tea in Britain's North American colonies, partly because of the close association between tea and Britain, which exploited its American subjects—although not in the manner it exploited enslaved people in the Caribbean. The Boston Tea Party of 1773 made tea a symbol of colonial control and of taxation without representation, and coffee houses became hotbeds of revolution, establishing an association between coffee and politics that survived long after the American Revolution in cities like New York and Philadelphia.

Coffee, like tea, earned an early reputation as a sober drink, linked with temperance. Both beverages also developed an association with free, liberal talk, and thus attracted critics and enemies, notably rulers who feared their subjects convening in venues outside their control. Almost outlawed in England but never cast down from a position of social prominence, coffee was the centerpiece of social spaces where people might meet friends and strangers, profit from conversation or find solace from the pressures of work or home. The social theorist Jürgen Habermas has identified coffee houses as an important part of the development and spread of what is commonly called "the public sphere," beginning in the mid-seventeenth century in England.[7] A conversational space between government and the individuals who made up the bourgeois public, the public sphere admitted people from different backgrounds and conditions of life, and gave them an opportunity to discuss the political and economic conditions under which they lived. Even as business deals were sealed in coffee houses, men exchanged news and opinions about governance. Coffee house sociability was various in kind, but it was always more sober than the kind of socializing that went on in taverns under the influence of alcohol, and coffee houses took on associations with information exchange, even as critics associated them with time-wasting and idleness.

By the eighteenth century coffee produced wealth for colonial countries such as Holland (which had colonized Indonesia) and France and Portugal, which held colonies in Africa. However, by the end of the nineteenth century, Brazil, which had been independent of Portugal since 1822, had started to produce coffee. Brazil would eventually become the largest coffee producer in the world. In the early twentieth century Japanese farmers were brought to São Paulo to work in coffee, and some who returned to Japan created the world's first coffee shop chain, called the Cafes Paulista.

Coffee's success in Japan is a story unto itself.[8] While coffee arrived in Japan in 1549, brought by Portuguese missionaries and traders, it took centuries for coffee drinking to become popular, and even overtake tea as a daily beverage for many Japanese. The world's third-largest coffee importing country, after the United States and Germany (which turns much of its imported coffee into "coffee products" like syrups), Japan has become an exporter of coffee techniques and trends. In a contemporary Japanese *kissa* or coffee house, the "pour-over" method of coffeemaking, can entail a kind of performance; it is not quite a tea ceremony but conveys a similar sense of hospitality. While espresso machines can be found all over Japan, a pour-over is the essential *kissa* drink. The barista grinds the coffee at the exact moment the water comes off the boil and begins to cool. She pours the water slowly and meticulously in a spiral pattern over the grounds, which sit in a filter holder over a glass pot, perhaps with a wood neck. This style of coffee, noted in the older coffee houses, is said to be "hand-made"—and thus has more cultural cachet than espresso, said to be made at a distance, through the intervention of a machine. Pour-over coffee shares "hand-made" status with siphon coffee, a technique that arrived in Japan with Dutch traders in the eighteenth century. Espresso, made popular in Japan by Italians, but most particularly by the arrival of American chain cafes at the end of the twentieth century, has its own Japanese adherents. For some of them, espresso can be "hand-made" too, depending on how precisely one uses it. "I have made the espresso machine," one Japanese coffee man said, "into an extension of my arm."[9]

Wherever people drink coffee, they tend to attach social functions to it—and indeed, there is a coffee ceremony in Ethiopia itself. Sharing coffee (*buna tetu or buna inibila,* in Amharic) is synonymous with socializing. The performance is said to have emerged in Southwest Ethiopia, but now is a regular event almost everywhere. A woman usually performs the act, which may include roasting green beans in a pan over an open fire, and then grinding the beans with a mortar and pestle. As in the Japanese tea ceremony, the goal is to create a good cup for a friend, and the steps take time. The grounds are mixed with hot water in a clay pot with a straw lid, stirred, sieved several times, and poured continuously over cups on a tray until all are filled. There are a series of cups to drink, some of them including sugar, others salt and butter. Snacks are important; popcorn, served with coffee, is a sign of hospitality. Though coffee first grew in Ethiopia and Yemen, it took some time for the high quality of Ethiopian coffee to receive recognition. Specialty coffees range in their identity and character, and particular beans are often thought to express the *terroir,* literally the soil, of a particular place. Aficionados of Ethiopian coffees know to look for "tones of blueberry" in the Yrgacheffe, and know which beans to roast light, and which can sustain darker roasting. The surge of interest in Ethiopian coffee among baristas and coffee tourists has left locals bemused. Their tastes and their methods are very different from those of visiting "specialty coffee" experts, though they value their beans as highly as the foreigners do.

Authenticity in Panama

I WAS IN A FOREST, high up on a Pacific Rim mountain ridge, and a man with whom I didn't share a language showed me how to twist a coffee cherry off its branch. We weren't in a simple forest. We stood in a coffee farm planned so that the coffee plants grew between trees and bushes and vines, protected by the shade (a rogue sunbeam found my neck). Benjamin, the English-language name of the Gnäbe tribesman who was showing me how to pick coffee cherries, seemed to know every square foot of it. Pointing at one cherry, then another, he indicated that I should look for fruits that were red all over, showing only a tiny bit of white at the stem, a sign that they would come off easily with a twist. We slowly filled a plastic bucket. Once processed, this coffee, called *gesha,* would fetch a high price from roasters. When roasted and brewed, it would win high ratings from coffee experts, who note its unusual flavor profile. Panamanian *gesha* coffee has quickly climbed to the top of international competitions. *Gesha* is a particular coffee varietal, a plant that grows slowly and produces fewer cherries than its more fecund cousins, and thus has been less popular with large-scale growers, like the ones working in Panama's lowlands, or in Brazil, or in many other places in the world where commodity coffee grows. *Gesha* is for the specialty market, which makes up a tiny percentage of the coffee enjoyed around the world each year. This happens to be the percentage close to my heart. That's what brought me to Panama. I was looking for something rare.

I was lucky to score an invitation to join a group of specialty coffee growers in Chiriquí Province, in the western highlands of Panama, along with a few other food and beverage writers. I jumped at the opportunity because except for one visit to a coffee plantation in Hawai'i, I had never before "gone to origin," as such trips are called in industry slang. This pilgrimage has become something like a *hajj* that certifies a coffee person's seriousness of intent. Coffee buyers, who travel from farm to farm working directly with growers, see a world of coffee production most coffee drinkers never will. The conditions that produce flavor are also conditions of labor, of environmental management, of processing. Our pleasure rests on other peoples' work. I wanted to taste coffee where it's grown, to put my hands in the soil, to feel the particular mists that land on the coffee plants— Boquete, among other coffee-growing towns in Chiriquí, enjoys a rain of almost misty fineness called the *bahareque*; in Japanese, such rain is *nuka-ame* or "rice-bran rain." I wanted to see if the idea of *terroir*, that taste expresses something in the soil, held truth. I was looking, even though I know better, for authenticity.

But "authenticity" is tricky. It's a word with old roots, starting with the ancient Greek *authentikos*, which means "genuine" or "principal." In Latin it became *authenticus*, and then took on other meanings in more modern languages, including connotations of authority and canonicity. Thus we search for the canonical *cacio e pepe*, the official *béchamel*, or "real" *nuoc cham*. The term implies that if you took a range of examples of a kind of thing, such as Panamanian *gesha*, you would find that some of them were closer to a Platonic ideal than others. The term "authentic" wouldn't need to exist if it weren't for the existence of approximations, copies, emulations, and downright fakes, or at least, things that a speaker or writer would like to tag and denigrate as such. "Authentic" suggests a certain anxiety about copying or being copied, or a fear of the ersatz. It's a term widely used by "chowhounds" who hunt for the "most authentic" version of a dish, be it searching Los Angeles's Koreatown for a black goat stew, or asking why a certain pizza seems to epitomize the New York style, or why a bagel studded with blueberries seems upsettingly "inauthentic." Authenticity is a sorting mechanism, a value word, and a term of praise, just as "inauthentic" is a purist's term of scorn. Taken to extremes, "authentic" makes a fetish of the social and environmental conditions that make an ingredient or dish possible.

In Boquete, coffee growers have analyzed the way the *bahareque* slows coffee cherries' development, which keeps them on the plant longer and allows them to accumulate more sugar. Panamanian *gesha* coffee is the product of happy chance, a plant winding up in a climate that produces flavorful cherries. Roasted light, it carries flavors I've never found in coffee before—from a tea-like smokiness to something like grapefruit peel. It changes my sense of what coffee can be. But none of this is authenticity, for authenticity is a quality we project onto things (food and drink included), rather than something things possess.

I am curious why so many people use the word "authentic" so often, in reference to food and drink. Some answers spring to mind: in an age of industrially processed ingredients, each package of flour is identical with the last, perfectly machine-ground and predictable in its behavior when you bake it into bread. Perhaps there is something appealing about unique ingredients with stories attached to them. By working with them and tasting them, we might learn the terms of production of the things we consume, terms that are usually impossible to know. In some circles such ingredients could also give us more cultural capital, just as a hand-carved wooden spoon is more unique than one stamped out of a metal plate, suggesting a premodern peasant vernacular rather than a modern industrial one. Oddly, under the right circumstances industrial things can have cultural capital too, when they manifest the "authenticity" of contemporary (and thus industrial) foodways. At a potluck dinner in San Francisco I watched with something like morbid curiosity as a woman arrived carrying a small purse, out of which she removed three cans: one of beans, one of cheese, and one of fried onion rings. She baked them in our host's oven, producing what she called Midwestern hot-dish, more alien to me than the samosa I once bought on the street in Delhi, but just as "authentic."

My sense that culinary authenticity is a kind of philosophical dead end doesn't address the idea's persistent appeal. We can dismiss the hunger for authentic versions of dishes on the grounds that authenticity doesn't exist, but people will continue to hunger. "Addiction to authority" is one of the phrases the philosopher and critic Theodor Adorno used to describe the mindset of authenticity.[1] Just tell us where to get our pizza, our bagels, and yes, our coffee. To restate my point: authenticity may not exist, but its existence does not matter for practical purposes, since it persists as a belief, a belief often fervently upheld, and for that reason we can never ignore it. Rightly or wrongly, our age values the *authentikos*, the genuine, amidst industrial standardization, widespread travel and migration, and an unprecedented level of contact between cooks and eaters of different cuisines. We should continue to ask why, recognizing that the issue of authenticity is a social issue that only appears to be a philosophical one.

CHAPTER 6

Colony and Curry

HERE IS A BRITISH COLONIAL recipe for Mulligatawny soup, presented in the 1861 edition of *Mrs. Beeton's Book of Household Management*:

> 2 tablespoonfuls of curry powder, 6 onions, 1 clove of garlic, 1 oz. of pounded almonds, a little lemon-pickle, or mango-juice, to taste; 1 fowl or rabbit, 4 slices of lean bacon; 2 quarts of medium stock, or, if wanted very good, best stock.
>
> *Mode.* Slice and fry the onions of a nice colour; line the stewpan with the bacon; cut up the rabbit or fowl into small joints, and slightly brown them; put in the fried onions, the garlic, and stock, and simmer gently till the meat is tender; skim very carefully, and when the meat is done, rub the curry powder to a smooth batter [ed: a roux]; add it to the soup with the almonds, which must be first pounded with a little of the stock. Put in seasoning and lemon-pickle or mango-juice to taste and serve boiled rice with it.[1]

And here is how novelist William Thackeray depicts an English encounter with Indian food, taking place just a few years later:

> 'I must be very quiet,' thought Rebecca, 'and very much interested about India'. . . . 'Give Miss Sharp some curry, my dear,' said

Mr. Sedley. . . . 'Do you find it as good as everything else from India?,' said Mr. Sedley. . . . 'Oh, excellent!' said Rebecca, who was suffering tortures with the cayenne pepper. 'Try a chili with it, Miss Sharp,' said Joseph, really interested. 'A chili,' said Rebecca, gasping. 'Oh yes!' She thought a chili was something cool, as its name imported. . . . 'How fresh and green they look'. . . . She laid down her fork. 'Water, for Heaven's sake, water!'²

There is a great distance between the hot chilis that Becky (Rebecca) Sharp ingests in Thackeray's 1847–48 novel *Vanity Fair* and the mild Mulligatawny soup described in *Mrs. Beeton's Book of Household Management,* a book that codified the blander culinary culture of domestic Victorian England. ("Mulligatawny" is from the Tamil; *molagu* is pepper, *thanni* is water). Call that distance the gap between the empire's reach and the English home, between an "exotic" world of conquered peoples and the safe domestic space of the hearth. Thackeray's scene captures the gap with a telling irony: a young Englishwoman, full of social aspiration, hopes to attract a returned English operative who worked in British India. Marrying him would raise her social position. Her target, Jo Sedley, is a member of the Raj, the term for Britain's imperial reign over much of India, which began under the auspices of the British East India Company in 1757 and passed to direct British rule in 1858. But Becky's efforts expose her combination of strategic enthusiasm and woeful ignorance of her intended's more cosmopolitan gastronomic experience. Of course, not every "Anglo-Indian" (meaning a British person living in India for an extended period of time) "went native," bringing home Kashmiri shawls, elephant-foot umbrella stands, and a taste for South Asian foods. This helps to explain the development of Mrs. Beeton's Mulligatawny soup, a dish mild enough for the average British palate, but still recognizably South Asian in inspiration. It evoked India and the Raj but would not offend, or inflame, English mouths.

The terms "colonialism" and "imperialism" are often used interchangeably, but they describe different political and military phenomena. Sometimes historians and social scientists define imperialism as the deliberate expansion of one state's rule over new territories; as noted in chapter 2, the English term comes from the Latin *imperium*, or rule. Colonialism, which comes from the Latin *colonus*, or farmer, is the establishment of settlements in new territories for the purpose of growing crops or extracting other resources. Colonialism, in other words, seeks economic gain first, whereas imperialism seeks political control. In many cases, such as that of the Raj, early colonialism gives way to later imperialism, and imperialism eventually became a doctrine in its own right. The British imperialist Cecil Rhodes, for whom the British colony Rhodesia was named, declared that he wanted to "paint the map red," and late-nineteenth-century maps and globes did indeed become pinkish to signify the British acquisition of territories throughout the world. By the time of the "Scramble for Africa" in the late nineteenth century, when European powers greatly expanded their African holdings until they controlled some 90 percent of the continent, imperialism had become a contest for dominance in which European rivalries played out on a global stage, with natural resources an important motivation for empire. This chapter examines the culinary effects of modern European imperial and colonial expansion, looking in turn at the British, Dutch, and French cases. These empires were short-lived when compared with ancient Rome, lasting only a couple of hundred years whereas Rome endured for over five hundred. But modern technology facilitated the Europeans' reach, and their modern empires helped to reshape the way the world eats.

The Sun Never Sets on the British Menu

British rule over most of the Indian subcontinent began with the arrival of the East India Company in the early 1600s. Trade led to wealth, and wealth, supported by military force, led to rule. By 1757, much of India was in the control of the British East India Company. By 1858, the Crown had taken control and much of India had become a colony of Great Britain. British culture disseminated through the behaviors of officials and through the institutions they ran, including the Indian Civil Service, the educational system, and other agencies. They introduced British social practices and foods (for example, afternoon tea was observed in the Civil Service) and such hybrid foods as "Gentleman's Relish" eventually appeared in middle-class Indian households. Created in 1828 by John Osborn, and made of mashed dried salty anchovies, butter, herbs, and spices, this paste reflected nineteenth-century British ideas about nutrition and flavor. Also called *patum peperium*, it traveled easily in its handsome ceramic pot, didn't spoil quickly, and spread on toast it became an easily prepared savory item—a necessary ending to a proper upper-class meal.

The foods of the British Empire included items from the American colonies, as well as from Britain's East African and Caribbean holdings and other colonies across the world, but it was "Indian" food, with its enormous regional variation, that had the greatest impact on the diet of the homeland. Mrs. Beeton, author of the *Book of Household Management*, was considered an authority in many English Victorian households and as such, was able to interpret and reconfigure Great Britain's imperial foods as they came home to Little England. Mulligatawny soup was not, strictly speaking, "Indian," but it was evidence of the tentative acquisition of "Indian" tastes by Anglo-Indians and their compatriots in England. The use of "curry powder" in this dish is a sign of a "native" foodstuff transformed: the soup, thickened with ground almonds, is actually closer to a hearty Victorian cream soup than to any of the soups of India.

British control over the Indian subcontinent, while not all-encompassing—there were "islands" of princely states which were at least semi-autonomous—was extensive and long-lasting. The India

Office in London created the structures of governance, and British district commissioners, who had the most contact with local people, sweated in their bungalows with scarcely a *punkah-wallah* (a fan-operating servant) to pull the louvered canvas sails that cooled their residences. They managed by accommodating in local ways to the heat and food (sometimes taking local women as "wives" as well) in small corners of India during the Raj. And while returnees to Britain might boast of their acquaintance with "real" Indian food, the British often maintained their own foodways as best they could while in India itself, teaching their Indian cooks (*khansamar*) to make a rib roast and boiled vegetable side dishes for a midday dinner. At this very English meal, Anglo-Indians would dress as they would have at home, in suits, waistcoats, and cravats, corsets and high-necked long dresses, and all this in the hundred-degree noontime Indian heat. While some were able to retreat to the cooler hill stations during the summer months, not all were so lucky, and had to stay on the sweltering plains. Heroic attempts to preserve customs away from home had political meaning. Food and formal clothing expressed identity—"we will be British, and keep our ways no matter what the struggle costs us"—and character, and power—"we are able to do this extraordinary thing, make these sacrifices of comfort, because we are made of the strong stuff that made us rulers of this empire." Capacity to remain British in all things was proof of legitimate rule. Furthermore, the British saw their manner of eating and drinking as a civilizing influence. As one colonial operative noted, the introduction of a regular English tea would be a sign of progress among the natives: "When they have Tea, they will want Sugar, Tea Cups—they will want a Table . . . then . . . seats to sit on. . . . European customs in a very short time will be wholly introduced."[3]

Older colonials felt that "eating Indian" was tantamount to "going native" or "letting down the side," a form of cultural treason. The phrase "plunging into the bazaar" was used to describe a British colonial who'd left off the constraints of British "civilization" and taken on the behaviors, dress, and apparent "chaos" of the locals, with the bazaar a symbolic teeming maelstrom of Indian custom and lawlessness. The empire struck back, however, as, gradually, Indian foodways found their way into English kitchens both on the subcontinent and in the homeland. Though culturally sanctioned roasts dominated the British table, there were also "curries" created to the tastes of the British. Curry powder itself is an Anglo-Indian invention. Indian cooks and housewives would not use such a standardized mixture of spices, though there were mixtures such as garam masala, used especially in the north of India, and in the south, a sambar powder used by Tamils. Usually, each region, village, and household would have its own mixtures, and the spices would certainly not be the same for every dish. Seven or eight distinct spices might possibly be toasted, ground, and compounded into whatever mixture or paste was needed. The British "curry powder," like the "chutney" created by the eponymous Major Grey, was always more generic and uniform than what it emulated.

On returning to England, former colonial operatives were often socially isolated and, even if they hadn't committed the treasonous cultural crime of developing an affinity for the natives, they might be branded as "damaged" by the experience of living abroad. At the very least, returnees often missed their servants, most particularly their Indian cooks. Some went so far as to bring their servants back to the British Isles, putting them in a difficult position, for they would have felt more socially isolated than their masters by far. But gradually other Indians arrived in England, especially those who had served the Raj, and who had been somewhat "anglicized" in the process. "Indian" dishes such as Mulligatawny soup and kedgeree became popular in Britain. Kedgeree, or *khichuri,* or *kitchiri,* is a colonial dish of smoked, cooked, flaked haddock served over spiced rice, and usually served at breakfast. The *tiffin* (the classic Indian lunch pail consisting of nesting levels) came home to England, and with the "Indian-ish" dishes within it, it could serve nostalgia—as had the tins of Jacob's Biscuits and other preserves and staples that had come out to India in hampers shipped from Fortnum and Mason's in London. The colonial table, as Lizzie Collingham notes, was a "theatre of [changing] British identity."[4]

Dutch Imperial Adventures On the Plate

The sun never set on the Dutch Empire, much as it never set on the British. Both spanned the globe. Founded through the actions of a trading company, much as the British Empire was, the Dutch Empire began with Dutch mercantile skill, eventually backed by Dutch military force. The establishment of the Dutch East India Company in 1602 and the Dutch West India Company in 1621 institutionalized Holland's extensive reach. And the traders' maritime and financial power became state power when the Dutch Republic took control of the Companies' holdings.

Speed at sea had made the Dutch successful competitors to Spanish and Portuguese adventurers early on. The Dutch also had financial and informational advantages, for they benefited from an influx of merchants and bankers who had migrated from Portugal to Antwerp and Amsterdam. Many of these were Jews whose families had been forced out of Portugal in 1492.[5] Enriched by the spice trade, which helped to fund the internal development of Holland (famously, the Dutch engaged in massive geoengineering projects, building dams and reclaiming land from the sea), the Dutch developed the largest fleet of merchant ships in the world, commanding the Baltic, trans-Atlantic, and Asian routes. The Dutch East India Company conducted spice expeditions to the Moluccas and other Southeast Asian territories, and they eventually established control over sources of nutmeg, cloves, and more, first by controlling sea routes and then the lands where the spices grew, often lands the Portuguese had previously held.

The Dutch found help in a set of maps of Portuguese trade routes smuggled out of Lisbon by a Dutch seafarer in the late sixteenth century. Maps were strategically significant objects, depicting shorelines, deep coastal waters, tidal irregularities, and safe harbors. Trade and political and military control depended on maps, and private ownership of maps was often punishable by death in maritime nations. The Portuguese routes, kept secret for generations, led to spices, sugar, and tea. The Dutch went from working with Portuguese maps to targeting Portuguese possessions in Southeast Asia, the Americas, and Africa, and they gradually drove the Portuguese out of their Asian holdings, seizing land, enslaved people, and sugar plantations as they went. Territories seized included spice- and tea-growing regions such as Ceylon (now Sri Lanka) together with its rich capital, Colombo (now Sinhala), Formosa (now Taiwan), Cochin, and Mauritius. The Portuguese found this latter island with only Dodo birds living on it; extracting their guano from Mauritius helped the Portuguese colonizers develop a rich agricultural base in their islands.

Pursuing their political and economic rivalry with Portugal, the Dutch soon dominated markets for Asian products in Europe. In addition, the Dutch seized control of Caribbean islands such as Sint Maarten (St. Martin), Curacao, Aruba, and Bonaire, giving them the productive salt fields of these islands. Salt, one of the most basic elements of the human diet, became the basis for the prosperity of Dutch traders, who floated luxuries back to Holland. Much as the Portuguese had done, the Dutch drank tea both for pleasure and as medicine, and Dutch physicians working for the Dutch East India Company were known to prescribe it to their patients.

The Dutch Golden Age spanned a century between 1575 and 1675 and saw a great increase in Dutch fortunes, as well as Dutch power around the globe. Literacy was high, engaging with the arts became a social imperative, and the arrival of immigrant talent enhanced native industry. Sephardic Jews from the Iberian Peninsula, Protestants from France, and others found Holland welcoming. Long a group of allied provinces, Holland only became the Kingdom of the Netherlands, as it is still called today, in 1815. Holland had, in fact, sometimes been held together by its power over its colonies, which exerted a politically stabilizing force at home. Yet Holland had little to call a "national" cuisine. It was hard to say what constituted "Dutch" food and what traits distinguished it from the foods of other lands. Featuring Northern European bread styles, an emphasis on vegetables and eventually potatoes and tree fruits as well, Dutch cuisine was a collection of homey, unelaborated domestic dishes. Commercial fishery focused on herring, which one writer said "determined the destiny of empires"[6] because it could be pickled, dried, and salted, and it traveled well, enhancing long voyages as well as long winters at home. More than the herring itself, Dutch ways of preserving fish were influential in keeping crews healthy and alive on months-long trips. Thus the requirements of long ocean voyages, particularly the need for food that did not spoil, led to changes in diet, and benefited later explorers, such as Captain Cook, who even introduced fermented foods on board, such as the antiscorbutic sauerkraut.

Dutch cooking tended towards simplicity, but the Dutch nevertheless readily adopted the spices that their merchant ships brought back. Their widespread use of spices was evident in cookbooks such as *De Verstandige Kok* (*The Sensible Cook*) published in 1669, which took full advantage of the exotic ingredients coming into Holland, offering dishes that featured turmeric and quince, coriander and pepper. However, by the nineteenth century, Dutch cooks had begun to eschew more stimulating ingredients in a trend towards ascetic frugality. The Dutch refer to "those who stay" and "those who travel," and divide their cuisine into two distinct categories: today the "home" menu is dominated by cheeses, potatoes, cabbages, chicken, and baked goods, while "exotic" items now found in restaurants or in any Dutch supermarket include galangal, cinnamon, *sambal oelek, satay* sauces, and various *ketjaps* (condiment sauces) enjoyed by even the most stay-at-home family.

As has so often happened, foods traveled from conquered lands to the conquerors' homelands as the plates of the rulers reflected the culinary ideas of those they ruled. The "travelers'" menu thus eventually came home. The Dutch counterpart to the British Mulligatawny soup and chicken tikka masala is *rijstafel,* or "rice table," a meal that draws inspiration from Indonesia but is not natively Indonesian. The style and service of a *rijstafel* was pure power theatre. It had its origins in a rather ostentatious colonial banquet eaten by the Dutch in Indonesia, and was made up of as many dishes as the host could afford. In fact, a colonial Dutch household in Indonesia would serve as many dishes as they had "boys"—servants who each would carry in one dish. A forty-"boy" *rijstafel* was not uncommon. The *rijstafel* had roots in Western Sumatra but was itself very multiethnic. From Java came *sateh* (or satay), from Sumatra, *rendang,* a spiced beef dish, and from local Chinese cooks *babi ketjap,* or pork belly cooked in sweet soy sauce. The "*ketjap*" in this dish is the ancestor of ketchup or catsup, which later, in the United States, became a tomato-based product. *Ketjap* had its origins in a variation on soy sauce, often containing fermented fish sauce or shrimp paste, and could be made of other produce, like tamarind, or, in England, walnuts or mushrooms.

The Dutch interest in food was also evident in paintings. During the Dutch Golden Age, at the height of imperial power, still-life paintings expressed pride in wealth and influence, often depicting foreign, tropical items which symbolized territories under Dutch control. In what appeared to be calm, European domestic scenes featuring kitchen tables or cloth-covered sideboards, exotic foods would appear. A small paring knife and a swirled peel of a lemon (a fruit that had to be expensively transported from Caribbean possessions) demonstrated, in artfully casual ways, the reach of empire. Often painters would show a cornucopia in their paintings, with ripe fruits and nuts tumbling out in profusion, indicating uncontainable wealth. Paintings of this period were very carefully detailed and sometimes served as botanical illustrations describing rarities. The paintings often also contained symbols of the Dutch mastery of, and dependence on, the sea: a whole fish might be draped over the side of a table, with a basket of oysters and clams nearby. Hunting prowess was shown through braces of hares or game birds. But such paintings were not simple celebrations. They also contained morality tales about gluttony and mortality and the transitory nature of ownership—and life itself. A bowl of ripe fruit often shows one apple or orange in a state of decay. Power, like the apple, might contain its own demise in the form of rot or a worm. Food, while representing conquest, was also an ideal subject for representing the passing nature of empire, which functioned as a word of caution: guard it well while you can.

The Sausage and the Glory That Was French Cuisine

Many years ago, the authors of this book were caught up in a surging crowd of James Brown fans at an outdoor concert in Paris, and one of us tripped and fell over an already felled sausage cart, landing face down in bright red uncooked sausages. Smeared with the fatty red dye and suffering a scraped ankle, she protested to the savior who lifted her from the grease, saying, "No, no, wait! Don't you see, these are *merguez!*" The sausages, a colonial food come home to Paris, were more important than escaping a crowd of Algerian James Brown devotees. The *merguez* sausage, often made with lamb or lamb and beef, spiced with cumin and chilis and served with harissa (red pepper paste), reminds us not only of the French colonization of North

Africa, but of the inroads that North African cultures have made in colonial France—often through the immigration of former French colonial subjects. And yet the fact that the *merguez* remains exotic within France illustrates something distinctive about the French imperial culinary experience: even as colonial encounters transformed foodways within the "hexagon" (geographic France), many French denied that this was happening, as if French culture and civilization were pure, unchanging things.

The French Empire was more precisely two sequential French imperial periods: one that began in the sixteenth century with the seizure of land in North America and the establishment of colonies, and concluded with the end of the Napoleonic era in 1815; and another that began with the conquest of Algiers in 1830 and then extended to include much of Northwest Africa, Indochina, and beyond, lasting well into the twentieth century. Often, French imperialists used the idea of a civilizing mission—*une mission civilisatrice*—to legitimate their political projects. During its two phases of imperial control, France's holdings reached from North America to North Africa, and from West Africa to Polynesia; it encompassed the Middle East and half of India, and included islands of great worth in the Caribbean Sea and Indian Ocean. As Van Troi Tran notes, at grand late-nineteenth-century expositions in French cities, parades of natives representing all the ethnicities under French control would demonstrate the empire's power and scope.[7] These natives, taken from their homes, would also act out their "daily lives" on small diorama-like sets. Part of the point of this display was to inculcate a sense of superiority among the French at the expositions. Did these natives eat raw food? Might they even be cannibals? In any case, the natives were backward and needed civilizing. If they could make progress, presumably that progress would include a change of diet.

The French occupied much of the Maghreb in North Africa, including Algeria, Morocco and Tunisia from 1830 to 1962. Much as

Indian foods changed the tastes of the British, couscous and other North African staples became part of the diets of French colonial operatives, who then brought them back to France. Yet figs, dates, and rosewater did not fundamentally alter French ideas about what counts as French food. France's core was (and remains) Paris, and its restaurants and chefs were codifiers of culinary civilization, and sources of national pride. They acquired that status as early as the eighteenth century. Until then, individual chefs were generally little known. Antonin Carême (1784–1833) and Auguste Escoffier (1846–1935), among other famous chefs and writers, established themselves as voices of *haute cuisine*, and arbiters of French culinary distinctiveness. Within the hexagon, France's culinary identity was not monolithic. It contained regionalisms, many of them based on a sense of local *terroir*. But that was an interior story, a feature of French life, rather than part of the ideology of French colonialism; beyond the hexagon, a more singular view of French culinary identity predominated as part of a "universal, secular 'culinary civilizing mission.'"[8] To cook and serve "French food" (as opposed to the food of any one part of France) became an imperial imperative among the French abroad, just as the British, in India, insisted on their own cuisine.

The crops grown in French colonies reflected French tastes. Although crop plants had to fit the local ecology and climate, they were inevitably planted because they also suited French diets and cuisine. In territories such as Algeria and Tunisia, which had large Muslim populations that did not drink alcohol, French colonials nevertheless planted grapes and eventually produced enough to support a large wine industry. Far-flung outposts of empire were encouraged to grow and eat "French:" bread rather than rice or cassava, and meat and vegetables, all following French preparations, however out of context and expensive to prepare. In French territories even today, such as St. Barthelemy in the Caribbean, many of the ingredients are flown in from France—even fresh fish.

The fallen raw *merguez* on the pavement at the Place de la Republique in June of 1995 was the street food of immigrants, but also an item desired by gourmets, an "ethnic" food given celebratory fanfare at festivals in Marseille.[9] These sausages also traveled (ironically, as if under a French passport) overseas, and artisanal butchers in Vermont and Wisconsin make them, invoking not the North African roots of these sausages, but their adoptive French-ness. Though the French sense of French cuisine remains restrictive, everyday French food practices are more inclusive than they once were. Street foods like *merguez* or meals of couscous, "Indochinese" noodles and "creole" fish stews, have entered everyone's vocabulary and diet, and foods from outside France (especially foods from Japan) have influenced high cuisine chefs in France. This means that cultural regulatory mechanisms are gradually becoming less restrictive, giving chefs permission to adapt, borrow, and learn from dishes around the world.

The Icebox

RUNNING BEHIND THE TRUCK with its open back door, as melting water dripped onto the road, I finally caught up with the iceman as he made his next stop. He took a scarred, wood-handled icepick and chipped off some shards from a big block of ice. He dropped them in my enameled tin cup. When my cousin caught up, panting, he gave her a few shards for her cup, too.

Every four or five days, the iceman would drive up to the cottage on the Minnesota lake where my family spent three months a year, the mosquito months. He was there to deliver ice for our icebox, a bulky, thick-walled structure in a small pantry off the kitchen. This box was lined with zinc, and insulated with cork, little bits of which we'd sometimes find strewn on the floor. My grandmother Lena governed the kitchen and she didn't have any patience with newfangled refrigerators, though her son-in-law, my uncle, ran an electric appliance store in Minneapolis, and my aunt kept pleading. My grandmother had her own ways of keeping food: canning, preserving, pickling. Cooking was at least as much about keeping and protecting the food as it was about flavor.

The fish Uncle Dave caught had to be cleaned right away, on a wooden board nailed to a tree behind the house, and then iced down in a bucket, if we weren't eating it that night. We cleaned and ate the vegetables from the garden the same day we picked them. We saved the icebox for keeping milk, cheese, eggs, and butter fresh.

When we finally did get a refrigerator, it meant we could store cold cuts from the Twin Cities, leftovers from the meals we made, and even pickled herring, which technically didn't need cold storage. And, many years later, after my grandmother passed on, there was a box freezer for Uncle Dave's fish.

The flavor of Granny's dill pickles, the chill of the air coming from the icebox on a very hot day ("shut that door! The ice will melt!") are sensory memories. They take me back to my family's practices, to our small, household-sized version of a larger culture, all at a specific historical moment. Memory is historically unreliable but full of personal meaning. Tinged with pleasure and loss, indulgence and hurt, memory has its own truth. Food memories can connect us not only to our past, but also to other people whose memories might resonate with our own. Sometimes, when speaking with other people of our own generation or even of our own family, we hear something that surprises us, or that clashes with our own recollections. Perhaps we have misremembered something? Memory's truth is no replacement for investigation.

I spoke with a friend whose mother had insisted on a dishwasher, and with another friend who brought out her mother's manual meat grinder, used to make "real" cranberry-orange sauce instead of using a food processor; we're all bouncing between technological generations in the kitchen, inconsistent in our choices, motivated sometimes by nostalgia, sometimes by a desire for efficiency. Once, mixing a great deal of batter for fruitcakes, more than would fit in a standing mixer, I remembered how my grandmother, despite her arthritis, would place a giant bowl on the floor and kneel to stir. So, squatting down on the floor to mix the stiff fruitcake batter with my hands, in a kettle once used to bathe babies, my body itself a kitchen tool, I thought, "oh this is cooking!" I felt some pride in that. But did my grandmother actually make dough that way?

The refrigerator meant that you could now buy or grow more than you could immediately use, and bag and freeze it, without brining, pickling, salting, or canning, methods that took time and attention. When canning, you had to be sure the seals on the jam jars were tight or the food inside might get contaminated. The refrigerator also saved daily trips to provisioners, kept milk longer and more safely, and made it less urgent to use up leftovers. The home cook could think more about pleasing palates than about food safety. As home canning, preserving, and pickling have become less important, they have become nostalgic hobbies. As I write, there are citrus rinds boiled in sugar syrup drying on trays on my radiators, quite unnecessary but pleasing: their aroma advocates for the "cottage" methods of preservation. Granny Lena's resistance to the electric refrigerator, however, did not mean that she didn't love the little boxes of Jell-O that sat in her pantry. She lived with her choices, not bothering to call them "tradition" or "progress."

CHAPTER 7

Food's Industrial Revolution

From 40 to 60 years ago, all the northern and western, and a part of the eastern tracts of the county, were sheep-walks. . . . Much of it was in this condition only 30 years ago. The great improvements have been made by means of the following circumstances.

FIRST. By enclosing without assistance of parliament.

SECOND. By a spirited use of marle and clay.

THIRD. By the introduction of an excellent course of crops.

FOURTH. By the culture of turnips well hand-hoed.

FIFTH. By the culture of clover and ray-grass.

SIXTH. By landlords granting long leases.

SEVENTH. By the country being divided chiefly into large farms.

ARTHUR YOUNG, *The Farmer's Tour Through the East of England* (1771)

IN 1770, THE ENGLISH WRITER and sometime farmer Arthur Young (1741–1820) toured the countryside. He recorded his observations on agriculture in *The Farmer's Tour Through the East of England,* one of many books he would produce on the transformation of farming in the British Isles. Young took particular note of a practice called "enclosure." Though enclosure was already well established in English and Welsh farming, promoters increasingly discussed it as a way to improve agriculture, making yields larger and less labor-intensive.

Under enclosure, fields previously used by an entire community under common agreement (regardless of who held the title) fell under a single landowner's control. The enclosure movement progressed over many decades in England and across Great Britain, and it had counterparts on the Continent as well. Enclosure helped prepare the way for the modernization of agriculture between 1700 and 1900, when foodways around the world were fundamentally transformed in economic, cultural, and social terms. Most immediately, it did make British agriculture more productive; the *Encyclopedia Britannica* of 1797 did not exaggerate when it boasted, "Britain alone exceeds all modern nations in husbandry." As Robert Allen points out in his *Enclosure and the Yeoman,* at the end of the eighteenth century English farms were about 50 percent more productive, per worker, than their counterparts on the Continent.[1] Over the course of the eighteenth century, Britain became the greatest commercial power in Europe, and in the nineteenth it became Europe's leading industrial nation.

Enclosure did not singlehandedly catalyze the dramatic technological, social and economic changes we often call the "Industrial Revolution" (often dated from around 1760 to around 1830). However, the transformation of agriculture was a significant driver of the Industrial Revolution, and enclosure was how it began. The consolidation of land in the hands of a few owners made it easier to change farming practices, to try new crops and drop less beneficial ones, or to adopt newly available farming equipment. Farmers have reason to be conservative. Rapid change means risk, and deviating from time-worn methods may mean losing a year's harvest. Prior to enclosure, an entire community had to agree on shifts in agricultural practice. After enclosure, individual landowners could decide to adopt new drainage systems, or the widespread distribution of clover, a crop especially useful for maintaining or improving soil fertility. Farming started to change faster.

The enclosure process actually began around 1500, at which point 45 percent of land had already been legally shifted from the old communal system into the hands of fewer landowners. Thus, as of 1700, only about 29 percent of land remained open, and that would shrink to 5 percent by 1914. At the time of Young's travels, most cases of enclosure took place through acts of Parliament issued at the request of the principal landowners of each village. Though they usually profited by enclosure, many of these landowners acted on the belief that with fewer, larger farms one could more efficiently increase gains, understood as the sum of wages earned by agricultural workers, profits earned by farmers, and rent earned by those landowners who rented their land out to be farmed. The agricultural revolution in Great Britain was essentially institutional, driven not by technological innovations like the famous steam engine but rather by placing decision-making power in the hands of fewer and fewer persons. The enclosure movement drastically increased the inequality between those who owned the land and those who farmed it. As Allen puts it, "by the nineteenth century, the landlord's mansion was lavish, the farmer's house modest, the labourer's cottage a hovel."[2]

Industrialization began in England and soon spread to continental Europe. For our purposes, we define industrialization as the shift from an agriculturally-based economy to one with a manufacturing base. Modernization, which presumes industrialization, is a broader term: it involves urbanization, reorganizing society around the goal of productivity, a tendency to de-emphasize the family as a social unit and to promote the individual as the most salient social unit instead, and what the sociologist Max Weber called "rationalization," a focus on calculated goals as opposed to values conveyed through tradition. Great Britain's industrialization did yield growth and progress in many senses, but when viewed from the perspective of workers, the period looks less like a triumphant surge forward. The British government tended to pass legislation that benefited landowners, inventors who filed patents (especially after the national Patent Office was established in 1852), and other businesspeople. Great Britain's industrialization led to Charles Dickens's social landscape, with its orphan workers and poorhouses, and it indirectly produced generations of social critics for whom industrialization, and modernization in general, had led not only to class warfare but also to a dehumanized form of everyday life in urban mass society. Among the many paradoxes of modernization is that within the "developed" world it has given more people access to more resources, even as it increases the distance between rich and poor.

The period of industrialization was also a time of massive enrichment for the fortunate, as well as a time when urbanization proceeded at a rapid clip and social life changed in many ways that are still with us today. The workforce was subdivided into more specialized categories than it had been before, producing a fore-glimmer of our contemporary division of labor. Crucially for the transformation of cooking and eating, workplaces split off from the domestic sphere, a social arrangement without which our contemporary food practices, both within the home and outside it, would never have emerged. While many women and men still worked in their homes, the practice of going from home to a factory or other workplace became widespread, and the family itself became less important as an organizing principle of social life—though many still took their midday meals at home. Not only was the household displaced, so was the seasonal timetable of the working year. The cycle of growing and harvesting regulated farm work, but the factories knew no natural timetable, often defying even the human need for rest.

The new division of labor not only transformed workplaces and domestic life, it also greatly accelerated the business of writing and selling cookbooks, whose chief consumer in the late eighteenth and early nineteenth century was a new kind of person: the middle-class woman, manager of a household. The idea that housewives (many of whom lost their cooks and other servants to the factories) needed manuals to teach them to cook, clean, and treat minor injuries and illnesses also appeared, as if materializing out of nowhere. Perhaps one's grandmother could cook, but she was not a "scientific" or "modern" cook, and this meant she had no authority; that had to be found in cookbooks. At the same time, women began to work outside the home in unprecedented numbers. This made it necessary to find new strategies to provision a household with food and to ensure cleanliness, and all this on a daily basis. The practice of eating in restaurants was not itself a product of industrialization, but it received a great boost from the new division of time between home and workplace.[3] Restaurants served a purely practical function on the one hand, providing food for those with no time to cook, but they also served what historians sometimes term a "gastronomic" function. They offered food that became a benchmark of culinary change, informing diners about current trends, and shifting their expectations for quality. This was not chiefly an elite phenomenon. Modest establishments and street-side stalls served food that marked shifts in food practices, and effectively educated all kinds of people about the types of dishes that were possible or desirable. Notably, this was also not a uniquely modern phenomenon. Across Europe and the Mediterranean world more broadly, street kitchens had influenced tastes for centuries, all the way back to the Roman Empire.

New industrial processes for producing and preserving food also altered the way people cooked and ate. Aspects of cooking, like the preparation of basic sauces, could be outsourced to industrial producers. The markets for many traditional "food crafts" such as brewing, baking, and butchering were transformed by the new scales of production. White milled flour, formerly only available to the very rich, became an everyday sight. While eating preserved food had been a feature of human foodways for thousands of years, the arrival of canned foods (invented in 1809 during the Napoleonic Wars) made it ubiquitous through the developing western world. By such technologies modernization vastly expanded the range of foods we can access while placing us further from the places where our food is grown.

In many countries, the advent of the railroads dramatically changed foodways by allowing merchants to send ingredients far from their origins. Eating seafood in Paris, for example, was made easier and more common once trains crisscrossed the country. Eventually, steamships connected food producers to consumer markets across oceans and borders, continuing and accelerating the global exchange of ingredients and dishes. Meals eaten out of doors at night in the great cities of Europe were illuminated by gas lamps and, in time, by electric lights. In Japan, the advent of trains in the last third of the nineteenth century made fish a common food throughout the country; before this time, fresh (or raw) fish was not consumed except in seaside towns and cities along Japan's coasts.

Some of the developments in agricultural practice described in this chapter, including the science of artificial nitrogen fixation, paved the way for the massive population growth of the twentieth century, as well as for the twentieth and twenty-first centuries' crises of malnourishment and starvation, which often result not from famine but from uneven food distribution. In parallel with these developments, modernization meant that food production and distribution began to be shaped by market forces in historically unprecedented ways. Food riots sprang up in towns and cities during Britain's eighteenth-century industrialization, produced by the breakdown of traditional arrangements through which all members of a community could expect to receive some bread or other foodstuffs. The legitimacy of the market as a means for distributing goods started to threaten the legitimacy of the community as a source of entitlements and security. In a loose sense these riots, more than simple "rumblings of the belly," anticipated the extreme inequalities of food distribution seen in later centuries, even in the wealthy and developed West.[4] Farmers became vulnerable to market forces in a way they had not been in previous generations, when farming had been practiced as a strategy of subsistence and communal welfare.

The Agricultural Revolution and the Industrial Revolution

An earlier view of the Industrial Revolution in Britain, as a suddenly surging "wave of gadgets" which led to ongoing technological progress and economic growth, has now given way to a more nuanced view. Historians today disentangle the effects of inventions, new practices of labor organization, government regulations, and economic changes, and observe how these different forces worked in concert. Some have used economic data to depict the change as slow-burning, not really a swift "revolution" at all, while others suggest that despite its qualitative transformation of daily life, and despite its massive effects on localized parts of the economy, the Industrial Revolution did not have such profound effects on the British economy as previously thought. Furthermore, economic historians draw on a range of sources in order to put forward various other arguments about the mid-eighteenth to the mid-nineteenth century in Great Britain: that its distinguishing feature was not really generalized progress but class struggle (in keeping with the social critics' version of the story of modernity); that the structural changes in British life were not really accompanied by rapid economic growth; and so forth. Some have even argued that, in the early stages of the Industrial Revolution, increased agricultural productivity was far more important than technological inventions considered on their own. As the overall percentage of male laborers who worked on farms declined substantially between 1700 and 1850, many workers were freed up to labor in the factories and workshops of the new industries. Without the agricultural revolution, its industrial counterpart would have had to find a different work force.

The "wave of gadgets" included the steam engine, the railroad train, gas lamps, Richard Arkwright's "water frame" or water-powered spinning machine, and, in one instance of an invention that did change agriculture directly, Jethro Tull's famous seed drill, a horse-drawn innovation which planted seeds far more regularly than hand-sowing could. Factories sprang up around the country, a mining boom was aided by steam engines that could extract water from mines, and trains carried raw materials to factories and then finished products to cities and markets. As production accelerated, the use of fossil fuels increased, and the lands where coal was mined were stripped bare.

As the factories grew, so did consumer interest in their products. It is no stretch to say that the rise of modern consumer culture is a direct result of industrialization. From the perspective of economic history, the Industrial Revolution meant that other sectors began to outpace agriculture as the most important drivers of economic growth, and the condition of Britain's gears began to be as important as the condition of her soil. But, as mentioned earlier, it was the agricultural revolution that led workers to move in from the countryside and fill the new factories.

In his travel writings in the late eighteenth century, Young praised those farmers he considered excellent in their efforts to "improve" the land. He took careful note of one set of new farming techniques, the influential "Norfolk System," named for where it first took hold towards the end of the seventeenth century and growing increasingly popular in the eighteenth. As Young put it, "No small farmers could effect such great things as have been done in Norfolk." The central elements of the system included the addition of clay or marl to soil that was too sandy to be farmed, as well as grazing animals on the fields so that their dung would serve as fertilizer. It also meant the practice of tenant farming: many of those working as farmers were not landowners, but tenants paying rent on the land they farmed, and much of the money made in agriculture was made by landlords, the ultimate winners of the enclosure movement. Additionally, at the heart of the Norfolk system was a four-course planting series lacking a "fallow year." In the first course (first year) wheat would be planted, followed by turnips in the second course, then barley, clover and rye in the third. Animals would graze on the clover and rye during the fourth year, and the turnips served as animal fodder during the cold months of winter. Not only did the Norfolk system eliminate fallowing and thus boost productivity, but by incorporating turnips and clover into the crop rotation it ensured that animals were fed, that their fertilizing dung was exploited as a resource, and that the soil was revitalized by clover.

The increased productivity of the Norfolk system and other innovations made more food available, which in turn tended to increase the rate of population growth and made continued improvements to agricultural production all the more vital. As T.S. Ashton put it, the problem of the eighteenth century was "how to feed and clothe and employ generations of children outnumbering by far those of any earlier time."[5] Not only in Great Britain but in Western and Central Europe as a whole, the period saw a massive "resource rush" often consisting—as it did in the emerging modern nations of Italy and Germany—in draining swamplands so that farms could be established; this was one of the themes of Goethe's great play *Faust*, finished in 1831, which describes the protagonist's efforts to master the forces of nature themselves, to make the sea and land serve humanity as sources of power, and describes Faust's crimes against the residents of the land he sought to exploit.

In some cases, as in that of Great Britain, intensified farming meant planting more grain and devoting less land to livestock. The result was that many peoples' diets began to feature more grain and less meat. Average per capita meat consumption in Europe declined during the transition from the medieval period to the modern. The grain-fed populations of Europe seem to have become smaller in stature during the late eighteenth to the early nineteenth centuries, and grain consumption only peaked during the last quarter of the nineteenth century.[6] Notably, the more dependent on a single crop or single type of crop Europeans became, the more they grew vulnerable to shortage or famine due to crop failure. The emphasis on grain production also contributed to a pan-European phenomenon: bread became a symbol of sustenance, and the default unit by which to measure the quality of a diet.[7]

Early modern Europe was essentially rural and the lifeways of its inhabitants were timed by the harvests. European cities were not the heavily populated spaces they are today, and some 80 or 90 percent of the Continent's population still lived in the countryside. Not only did Europe's population (both in Great Britain and the continental states) more than double between about 1500 and 1800, going from 80 million to 180 million, it urbanized dramatically. David Clark has identified two major "urban revolutions" in world history, the first coinciding with the development of agriculture, the second with the Industrial Revolution.[8] As mentioned earlier, one reason for the increase in population was the increase in agricultural yields; another was a growth in employment, which meant that people tended to marry and produce children at a younger age, leading to more children produced over a lifetime. The move to the cities was largely due to the factories, which employed ex-farmers forced out by enclosure. And industrialization led to the development of the Midlands and the growth of Manchester, Birmingham, and Leeds, which in the eighteenth century had been essentially rural locales but now became the heart of industrial England.

As the pace of production and commerce increased, the city served as an important social matrix for economic growth, a place where workers, inventors, businesspeople, and merchants all lived relatively close to one another and could communicate readily. This was not a uniquely modern phenomenon; even in the feudal medieval period, many European cities had been most important as places where merchants could effectively operate without undue interference. The city had served as a kind of engine of economic progress long before the physical engines of the Industrial Revolution began to hum. In fact it is possible to argue that urbanization both was produced by, and helped to produce, the Industrial Revolution, because it was in cities that people could form the complex and constant social relationships that drove innovation. It was in cities, with their factories and working men's organizations, that Britain's eighteenth- and nineteenth-century culture of mechanical aptitude and innovation took shape. Said aptitude was not held only by elites, such as the educated members of scientific societies; it was also the possession of everyday machinists whose daily efforts made the Revolution possible. In turn, technological development increased the pace of urbanization, a process that never stopped, and is still ongoing in the early twenty-first century.

Modernizing Cuisine

Cuisine underwent its own kind of modernization, and so did the tastes of European consumers. French cuisine led the way, and the case of French cuisine's modernization matters because it dominated Europe until the nineteenth century; in late seventeenth- and early eighteenth-century London one could even find French cooks in common taverns. Vegetables enjoyed a new visibility and became a prominent part of many peoples' diets. At the same time, the range of animals deemed suitable as food shrank, and herons, peacocks, and swans disappeared from banquet tables. Goats and sheep vanished from the diets of the wealthy, though the poor still ate them.

French cookbooks, as they emerged in the early modern period, began to mention not just the animal from which meat was desired but also the cut of meat preferred. This was a new innovation, which led to the idea of serving, as a dish, a particular cut of meat: tongue, hip, kidneys, tripe, and steak. Lists of ingredients in recipes became more specific, measurements more precise. Just as the number of animals deemed appropriate for cooking decreased, so did the range of spices considered proper to use. But one of the most recognizable tendencies in Western food, namely the assignation of sweetness to the end of a meal, arose only with French cuisine's modernization. Previously, it had not been uncommon to see sugar in meat, soup, and other courses. Eventually, however, sweet and savory seemed to stand in adversarial relation.[9] The influence of French cooking throughout Europe was profound, as a glance at the non-French cookbooks of the seventeenth and eighteenth centuries shows, but naturally some national differences persisted. For example, the British judged national cuisines by their beef, whereas in other countries, such as Italy or France, the important question was the quality of their bread.

Collections of recipes appeared before Johannes Gutenberg's introduction of moveable-type printing in 1450. In thirteenth- and fourteenth-century Europe, these collections were usually the work of professional cooks, and they were more directly practical and instructive than the literary productions of Apicius and other ancient writers on food. The advent of printing naturally increased the rate at which technical publications about food could appear and find readers. Some early printed works on food included Vittorio Lancelotti's collection of menus *Lo Scalco prattico* of 1627 and Pierre de Lune's *Le Nouveau et Parfait Maître d'hôtel* of 1662. In almost every case, early cookbooks were the works of cooks who found wealthy patrons, whose money enabled cooks to create elaborate dishes in the first place and then to publish books in which they described them. The modern cookbook did not develop as a distinct genre of its own at first, but rather emerged out of literatures of dietary advice which was also effectively medical advice. Early cookbooks often contained instructions for making sweets and cosmetics, especially if they were written with a wealthy female readership in mind. Indeed, the sixteenth century had seen the emergence of many works devoted to the codification of recipes for preserves, ranging from pickles to sweet jams made out of sugar or honey, called in French *livres de confitures*. The first cookbook printed in France was entitled *Le Viandier* (see chapter 3), and it was reprinted perhaps twenty-three times between 1486 and 1615.[10] Like many other early cookbooks it was a compendium of recipes published previously, including some from as early as the medieval period. The first English-language cookbook we might recognize as modern appeared in 1747: this was the *Art of Cookery*, by one Hannah Glasse, published in England. Among Glasse's contributions was to send the message, through recipes for pastries, that sugar was now an everyday commodity, and not for the wealthy alone. One of the most interesting aspects of the growth of the cookbook was simply that it introduced a new means of engaging with food: reading and writing. This meant not only that information about food became a commodity of sorts, in which cookbook authors traded, but also that the pleasures of the table could be enjoyed in a literary form. But it is also crucial to note that, prior to the rise of the middle class in Europe, which placed literate cooks in the kitchen in previously unheard-of numbers, cookbooks were not read by the same people who did the actual cooking.

After cooking, of course, one must clean. As expectations for new efficiencies in the kitchen rose, so did standards for food preparation at home and standards for home and personal maintenance. Late-eighteenth- and early-nineteenth-century cookbooks also provided "receipts" for making soap and other cleansers, both for the benefit of the woman of the household and for her (usually less literate) servants. In addition to colonial groceries such as tea, coffee, chocolate, and sugar, Britons and other Europeans began to import fats to make soap, including peanut oil, which the French imported from colonial Senegal, and coconut oil, which the British brought from India. This was done to answer rising demand for soap and other cleaning products on the European market; in nineteenth-century England soap use had tripled, going from around 24,100 tons per year to over 85,000. The sources of animal fats that had previously fed the soap industry were inadequate, given this scale. Europeans also imported more culinary vegetable oils, such as olive oil, with the welcome consequence that they began to consume more vegetables in the raw, in salads.

Nitrogen and a New World of People

While the farming "improvements" that Arthur Young surveyed did much to make British farmland more productive, they could not overcome the natural limits of soil fertility. The practice of letting land lie fallow for one or more growing seasons, of using fertilizers natural or artificial, and of rotating crops, have all been employed by farmers around the world, often in conjunction with one another. Mayan farmers used fields for a single season and then allowed them to lie fallow and become fertile again, sometimes slash-and-burning fields to clear old growth. In Han China farmers divided fields into three furrows, which left strips of land—"peaks" between furrows— unplanted and thus fallow, allowing them to regain their fertility. For thousands of years the soil rejuvenation process was managed not only through fallowing but also by means of the very crops farmers planted: clover and other beans have been prominent in almost every successful agricultural community in the world. Columella, a first-century CE Roman commentator on agriculture, advised farmers to use the Lucerne, or medic clover, which they fed to animals, and

Chinese farmers have long placed beans in their rotations of crop plants.

It was not until the development of modern chemistry that scientists began to understand what farmers had been doing since time immemorial. Fallowing, planting legumes, and using manure as fertilizer are all important parts of a process called nitrogen fixation.[11] One of the basic constituent elements of living things (others include carbon, oxygen, sulfur, hydrogen, and phosphorus), nitrogen forms a critical part of amino acids, which are in turn constituent parts of proteins, and nitrogen is also contained within nucleic acids.[12] Nitrogen fixation is worth dwelling on because, simply put, our contemporary farmlands could never provide enough food to support our current population levels without industrial-scale nitrogen fixation. Nitrogen (strictly speaking, dinitrogen gas) makes up about 80 percent of our atmosphere, but in its gaseous form it cannot be absorbed or processed by plants or animals. The molecular bond between the two nitrogen atoms of a molecule of dinitrogen gas must be broken, yielding a "fixed" form of nitrogen, before plants can take it up from the soil and use it. Without human intervention this takes place through what is usually termed "biological fixation," not actually done by crop plants themselves but by microorganisms in the soil that can convert dinitrogen to ammonia. Critical in this process (and thus critical to agriculture) are rhizobia, bacteria that attach themselves to the roots of plants and exist symbiotically with them. The most common plants that rhizobia "choose" are legumes such as beans and clover.

Progress towards industrial nitrogen fixation effectively began with the discovery of dinitrogen gas, achieved in 1774–75 by the English clergyman and natural philosopher (as scientists of his day were known) Joseph Priestley, who is more famous for his discovery of oxygen. Nitrogen itself had been discovered, or more precisely, isolated, by the Scotsman Daniel Rutherford in 1772. The full importance of this discovery for agriculture would become clear a century later when, in the late nineteenth century, scientists successfully transformed dinitrogen into ammonia.

The nineteenth century in Europe had seen a rush to import "fixed" nitrogen in a surprising form: bird guano, brought in by the shipload from Peru and other places where large, productive flocks gathered. The efficacy of such fertilizer had long been understood throughout Latin America, and the first Spanish conquistadors commented on it in writing. The Prussian naturalist Alexander von Humboldt examined a sample of guano brought back to Europe in 1804 and found it to be high in nitrogen and phosphorous, effectively confirming earlier Spanish observations of the efficacy of this method of fertilization. Soon guano became a mainstay of the Peruvian economy; British importation of the stuff began in 1820 and reached extremely high levels by the mid-nineteenth century, as did guano imports into the United States. While guano does indeed seem to have bolstered British agriculture during those peak years of imports, dependency on one source had terrible consequences when Peru's supply dwindled, eventually bottoming out in the 1880s. British farmers were able to use another imported fertilizer, saltpeter (nitrate) from Chile, but Peru's economy was crippled, and European scientists searched for an industrial process that might ensure the availability of nitrogen for agriculture. In 1898 the chemist Sir William Crookes captured the widespread sense of alarm in a volume called *The Wheat Problem*. As he put it, "The fixation of nitrogen is vital to the progress of civilized humanity."[13]

While Crookes meant only modern, developed countries when he wrote "civilized humanity," the industrial process of fixing nitrogen would affect the entire world. What we commonly term the Haber-Bosch process was first demonstrated by the German Jewish chemist Fritz Haber in 1909 and then scaled up for industrial production by the firm BASF in 1913. This process made ammonia out of dinitrogen and dihydrogen by passing these gases together over a catalyst at great pressure and heat. Notably, during the First World War the ammonia generated by the process was used to create nitric acid, and nitric acid was then used to create explosives. Haber himself became a weapons designer, catalyzing a kind of arms race in chemical weapons which led to the development of mustard gas. A hundred years after the Haber-Bosch process was pioneered, ammonia factories fix a hundred million tons of nitrogen per year, about equal to the amount fixed each year by natural biological processes. And industrial agriculture uses more and more artificial fertilizer; if in 1960 worldwide fertilizer usage per annum was roughly ten million tons, by 2001 it had gone up to eighty million tons. This increase is even greater than that of our global population, which was about three billion in 1960, and a little over six billion in 2001. As of this writing roughly eight billion people share the earth.

Through industrialization and modernization, food supply chains lengthened, our agricultural productivity increased, and the range of staple foods we consume grew more limited even as the range of foods available from around the world (for those living in metropolitan hubs, and especially in the West) grew. Immigration into the United States made that country a kind of social laboratory for mixing cuisines and incorporating new ingredients into them. And as the pace of daily life increased throughout the developed world, foods changed shape to accommodate the public's shifting needs. Perhaps the most familiar example of this change, for Westerners, is the industrial loaf of white bread, almost aerodynamic in form and available pre-sliced for extra convenience. By thinking about it we can "materialize" many of the questions of this book's closing chapters. In medieval England many workers had eaten as many as 70 or 80 percent of their daily calories in the form of bread, with bread's alcoholic cousin, beer, serving as an important supplement. While their nineteenth- and twentieth-century counterparts usually consumed a smaller percentage of their daily calories as bread, they were still enormously dependent on it, and factory production met their needs by taking up the task of baking. The factory gave bread a new incarnation many could associate with progress: standardized white loaves made with flour refined through industrial processes. Bakers learned to tame a form of nature, namely yeast, and turn it into something that production lines could manage. Soon working people could eat soft, pillowy bread made with white flour, something previously enjoyed only by the wealthy. Such bread became a symbol of plenty. How, then, did white bread eventually go from representing abundance, to representing poverty and ill health, a transformation that would take place in the late twentieth century? This is a modern question. In our next chapter we will explore a few answers.

Bricolage

SLICE A PASTRY IN HALF and you get an idea of what happened
in the oven. Breaking apart a croissant at Bricolage, a bakery-café in
Tokyo, we see laminations, scores of pastry layers created when the
heat of the oven hit alternating layers of dough and butter. The water
in those layers evaporated, and the steam puffed up the pastry. To set
up the conditions for this effect, the pastry chef creates layers of lean
pastry dough and butter through a sequence of rolls or turns. Laminations are widespread in pastry, and do not always act the way they
do in croissants; the laminations in Portuguese custard tarts called
pasteis de nata, visible in the tart's underside and rim, produce a
flakey crunch. Travelers to Japan used to experience surprise at the
high quality of Japanese croissants, the fact that they are "*plus francais que les croissants francais,*" but now it is common knowledge that
Japanese chefs apply themselves to mastering skills from all over the
world. A short walk from Bricolage is a pizza shop called Frey's,
whose pies meet the very high standards of the Associazione Verace
Pizza Napoletana, which has accredited more pizza in Tokyo than in
any other city in the world.

Are croissants Japanese? It is hard to answer "yes," but the ones
made by the pastry chefs at Bricolage are as good as any we've had.
Are croissants French? It is hard to answer "no," but one ancestor of
the French croissant is actually Viennese: it's called the *kipferl,* a cres-

cent of non-laminated dough made as long ago as the thirteenth century. The shape made its way to France in the nineteenth century, and the production of pastry dough received a major boost from industrialization; to produce croissants and other pastries *en masse* requires a dependable supply of standardized ingredients. The foods that we assume typify a place, or a culture, are not eternal absolutes. The idea, and the ingredients, had to come from somewhere, and perhaps not from the place most closely associated with the dish. Is pizza Italian? Yes, but the tomato didn't reach Italy until the sixteenth century.

Bricolage means "building with what you have." It derives from the French *bricoleur,* or handyman, but suggests an improviser willing and able to work with whatever's at hand. It's a common term in the arts. The Watts Towers, a set of spires built in Los Angeles by an Italian immigrant construction worker named Sabato Rodia, are one example. So, arguably, is a pizza topped with whatever you have in the fridge.

Claude Lévi-Strauss brought the term bricolage into widespread usage in his 1962 book *La Pensée sauvage* (*The Savage Mind*), where he used it to think about myth. A culture's system of mythic thought might include elements borrowed from other, prior, cultures. Lévi-Strauss juxtaposed the *bricoleur* against the craftsman and suggested that the former used more "devious" means to achieve his ends; craftspeople work in more predictable ways, using traditional techniques. Yet the line between craft and bricolage may not be so clear, because the supposedly stable traditions associated with craft are always changing, perhaps through the kind of improvisation that the term bricolage calls to mind.

The croissant itself was a kind of bricolage completed not by an individual *bricoleur,* but by generations of them. The classic French pastry combines pastry dough with a shape whose origin is hard to know for sure. According to some, the shape began in Vienna, first made to celebrate the defeat of the Ottomans who laid siege to the city in 1683; the crescent was on the Ottoman flag, and so to eat a crescent was a symbolic commemoration of victory. But crescent-shaped baked goods exist elsewhere in Europe and are sometimes thought to mimic the shape of the moon, a holdover from pagan celebrations. The pastry chef, like the *bricoleur*, makes layers. At Bricolage, a few pigeons wait nearby, eager to see what we drop.

CHAPTER 8

Twentieth-Century Foodways

Or, Big Food And Its Discontents

BY THE EARLY TWENTIETH CENTURY the food markets of the West seemed like beacons of prosperity to recent immigrants from poorer countries. Russian Jews living on New York's Lower East Side were often dazzled by the variety of goods sold from pushcarts. Almost a hundred years later, the supermarket is a marvel, but unrecognized as such because it is so commonplace. The central aisles are filled with canned goods, sauces in bottles, boxes of cereal, sacks of flour, sugar, and other processed dry ingredients, bags of snacks, refrigerated cases filled with frozen foods. Time seems to flow differently through the foods on display, many of which are filled with preservatives to guard against decay. Only at the periphery of the store are there stacks and pyramids and machine-misted cases of fresh fruits and vegetables, shipped in from far-away farms at considerable cost in gasoline, human labor, and carbon emissions. If this supermarket is in a European Union country there may be warning labels on fruits and vegetables grown from genetically modified seeds, or they might be banned altogether. In both European and North American markets, foods grown "organically" are labeled to distinguish them from "conventionally" grown produce; farms that wish to use the "organic" label usually go through a difficult and costly multiyear review process, after which they can sell their produce at a higher price. Even if supermarkets are only centrally important for consumers in the developed world, they have become symbols of gastronomic modernity.

You can read the supermarket like a record of the massive transformations of agricultural practice that took place during the twentieth century. Each of the products lining a supermarket's shelves tells its own story, as in the example of industrial white bread, or canned bamboo shoots, a product whose presence is due not only to the development of canning, but to the spread of Asian immigrant groups who need bamboo shoots for their cooking. Some products—such as potato crisps flavored with Indian spices—result from globalization, as flavors and shapes from different culinary traditions meet, either to good or bad effect depending on one's tastes. Heavily processed sugars and white flours, which contribute to diabetes and other diseases associated with the Western diet, would not be possible without the advances of industrialization. ("Western diet" is a crude but dietetically evocative term; it generally means a diet disproportionately high in carbohydrates, processed sugars, and animal fats.) It would be nearly impossible for an individual to fully document the path each item traveled to reach the supermarket, and to account for its effects on the economies and environments it traversed along the way. As impressive as they are, supermarkets are just nodes in the mighty food network that modernity created. And, of course, many supermarkets around the world are decidedly modern but not Western; the products on their shelves will tell stories about the forms of agriculture and supply chains that serve non-Western diets.

In some ways the supermarket fulfills many industrial-age North American and European visions of what the future of food should look like. In today's Western supermarkets food is plentiful, and it has been produced, shipped, stored, and presented for sale through carefully controlled means. Foods are standardized. Even foods that should be irregular because of natural differences in growth or the activity of microorganisms, like yeast-raised bread or cheeses, are far more predictable in shape, flavor, and texture than they were a few hundred years ago.[1] Industrial loaves look more like identical twins than like cousins. This kind of standardization does not mean that variety has been ignored. Those regularly shaped loaves of bread are available in organic wheat, rye, refined white flour, rice flour, and sometimes gluten-free varieties. The customer's power to choose has been maximized, but care has also been taken so that choice items will always match the one the customer previously purchased. Customers live, shop, and eat in a world of unprecedented predictability. Moreover, the breads, buns, and bagels on the shelves span the globe. Their flavors intermarry: saffron hot cross buns, cranberry bagels.

And the packaging! In 1970, the architectural historian Reyner Banham wrote an entire essay on the relationship between the crisp, or potato chip, and its bag.[2] His insight was that they functioned as a designed unity, "operated" by ripping the bag and crunching its contents: "You tear the pack open to get at the contents, rip it further to get at the corner-lurkers in the bottom, and then crush it crackling-flat in the fist before throwing it away." And all this with emotional consequences: "It's the first and most familiar of Total-Destructo products and probably sublimates more aggression per annum than any quantity of dramaturgical catharsis." Banham understood that industrialization had opened up whole worlds for product designers, and that our snacking and dining often begin with a set of physical actions and auditory experiences choreographed in the offices and laboratories of big companies. Those actions and experiences—especially the crackling, crunching sounds—are part of food's pleasure, and part of snack foods' addictiveness. Banham made the further claim that packaging, in the later twentieth century, had become one of our vernacular technologies, expressing our values and way of life, much like the oar in the hands of an ancient Greek sailor, or the ax handle or plow in the hands of an eighteenth-century English peasant.

Self-service supermarkets, which began to appear in 1916, may be matched only by the fast-food restaurant as an icon of plenty around the globe. Those restaurants are themselves historically linked to the highways and other transportation networks of the modern world, having gotten their start as roadside spots for refreshment.[3] However, both supermarkets and fast-food chains are routinely criticized for contributing to one of the downsides of caloric abundance: most consumers in the developed world have access to more calories per day, on average, than their ancestors ever did before, and this is a contributing factor in the growth both of waistlines and of our collective "disease burden." If the most prominent diseases of earlier eras were communicable infections that infiltrated the body from the outside, the most prominent ailments of the early-twenty-first-century Western world include diabetes and heart disease, which are related to industrial and social conditions but, physically speaking, attack us from within. The billions of hamburgers sold by McDonald's have certainly played a role in this, as has the French fry (about 50 percent of the potatoes harvested worldwide, each year, become fries). Notably, however, McDonald's and its counterparts also sell food cheaply enough that they are the only restaurants many poorer consumers can frequent, and McDonald's can do this because it purchases cheap, low-quality ingredients, many of which are produced with help from government subsidy programs.

The popular food writer Michael Pollan encourages consumers to avoid the central aisles of supermarkets because they contain the highly processed foods that the machines of the Industrial Revolution, or their descendants, gave us.[4] Industrial processes have been good for more than standardization, variety, and the shelf life of foods; they have also packed more calories into foods, and heavily-processed grains are more readily metabolized than their less-processed counterparts. Many of us, living in a postindustrial society in which our jobs are sedentary, consume far more calories than we need, and in fact we are malnourished; the dynamics of our malnutrition simply differ from the dynamics of malnutrition in preindustrial societies.

Fast food and the western diet have gained more than a mere foothold in the developing world. McDonald's thrives in China and India (often serving vegetarian or chicken patties rather than beef in the latter), and McDonald's analogues exist in other places, such as Iran, where different chains bear the names MashDonalds and McMashallah. Ironically, when McDonald's arrived in Japan in 1971 in the first flush of what was called Japan's "economic miracle," Japanese customers went to "Makudonarudo" for snacks, not meals; after all, a "meal" must include rice. One of McDonald's competitors, Mosburger, solved the problem by placing a burger between two patties of rice.[5] Japan's economic emergence was not built on Western imports, either of food or of business models, but the efficiency of fast-food restaurants found many Japanese admirers. McDonald's expansion into Japan was part of a global campaign, and in 1971 the chain also moved into Australia, Germany, Guam, the Netherlands, and Panama. In China, McDonald's and other chains now fuel a trend towards childhood obesity, as parents of the "only children" formerly mandated by China's one-child-per-family policy gratify their offspring's wishes.

Pollan advises us to avoid the supermarket's comparatively unnutritious but caloric central aisles and instead shop from the fringes, where we can find fresh products like fruits and vegetables. The result would be a mostly fresh plant-based diet that often produces better health outcomes than a carbohydrate- or a meat-centric diet. But to eat mostly plants in the early-twenty-first-century West means considering issues foreign to nineteenth-century consumers: does one choose "organic" produce as opposed to "conventional" or "transitional" (and how does one interpret these often-deceptive labels)? Does one avoid plants that have been grown with the help of pesticides? Eschew "genetically modified organisms" or GMO foods, out of anxiety that genetic manipulation is bad for human consumers or bad for the surrounding natural environment? If "natural" means being unmodified by human hands, then food has not been natural since the advent of agriculture. Nevertheless, fears of "unnatural" or "franken" foods have cropped up among consumers whose families have been eating highly processed foods for generations. While genetic modification—whether to make crops cold resistant or vitamin-enriched or for some other purpose—has not been proven to be inherently harmful to human health or to the environment, many European Union consumers have been especially critical of the practice, and some US markets have also been resistant. The public profile of GMO foods cannot be fully separated from the business practices of companies such as Monsanto, which profit from patents taken out on GMO seeds, yielding complicated and troubling ethical questions about patenting life itself.

To critique supermarkets and fast food often means critiquing modernity. In 1998 José Bové, a sheep farmer, former philosophy student, activist, and member of France's largest farmers' union, attacked and demolished a McDonald's restaurant that had been under construction in the town of Millau. He was tried, convicted, and received a three-month jail sentence, but approximately forty thousand supporters turned up at his trial, and his conviction and jail time only enhanced his appeal as a leader. While anti-fast-food sentiment was common among European supporters of local farming and local food, the proximate cause of Bové's attack was the action of the World Trade Organization, which had supported US efforts to export to Europe beef from cows treated with Bovine Growth Hormone; not only globalization but the "Americanization" of beef was threatening European shores and stomachs. European resistance to such exports met US retaliation in the form of heavy import taxes on luxury products from Europe, including Roquefort, the very same cheese Bové produced on his own farm. Bové went on to become a leader in the anti-globalization movement, which stands against the global reach of free market capitalism and criticizes the influence of international corporations on national and international politics, especially when they push for the deregulation of markets.

Ten years before Bové's attack, protests against the opening of a McDonald's in Rome drew attention to a new organization: Slow Food, which promotes localism, knowledge of the origins of foods, and living and cooking at a less rapid pace than modernity often seems to demand. Appropriately enough, the organization's icon is a snail. Among Slow Food's many goals are establishing seed banks in which "heirloom" seed varieties can be stored, maintaining the diversity of plant and animal species, and combating big agribusiness's reliance on crop monocultures. Slow Food's insistence on locality has, perhaps ironically, globalized, and local chapters have opened around the world.[6]

Refrigeration and the Modern Supply Chain

At the core of most supermarkets stands a vernacular technology that pervades everyday life: aisles of refrigerated cases. As Nicola Twilley puts it, our food system exists because of a "vast, distributed artificial winter" that keeps foods unnaturally fresh and enables such feats of transportation as the distribution of bananas and orange juice throughout North America, the consumption of sushi in landlocked parts of Europe or Asia, and much more.[7] Call this the "cryosphere." What artificial nitrogen fixation has done for food production, refrigeration has done for distribution, leading to a food system very different from that of the nineteenth century.

Mechanical refrigeration was patented in 1851 but did not become widespread until the 1890s. Nevertheless, the use of ice to transport foods over relatively short distances was common—the "iceboxes" still visible in some older American homes attest to this—and ice-delivery men were once a familiar sight. The first (ice-based rather than mechanical) refrigerated railway car was built by the meat dealer George Hammond, operating out of Detroit; Franklin Swift created a better version in 1879, and his innovation helped to prepare consumers for the era of refrigerated meat and other foods that followed. Later refrigerated shipping containers, first developed in the 1950s and subsequently refined, and even the Styrofoam "coffins" in which sushi-grade fish is transported by airplane, are the descendants of Swift's car, as well as of the first refrigerated ships, used in the 1870s to transport meat across the Atlantic and Pacific for European markets. Ships like these later made the banana industry (among many others) possible; because of the pace at which bananas ripen, they have to be picked while still green and then, after the refrigerated journey to their destination markets, placed in a special ripening room pumped full of ethylene gas. Much as most coffee-drinkers have never seen a coffee plant, most North American and European consumers have never eaten a tree-ripened banana. The story of bananas also illustrates another dimension of food change in the twentieth century—while by the mid-twentieth century the banana had become one of the world's most popular fruits, only fifty years earlier, in 1899, the popular science magazine *Scientific American* felt obliged to publish instructions on how to eat one. Many of the things we imagine to be traditional or permanent features of our lives with food are, in fact, very recent arrivals. Foodways are in constant flux but quickly take on the appearance of permanent states of affairs.

The first refrigerated meats met mistrustful customers, eaters used to fresh meat that had not travelled long distances. In the United States, it was only during the First World War that eating frozen meat was "branded" as a patriotic act, part of maximizing the country's available resources for the war effort. By the 1930s, however, household refrigerators began to become common. Customers grew used to enjoying foods from all over, during all seasons of the year. By the third quarter of the twentieth century, Americans ate three times as many frozen foods as they had ever eaten before, and the processed-food business model flourished. Giant refrigerated storage tanks in orange-growing places like Florida and Brazil (which now produces much of the world's orange juice) have allowed orange juice to become a global beverage. And, as in the case of orange juice, refrigeration combined with transportation infrastructure has made it possible for a single region to grow the food for many others. In the United States a full half of the frozen vegetables and fruits we eat are grown in California—and a full three-quarters of the food we eat has, at some point in its production and transport process, been refrigerated. Refrigeration has had economic effects beyond the obvious ones having to do with production and consumption; the ability to extend the stored life of foods has led to the idea of food commodities as "futures" tradable on stock markets—thus the pork belly (1961) and commodity cheddar (1997). And its social effects are notable. Home refrigerators mean that families can shop only once per week if they choose, freeing time for other tasks. But if refrigeration's effects have been extraordinary, its relative invisibility is also important. Like so many other forms of infrastructure in the food system, including highways, trucks, trains, airplanes, shipping containers, and so forth, it is easily forgotten.

A Century of Nutritional Science

All the packages on our supermarket shelves display nutritional information, not necessarily written in language a layperson can understand. Like refrigeration, this is something so quotidian that its importance is usually overlooked: we live in a world used to breaking down foods both into constituent ingredients and into constituent nutrients, and we're accustomed to receiving dietary advice from credentialed experts (or from diet-fad-pushing quacks). As with refrigeration, it is a bit hard to imagine a world without calories, fiber, vitamins, or any of the other labels we use to describe the nutritious qualities of foods. But the "science of nutrition" only truly matured in the 1890s, flourishing in laboratories as well as in other circumstances in which investigators could hope to control the diets of a population—such as the front lines of military conflicts. And of course today when one thinks of "calories" it is easy to forget the original definition: the amount of a substance that, when burned, yields enough energy to raise one kilogram of water one degree centigrade. The "calorie" was born not in nutrition but in French scientific efforts to understand thermodynamic energy. Proteins, fats, and carbohydrates were among the first parts of food discovered, and the use of calorimeters (in which foods were burned and the amount of heat generated measured) was widespread. Many of the early nutritionists hoped to identify the minimum amount of nutrition it took for persons to live. They wanted to quantify minimum nutritional standards, something useful in providing aid to the poor, and they wanted to contribute to the efficient functioning of the workforce, often through educational programs for women in their roles as homemakers and cooks. The analogy between the human body and a machine, made by many early nutritionists, was hardly accidental. Some onlookers, such as the economist J. A. Hobson, predicted in the 1890s that "food science" would become a normative science, providing us with laws for eating.

In the early twentieth century the discovery of vitamins, whose absence was taken to cause "diseases of deficiency" such as beriberi, pellagra, and scurvy, led to a new round of experiments. Pre-vitamin nutritional science had focused on calories as the lynchpin of a thermodynamic model of metabolism; food was energy, and the body turned that energy into work while also replenishing itself. Suddenly there was a competition between nutritionists invested in energy and those invested in a new biochemical understanding of food that incorporated vitamins. Quality of food began to matter as much as quantity, and the notion of what counted as "plenty" started to shift. The human focus of most nutritionists in Britain and the United States remained the housewife—a figure who had already been the target of generations of experts on hygiene and domestic science from the mid-nineteenth century onwards. Now her kitchen was to become a laboratory and her understanding of the nutritional values of each foodstuff had to be perfect if her family was to flourish. Thus her role was effectively professionalized. However, a focus on the family as the crucial site of transformed cooking and eating practices developed simultaneously with a new focus on the individual's bodily wellbeing. Diet and health gurus populated the late nineteenth century through the twentieth century (just as they do the early twenty-first), and they appealed to individuals' desires to be free of excess weight or any number of health complaints. Not long after the discovery of vitamins, the first products sold on the basis of their enrichment with vitamins rolled into stores in Great Britain and the United States. The first enriched baby formula was sold as early as 1928. At the same time, and as late as the 1930s, products now known to be unhealthy, such as coca-cola and cigarettes, were promoted as health aids. Then as now, the promise of health helped to line the pockets of advertisers and agribusiness.

Dislocation, Tradition, and The Cookbook

Joe Strummer, founding member of the punk band The Clash, once sang of all the foods available on the high road of a cosmopolitan British city: *bhindi, dahl,* okra, Bombay duck, bagels, *empanada, lassi,* chicken tikka, pastrami. This is a partly Asian list and thus reflective of the dominant pattern of twentieth-century immigration to Great

Britain, but these are all foods one could expect to find somewhere in any global city worth its salt, or its chilis.[8] One of your authors spent many hours in the early 1960s searching for cranberries in Paris to serve alongside *une dinde* (a turkey) at Thanksgiving; she found a dusty can at a sky-high price in a fancy-goods store. Now such an exotic food is much more easily found.

The diversity of twentieth-century (and now, twenty-first-century) foodways in the developed world was (and is) unprecedented. Simply put, those who live in resource-rich parts of the world have access to a far wider range of foods than their ancestors could have dreamt of. Immigration to global hubs has brought together cuisines and inspired new dishes. In early-twenty-first century Los Angeles, food trucks turn out tacos and burritos filled with Korean bulgogi; in Toronto you can find pizzas topped with chicken tikka masala; in Tokyo there are inside-out sushi rolls adulterated with avocado, a California favorite that has been exported to sushi's mother country. The restaurateur Rocky Aoki, creator of the American restaurant chain Benihana of Tokyo, thought to be "Japanese" by many Americans, opened a location in Japan, where, marketed as Benihana of New York, it provided "foreign" foods that pleased many Japanese. The ironies of food's movement are many.

Migrants have always carried recipes, either in their memories or in their cookbooks. As Chinese laborers traveled to America to build the transcontinental railroad they brought their food cultures with them, resulting in chop suey and chow mein, not Chinese dishes, but riffs on them, using cheap ingredients available in North America. When Turkish workers reached Germany they made an institution of the doner kebab, and the appropriate rotisserie carts are ubiquitous on the streets of Berlin. Few things affected the restaurant culture of the late-twentieth-century United States more than the immigration reforms of the mid-1960s, which not only opened the country to more immigrants but also included provisions that helped to keep families together. Prior immigration laws had encouraged single men to travel to the United States to work without their families, returning home once they had made enough money. Families were more likely to start restaurants, and because of the relatively low overhead and the availability of family labor, this was a form of entrepreneurship within reach for many. With luck, the restaurants thrived and passed from one generation to the next.

Stuart Hall points out that from the privileged perspective of the powerful, one of globalization's effects has been to turn the world into a wonderful buffet:

> To be at the leading edge of modern capitalism is to eat fifteen different cuisines in any one week, not to eat one. It is no longer important to have boiled beef and carrots and Yorkshire pudding every Sunday. Who needs that? Because if you are just jetting in from Tokyo, via Harare, you come in loaded, not with 'how everything is the same' but how wonderful it is, that everything is different.[9]

But even comfortably polyglot and wealthy eaters may long for a certain stability of culinary identity. It might be a delight to eat fifteen different cuisines in a week, but it is also overwhelming. One of our primary ways to take shelter is to turn to a cookbook, treating it as a window into a singular, fixed, and authentic culinary tradition. The emergence of the cookbook as a humble literary genre did much for the establishment of codified national cuisines in Europe. Cookbooks established high and low food cultures and sometimes connected them, tying the court to the village.

Cookbooks have also become tools for the consolidation of national food communities around the world. Arjun Appadurai has described the functions of the cookbook for Indian readers in the late twentieth century. Cookbooks in India—in this case English-language books published and written for an Anglophone readership—helped a rising middle class to do two things at once: develop a culture of expertise in the kitchen as a marker of status attainment, and maintain their sense of tradition even as their daily lives became more modern.[10] Appadurai also notes two contrasting impulses in national cookbook literatures like that of India. There is the drive to emphasize the distinctiveness of local cuisines, on the one hand, and the drive to emphasize the unity of a national cuisine, on the other. This is especially significant in nations like India, made up of culturally distinctive states with their own ethnic, cultural, and religious diversity.

If the cookbook can be defined as a set of instructions for the recreation of dishes, it is usually much more. In Europe, the non-recipe material in cookbooks has sometimes included personal memoirs, lessons in etiquette for the upwardly mobile middle classes, and advice on staying healthy, cleaning house, and even hosting guests. And cookbooks have served as sets of rules determining what is inside, and what is outside, of a particular cuisine. Those rules do change over time, and by examining cookbooks used over relatively long stretches of time, perhaps fifty to one hundred years, one can start to track changes, such as the emergence of pork tacos in Mexico (native corn tortillas, invasive Spanish pork sausage).[11] Interestingly, in many cases—such as that of Mexican cookbooks—authenticity and tradition are closely identified with spices and sauces rather than with the ingredients that they season and flavor. Thus new proteins and vegetables can "go native," and tradition can travel and re-invent itself in new places where the available produce is different. Sometimes culinary identity is more attached to technique than to ingredients, as is the case in Japan. One chef, Matsuhisa Nobu, often says "give me local ingredients and, with Japanese technique, I can make Japanese food anywhere in the world." Nevertheless, by examining cookbooks we can get a sense of which ingredients a given culture decides to allow in, and which ones it never will or never can.

Contemporary (late-twentieth and early-twenty-first century) cookbooks often present their authentic and traditional character as a selling point for readers living in a globalized and ever-accelerating world. This nostalgic or romantic trend was not always dominant. Cookbooks have conveyed all manner of aspirations towards the future, including futures in which traditions are not preserved so much as amplified—as in Italian-American cookbooks in which meat and cheese are represented far out of proportion to their role in the everyday diets of actual Italian peasants—and futures in which nutrition and efficiency in the kitchen are paramount virtues. In the United States the 1960s saw the rise of cookbooks that revolved around the microwave oven, though the oven itself did not become widespread until the late 1970s. And before modern kitchen appliances, cookbooks had long been vectors for teaching cooks about new tools, from graters to garlic presses.

One of the most famously future-oriented cookbooks of the early twentieth century was not really a cookbook at all, but rather an art project conceived by some of Italy's boldest younger artists, the (notably politically conservative) *Futuristi* or "Futurists." The *Futurist Cookbook* isn't useful in the kitchen, but it illustrates one way cookbooks can position themselves relative to culinary tradition. Chief Futurist Filippo Marinetti hoped to supersede Italian traditions entirely, inveighing against that classic Italian means of transmitting wheat to the metabolism, pasta. Pasta, he insisted, weighed down Italians and made men effeminate. He recommended instead that Italians consume meats, especially aerodynamic (and phallic) sausages.

Actual Italian food innovations, like the espresso machine, had geopolitical meaning—the desire for colonies in coffee-producing lands; an appetite for aluminum obtained from colonial holdings in North Africa (the famous Bialetti stovetop espresso machines was made out of cast aluminum).[12] The Futurist call to reject pasta was similarly tied to global ambitions in a political climate of ascendent fascism. Eating less pasta would mean not importing as much wheat, beneficial for an Italy striving for greater self-sufficiency. Plus, sleeker and speedier Italians could compete more efficiently on the modern world stage. The *Futurist Cookbook*, like so many speculations about the future of food, is best read as a tense expression of anxieties about the present.

Cookbooks often present cuisines as authentic while acknowledging that authentic does not mean homogenously indigenous. A contemporary Vietnamese cookbook might describe *banh xeo* or rice-flour crepes, made with coconut milk but produced on the same hot griddle you could see on a Paris street corner, where the crepes would be made with wheat flour and served with butter and powdered sugar, or perhaps the hazelnut-chocolate spread Nutella. Southern Chinese influences on Vietnamese cooking include stir-frying, noodles, tofu, and the use of chopsticks; butter, baguettes, and coffee come from French colonial rule; peanuts and tomatoes originally arrived with European traders, souvenirs of the Columbian Exchange. And if modern Vietnamese cuisine were sampled in a strip mall in Southern California—say, in Orange County's huge expat Vietnamese community—there could easily be a bubble-tea store next to the restaurant, serving an originally Taiwanese tapioca-ball-enriched tea that fits the palate of Vietnamese and Chinese-Americans equally well.

"American" Flavor

As the global reach of the Golden Arches attests, the Westernization of the world's diet during the later twentieth century was indeed an Americanization. It was an extension of the dietary arm of American empire, which began with colonists seizing territory from the Native Americans and which later grew, after industrialization, through "gunboat diplomacy," unequal treaties, and the notion of "manifest destiny" propelling Americans and their interests south and west. The American imperial map would eventually range from Puerto Rico to the Philippines.

But what counts as "American" food has long been a puzzle. Tortillas and shave ice and sukiyaki are all American, but what can this mean? Such a statement, equally valid about all three foods despite their disparate origins, suggests the complexities of food history in the United States. Even as European colonists brought their own foodways to the "New World," they also imported enslaved Africans, whose foodways survived the terrible passage across the Atlantic. The presence of sorghum in the American South speaks to African influence, as do millet, peanuts, okra, kidney beans, and sesame seeds. Scots-Irish indentured servants may have made breads and cakes for English tables in the American colonies, but their own diets consisted of offal, potatoes, and other root vegetables. Scrapple, a crisply fried cake of pork bits, grains, and spices, arrived on American shores with Mennonite and Amish immigrants to Pennsylvania. It has a cousin in the pork-scrap pudding that Scots servants would have remembered from their home country.

American food history has long focused on the mixture of disparate food cultures within the continental United States. But American foodways have also changed, and gained texture, through American expansion. In 1898, as a result of the Spanish-American War, America found an opportunity for territorial growth as it tried to "liberate" Spanish possessions in the Pacific and the Caribbean. As a result, the Philippines would be under American control from 1898 to 1946, granted in the Treaty of Paris, which also gave the United States Puerto Rico; that island remains a protectorate or "unincorporated territory" as of this writing. These territories became sites for sugar plantations (the Philippines had in fact been producing sugar ever since Arab traders planted sugarcane cuttings there), and for growing other tropical products including bananas and pineapple.

Even as the United States acquired Puerto Rico and the Philippines, it gained Hawai'i in the same year. That territory would eventually become one of the most culinarily complex states in the country. The Hawai'ian diet is a very diverse one, including indigenous seaweeds, taro root (the source of *poi*, a traditional food eaten for holidays and at the community feasts called luaus), fish, and breadfruit, a large starchy fruit brought by Polynesians about 3500 years ago. But this set of "pre-contact" foods appears only occasionally in today's Hawai'ian diet—as ceremonial or ritual parts of a luau or as offerings at a spirit place or temple (*heiau*).[13] By contrast, everyday Hawaiian diets show the influences of Chinese, Japanese, Filipino, Portuguese, and mainland ("*haole*") American foodways.

There is nowhere better to observe these influences than in the "mixed plate," or "plate lunch," a classic Hawai'ian experience, especially when bought from a food truck or van near a park or beach. It always begins with several starches: two scoops of rice, and the same of potato salad or macaroni salad (or potato *and* macaroni salad). The plate may also include chorizo, a Portuguese sausage, chicken teriyaki (much sweeter than its Japanese antecedent), a Filipino *lumpia,* some Chinese glass noodles, perhaps a Polynesian *laulau* (a large burrito-shaped, pork or fish-stuffed, banana-leaf or luau-leaf-wrapped steamed item), *kalua* pig, *lomilomi* (massaged) salmon, ahi poke (marinated chopped raw tuna), and perhaps a square of *haupia,* a coconut gelatin dessert. All of these but the *haupia* might be piled precariously on a paper plate, to be eaten with the hands or, for tourists, with a plastic fork. This meal speaks to the last three centuries of influence in the Hawai'ian islands, reflecting the cuisines of people brought to the island to work the sugar or pineapple plantations. These workers, in the late nineteenth and early twentieth centuries, shared the contents of their lunch pails at breaks in the fields and processing factories. What they created was not a melting pot diet but rather a "buffet" diet, allowing the dishes of each of their cultures to stand together, only occasionally combining their ingredients and styles in new dishes. These dishes were not untouched by transport to Hawai'i. They were all sweeter than they would be in their originary countries, because of the omnipresence of the Hawai'ian sugar crop. Chicken teriyaki, Hawai'ian style, is as sweet as many desserts; indeed, it is as sweet as many apple pies, and just as American.

Nem on the Menu

RESTAURANTS WERE NOT PART OF MY CHILDHOOD. My family invariably ate at home. This was fairly common in the 1940s and 1950s in the Midwest. One consequence was that we did not eat "other people's foods," that is, the food of other ethnic groups. The most exotic things I ate, in my 1950s childhood, were stuffed grape leaves at the Minnesota State Fair, made by Greek vendors mostly for the benefit of other Greeks; I was one of the few non-Greeks who tried them. Only later, in my adulthood, after I had eaten at Chinese, Indian, and Persian restaurants, did I learn that there are finer distinctions to be made within each "ethnic" category: Szechuan, Madras, Persian-American. Menus became educational texts, offering me puzzles to solve: what were "starters" or "savories"? What was "offal"? I always knew what dessert was, but what was "*kulfi*"? Gradually, noticing these items became an obsessive habit. I started to learn more about "other people's" food. I adopted some of these dishes as my own.

When I trained as an anthropologist, I learned that restaurants were a perfect place to do fieldwork. After all, as a diner, I had a natural reason to be there. My hunger alone explained my presence. There is also a great deal to observe in restaurants: the dynamics of families, people's casual or formal dress, their conversations about a ball game, neighborhood politics, or a child's grades in school. The famous baseball player Yogi Berra was right to say "you can observe a lot by just watching," which readily becomes, "you can hear a lot by just listening," and on through all the ways of sensing and perceiving the world, and the foods, around you. In other words you can observe a lot by lending things your attention without preconceptions. And the menu offers an opportunity for conversation, which is useful if you're shy, as I was when I started my training. You can ask questions, especially if the restaurant isn't too crowded. Sometimes, if your server finds your curiosity charming, you can even get little tastes of things from the kitchen, and that's a fieldwork bonus.

At a Senegalese restaurant in Boston, Massachusetts, I was surprised to see an item called *nem* on the menu, among the appetizers. I asked the server if these were the same as the crispy fried Vietnamese rolls, called by the same name. How did they come to be on this West African menu? Our server brought the manager, who obligingly sat down and told us the story. When the French colonized Vietnam (which was part of French Southeast Asia and called Indochine), they brought in soldiers from another French colony, Senegal. They hoped the *tirailleurs Senegalais* (Senegalese riflemen) would serve as a more loyal and "objective" police force than the native Vietnamese could have provided. After all, the Vietnamese would have been monitoring their own people. When the Senegalese soldiers returned to West Africa, they brought back a taste for the delicious *nem*, which were eventually domesticated into the Senegalese culinary repertory, and some brought back Vietnamese wives as well. Years later, when Senegalese immigrants started restaurants in America, they put *nem* on their menus. Food's movements, sometimes via colonial exchanges like this one and sometimes because of random travels, demonstrate twists and turns of identity: Japanese tempura came from Portuguese influences, and sushi from Southeast Asia. The British Navy adopted curry as regular fare for its sailors, and the Japanese Navy followed suit, creating *kare raisu*, "curry rice," a Japanese version of the British Navy's dish. Just as the British version fed sailors from all over the British Empire, so did the Japanese version feed sailors from culinarily distinct parts of Japan.

In one of Boston's immigrant neighborhoods, a bakery caters to the local Vietnamese community's taste in bread. They bake baguettes for the well-known *banh mi* sandwiches, which according to one tradition always contains some Vietnamese pâté, salad, and mayonnaise, as well as cold cuts, seasoned with vinegar and pickle. Hang out long enough and you may see customers from other former French colonies: Algerians, Laotians, Tunisians, and Senegalese, as well as people from Mali and the Seychelles. French rule is over, but the soft power of French bread continues to unite people. And this really is softer, doughier bread than the crusty baguettes of Paris. Vietnamese French bread is spongy enough to soak up a mess of distinctly un-French sauce. Like the *nem*, this bread tells a story that is full of tragedy, tears, and bloodshed: the story of colonialism. Perhaps it shouldn't be delicious, then, but it often is. Pleasures that developed through colonial rule are nevertheless pleasures, and some of them—like *nem*—can stay with us, triumphantly assimilated, long after political fortunes have changed.

I never ate *nem* in Senegal. When I traveled there, my hosts brought me to homes where I was fed "indigenous" dishes: *thiebou-dienne,* for example, the national dish of fish, rice, and tomato all cooked together in the same pot. No one mentioned *nem*, though they were part of the Senegalese diet. Perhaps *nem* occupied a special category, domesticated but not thought of as quite Senegalese? I had to come home to eat Senegalese *nem*, in an expat restaurant in the city where I teach, *nem* made by a transplanted Senegalese cook who adapted the dish in her own way. We know things change, but it is sometimes surprising to catch change on the wing. It is difficult to identify a food by its origins or landing places. But complex pathways do not render a food's identity "problematic." They make things interesting. The baguette became a daily necessity in Vietnam but was greatly transformed—and made Vietnamese—in the process. *Nem*, brought from one colony to another as an unintended consequence of imperial personnel transfers, got domesticated in Senegal. Then the food of Senegal, including a trace of Vietnam, migrated to a third site, Boston, where an expat makes the dish in her own way. A humbling thought for someone with a need to categorize, to name, to create a geography of menus.

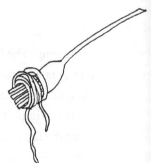

CHAPTER 9

Ways of Eating

THE LARGE, HIGH-CEILINGED WAREHOUSE is dark except for the fires of the small brick forges, about three of which are lit. We can make out small bins of coal next to the domed forges, with short scooping shovels leaning nearby. The smith sits *seiza*-style, on a *zabuton* (floor pillow) close to the open door of one forge. That door is about eighteen inches across, and we can see orange-red glowing coals through the opening. Doi-san, the *shokunin* (master craftsman) knife-smith, wears wrist-high gloves and a baseball cap, and ordinary glasses, but no other protective gear. His skill is his protection.

Doi Itsuo's workshop is in Sakai, a town near Osaka where knife-making is the signature profession, craft, and art. Doi's father, a legendary blacksmith, recently retired. He trained Doi, and Doi worked for him for over forty years before his retirement. Like his father, Doi specializes in blades, leaving sharpening and handle-making to others. A long road brought us to Sakai. It began with our interest in the cultural, moral, and practical dimensions of the actual act of putting food in the mouth—with literal ways of eating. This often involves utensils, those affordances of eating, and it often begins with cooking, and with the knife.

Sakai has long been a knife town. It was a rich merchant city in the fifteenth and sixteenth centuries, well located for trade over water. It was also a leading sword-making city, catering to samurai and aristocrats. Sakai's attachment to the sword outlasted a period of firearms manufacture; in the mid-sixteenth century, Portuguese priests and traders visited, and Sakai subsequently became Japan's leading gun-making town, but guns were eventually displaced by a baseline preference for swords. The sixteenth-century "great unifier," Oda Nobunaga, seized the town when it refused to give up its autonomy, and it only regained its wealth (if not its independence) later, under the leadership of Toyotomi Hideyoshi. In the Tokugawa Period (1600–1868), a long era of peace meant less demand for blades. Finally, when the Meiji government (1868–1912) made it illegal for samurai to wear their swords, sword-making all but ended, except for the manufacture of a few ceremonial swords with highly damasked blades. After World War II, Sakai became Japan's leading culinary knife-producing city, and craftsmen refined a process of metal lamination that had been used to make traditional swords. When lamination improved fine-edged cooking knives, this permitted Japanese chefs to establish a high aesthetic standard for their food, focused on clean cuts. Today, family-run workshops still specialize in blade forging, sharpening, or handle-making, the main tasks involved in finishing a culinary knife.

We hunker down at a safe distance to watch Doi work, as he pounds metal into blanks that will become knife blades. They consist of high carbon *hagane* (steel) sandwiched between softer and more resilient (more iron, less steel) *jigane* layers. Afterwards, we follow the resulting hardened blanks to his colleague's family workshop, nearby, for honing. Doi's colleague fits a blade into a wooden block, which he then places in a frame. Sitting on a stool in front of that frame, he uses it to lower the blade-to-be onto a turning wheel. Sparks fly. A jet of water flows over the wheel as he works, catching the bits of metal that come off the blank. A slurry of metal and water flies against the wall. It lands on a thickened layer of metal residue, creating an impasto, the oxidizing metal turning green in the air.

Gradually, he sharpens the blank into a blade. Before the Second World War, tasks were not so divided between different sub-contracted shops. Knife work, from forge-lamination to finish, was usually done in a single workshop. But now, we follow the blades to a third, final, workshop where the last craftsman fits each blade into a handle of magnolia wood with a bolster of water buffalo horn.

Traditional artisans in Sakai usually take at least four days to make a single knife, working almost entirely by hand. Doi tells us that his father objected when he invented a pounding device for the initial flattening of a blank. This was a simple foot pedal connected to a weighted overhead arm that could pound a red-hot blade with greater force than a hammer. But because the machine added a mechanical layer between man and product, it offended his father, who had a strict sense of what "hand-made" means. Only now that his father has retired does Doi feel comfortable using his device, though with a guilty laugh. After all, he understands the old way of thinking: the knife, an extension of a cook's hand, must start out as an extension of an artisan's hand.

In another workshop, ten thousand miles away, a different knife lesson continues. No forge here. Adam Simha, our teacher, studied metalworking at the forge but has decided to focus on a process called "stock removal," working with blanks that are cut from steel plates, shaped, and heat-treated. Simha is an expert at the process of reduction, which means taking a blank and effectively carving it on a big belt sander. The belts are studded with tiny shards of ceramic that remove material from the blank until a recognizable blade emerges. It is a mechanized process, but it is an artisanal process too, involving a precise coordination of hands, legs, hips, and core to manipulate the knife against the platen, a flat plate across which the sander's belt moves. The blade's angle against the platen is crucial, and tiny differences of emphasis or force against the platen have great consequences for the shape and material properties of the eventual blade.

Contra Doi's father, there is no contradiction between mechanical work and handwork; the machine might even act as an extension of the hand.

The belt sander, a drill press, band saw, and several other large machines dominate Simha's workshop. Our first impression on entering is "large machines for making small things!" And yet, as Simha manipulates them to hone a blade, there is something surprising that links his work, and his ethos, to Doi's. Showing us how to hold a blank up to the belt sander, Simha demonstrates how the process translates minute movements of the body into measurable differences on the eventual knife blade. We quickly learn that managing these machines means synching your body to them—not unlike dancing, except with an immobile, predictable, and very powerful partner. We're surprised by how close to the machine we have to position our bodies, legs up against a plastic bucket of cold water positioned immediately below the belt sander. One hand holds the blank by its handle, fingers curled forward around it, while the other holds the blade from below, thumb on the flat while the rest of that hand curls out of the way of the sander. The blank itself is crosswise to the direction of sanding. Simha tends to keep his arms locked against the sides of his body, and so we do too, legs in a wide stance, so that the system of the upper body is nearly motionless, and the action comes from a lateral movement of the hips. The result is a weird combination of stiffness and relaxation. Gradually we advance sanding belts, increasing grit number and thus fineness; the metal heats up faster as the blade gets thinner, and one of us burns his thumb more and more. The bucket of cold water becomes essential for cooling the blade as we work.

A stage of hand-sanding follows, using increasingly fine sandpaper interspersed with a spray of oil lubricant. Then we do a final round of belt sanding, to true the flats of the blade and add surface conditioning to the hand-sanded planes. Last comes the search for the right handle. Simha shows us the choices: acrylic, which is the lightest and most fragile material; wood, a traditional material that endures if you treat it properly; and fiberglass, which is heavy but tough, unlikely to break if you drop your knife. Pins and strong glue will hold the blade and handle together. Simha's creativity has even led him to use bicycle handlebar grips as knife handles. We opt for grey fiberglass, which we sand down to a classic shape. Our ultimate goal is a small tool modeled on a European oyster knife: a thick, short blade on a solid handle, an instrument capable of prying as well as cutting.

In Japan, the cutting posture of the *hochonin* ("knife person," synonymous with "chef") is crucial. The questions Simha asks a prospective knife-owner reveal a similar emphasis on the body. *How do you stand when you cut? What is the height of your table or counter? What are you cutting? Show me how you hold your knife.* One of us has been told that she cuts on a counter that is too high for her, while her lower back's ache probably comes from using a dull knife. She gets some relief after sharpening her knives and adopting a thick rubber floor pad to stand on while cooking.

The "textbook" description of correct knife use in Japan can sound very precise and formal. "In using a knife," Nozaki Hiromitsu explains, "the posture of the cook is most important. Lining up the right arm, bending the left arm in a semi-circle, you place one foot behind and to the side of the other, in a 45-degree angle to the counter. This frees up movement allowing for precision of cutting."[1] When we showed a chef this text, he laughed dismissively. Observing cooks in action, we rarely saw this posture. They were moving too fast, or the counter wasn't the right height, or someone was in their way.

The most significant question for a prospective knife owner is probably "what are you going to cut?" Is it a dense vegetable, like a daikon radish; is it a square of tofu, soft as a cloud; is it a piece of meat, of variable muscle-fat composition? Your answer will determine the knife you use. Of all Japanese knives the most versatile is the *santoku,* or "three-purposed" knife, which will cut fish, vegetables, and meat with equal ease. It is ground on both sides of the edge, unlike most Japanese knives, which are ground on only one. In this regard, the santoku more closely resembles the Western chef's knife. But we quickly learn that there are no absolutes in knife choice, and the local culture of origin plays a role, too. One striking example is the *unagi-bocho*, or eel-cutting knife. It serves the same purpose whether it is cutting in Nagoya, Tokyo or Osaka, but the knife will be strikingly different, as regional styles of knife-making and eel-cutting diverge. One young woman, raised in her family's eel shop in Tokyo, exclaimed at seeing a Kansai area eel knife, "how can they be so different when the eel is the same animal?" In fact, there are regionalisms in how one cuts: in the Tokyo area a fish should be cut from the backbone forward, because cutting from the stomach would appear like *seppuku*, samurai ritual suicide. In Kyoto, cooks prefer to cut from the stomach for their own aesthetic reasons. They are unaffected by the samurai culture that once dominated Tokyo, and more influenced by the imperial court culture whose seat Kyoto once was.

As we learn about knives, we start to appreciate the intricate and reciprocal relationship between technological change and culinary change. Reciprocal, because technology is not an engine driving history, but a set of human practices that responds to human needs; thus the Chinese cleaver. As food writer Bee Wilson points out in her book on culinary utensils, *Consider the Fork,* the cleaver (*tou*) expresses a beautifully economical relationship between materials and culinary outcomes.[2] Unlike Japanese knives, each highly specific (except for the *santoku*), the Chinese cleaver is a multitasker. A relatively small amount of metal makes a single, rectangular blade capable of very fine cuts and delicate work in the hands of an experienced cook. A *tou*-wielding chef chops food in small pieces that will cook rapidly in a wok over a small amount of fuel: wood and coal have often been scarce throughout Chinese history and cutting food into "stir-fry" size enables efficient cooking. Small pieces of meat and vegetable mingle easily with seasonings, becoming the portion of a dish called *t'sai,* served with *fan,* which is often rice, or wheat in the form of bread or noodles. Chopsticks are the only tool used both in the kitchen and at the table, as they are useful for food preparation as well as eating. They manage small bits of food more deftly than large cuts. By contrast, a traditional European kitchen boasts many specialized blades for specialized tasks, and the final division of meat at the table is left to the eater; the modern steak knife descends from a premodern tradition of carrying a personal knife with which to eat. Ways of cutting shape entire cuisines.

Japanese knives are regional, just as "Japanese" food is regional rather than a unified national cuisine. A visit to Scarperia, just north of Florence, shows us that this holds true in Italy, too. Scarperia was a medieval village founded in 1306 and, within a hundred years, it became known for its fine knife-makers. By the mid-sixteenth century, when European knives had the advantage of carbon steel as well as iron, Scarperia's workshops banded together to form a guild, organized around standards and quality to protect their artisanal heritage. But just as Italian towns all have their highly localized cuisines, often including shapes of pasta found nowhere else, Italian knives speak of their homes. Scarperia knife-makers have, in the past, made knives perfect for cutting the Chianina beef prized as *bistecca fiorentina,* the specialty of Florence. Just as local recipes are passed down through generations, so are traditions of knife-making, and of caring for blades.

As we walk through the village, we see small doorways that open onto workshops and sales rooms. Posters of knives illustrate a long history of shapes and styles—blades, handles, bolsters made of horn or metal. A young woman in one knife shop takes a keen interest in guiding customers through the variables. *What will you use it for? Show me your hand. Do you know you must keep the knife clean and dry? Will you promise? You can bring it back for sharpening and for new handles. What? You're taking it to America? Well, come back when it needs work.*

In our own modern period knives are mostly for preparing and refining the food that other utensils (sometimes including hands) convey to the mouth. But this was not always the case. Knives have often carried food to the mouth. In eighteenth-century England, for example, knives were the preferred way to eat fresh peas, which had come into fashion; previously, peas were mostly eaten dry and used for making pottage, which was eaten with a spoon. Forks commonly had only two tines and thus were not useful for picking up peas.[3] Many knives had rounded tips, safe for the mouth, and the peas they carried would roll down the blade into the open orifice. Once forks had four tines, however, the knife method started to look rather barbaric. Oddly, the spoon was not considered appropriate for eating fresh peas.

Every utensil is part of a larger system that includes agriculture, cooking and eating. By observing utensils, from their design and manufacture to their use, we can learn about that larger system, from crops to table manners. For example, while eating a steak usually demands a knife and fork, and eating *fufu* requires one's hands or a spoon, chopsticks are best used with food that has been chopped into small bits. The culinary system that demands the knife and fork involves a set of assumptions about what kind of piece of meat is desirable, and how an eater wants to take it apart and enjoy it; the culinary system based on *fufu* has its own ideas about the relationship between starches, other elements, and the hand-to-mouth trajectory; the world of chopsticks is, as we have seen, a world in which knife-work reduces everything to small bits (as with the *tou*) and this is often related, in turn, to a style of cooking (using, for example, the wok) intended to cook many small bits of food very quickly, to minimize the use of fuel. Even the most formal, lacquered chopsticks are the descendants of care, thrift, and invention.

Every affordance of eating makes possible the short, delicate journey from the world around us to the world inside us. Ways of eating cross the line into the personal space of our bodies via our mouths, and each culture imagines and understands that line in different ways. Our table manners have grown up, as it were, around that line between outside and inside, and if the rituals of eating (especially social eating) can seem unnecessarily elaborate from the perspective of simply getting one's nutrition, well, perhaps it is because of the sheer sensitivity of the line between world and mouth.[4] Eating is a liminal act: after the food crosses through the portal of the mouth into the body, it becomes the body. Keeping the food pure for this passage requires gestures of separation, and an echo of this idea remains in the modern industrial boast that a cellophane-wrapped food was "untouched by human hands" in its manufacture.

In the beginning, it must have been hands. Hands are an ancient eating tool, our first means for bringing food to mouth, but they are still one of the most popular devices for dining. And hand traditions are by necessity cleanliness traditions. Archaeologists have turned up hand-washing basins used by ancient Egyptians, Greeks, and Romans, as well as by Jewish communities. Even contemporary paper wrappers for pita-wrapped sandwiches or donuts express a felt need for separation, providing a barrier of some kind between food and one's presumably "unclean" fingers. In some cultural models for eating, hands are differentiated in their uses: in Hindu India, for example, the right hand only should be used for eating, as the left is traditionally assigned to cleaning after using the toilet. (It is interesting to see how many societies use euphemistic language like the Japanese *te-arai*, meaning "handwashing place," or even the American "bathroom," for toilets.) And in India as elsewhere hands are the primary utensil for eating, scooping up morsels of rice, dahl, or meat and vegetable dishes, or using a piece of naan (itself a temporary utensil) to couch some pickle. Eating with bread or other "scooping" foods provides a mediating substance between the "messy" food and the "clean" hand. It also joins a starch "staple" with a flavorful "side"— which in China would be *fan* and *t'sai*.

But hands have had an awkward place in the etiquette of the Western table. For preference, throughout much of Western European history, only the thumb and the two first fingers were used to convey food to the mouth. The margin between civilization and barbarism was measured in two fingers. Consider Chaucer's description of how the Prioress, in the Canterbury Tales, ate with her hands:

At mete wel y-taught was she with-alle:
She leet no morsel from hir lippes falle,
Ne wette hir fyngres in hir sauce depe.
Wel koude she carie a morsel and wel kepe
Thát no drope ne fille upon hire brist;
In curteisie was set ful muchel hir list.
Hire over-lippe wyped she so clene
That in hir coppe ther was no ferthyng sene
Of grece, whan she dronken hadde hir draughte.
Ful semely after hir mete she raughte.[5]

Chaucer somewhat satirically emphasized her delicacy, allowing the reader to imagine the coarser behavior of typical fourteenth-century tavern guests. The napkin is a tool of cleanliness and propriety at once, and it comes into play when Chaucer has his Prioress wipe her lip (presumably with a cloth). Manners, which are in essence rules for social behavior given by culture, founded on concerns about cleanliness, hospitality, and group membership, are full of meaning, for to have good manners demonstrates compliance with the social order in general. Manners are, in fact, public performances in which we assure one another of our good intentions and our participation in a common code. Manners can have moral force, with bad manners constituting a serious transgression, and good manners speaking positive volumes about a person.[6]

The napkin is not used in Japan, where table manners are meticulous and one's attention to others particularly important; before the meal you receive an *oshibori*, a cold or hot wet towel, to refresh and clean yourself before eating, but it is not customarily used as a napkin during the meal, even if it remains on the table or counter. Japanese visitors to Western tables have been known to remark on the habit of soiling a cloth with fingers and lips, finding it a little disgusting. But then, the custom of public tooth-picking after a meal, more common in Japan now than in the West, might seem out of place to Westerners, for whom tooth-picking is a private act. Napkins are also material for artistic expression in a table setting; treatises have been devoted to the many ways of folding a banquet or dinner party table linen square, before it is unfolded, placed out of sight on the lap, and, soon, stained with sauce.

Hands make their way even into the purest culinary temples. Watching a star chef in a restaurant kitchen, you will most likely see her use her hands, though the meal she prepares will be eaten with a carefully laid out sequence of forks, knives, and spoons. The feel of the food—a little finger pressure on a cooking chop will tell her when it is done—is vital to the product. Whether it is heat she tests, or texture or resilience, her hand is her best instrument. There is a lesson in the fact that the chef has a kind of permission to touch food that others will eat with utensils, permission granted by the workspace of the kitchen. There are ironies and contradictions in our cultural "grammars" of eating, and even as we use utensils to convey food to mouth in purity, all our senses engaged by the experience, we may allow ourselves to use our hands to lift a drumstick, or a radish dredged through butter and salt.

Conclusion

NATURAL HISTORY AND HUMAN HISTORY meet on the plate. Or to put it differently, a plate of food unites different timescales. There is the time the beans and rice take to cook, and the time farmers took to harvest and process them. There is the time those plants took to grow. But there is also the deeper and slower species-history of the plants, including the way humans domesticated and bred them, and carried them around the globe. Against that slow time, consider the comparatively fast time of human cultural change, generation to generation, different communities cooking their beans and rice in different ways, from a South Asian *dahl* to a Southern American dish of Hoppin' John. In less than a human generation food lineages can mix, producing new tastes and new expectations.

We think of this book as a toolkit for the study of food, rather than a complete catalogue of human foodways. This book offers no grand unified theory of how foodways change, or of food's cultural significance. Nothing, we think, explains everything—not biology, nor gender, nor geography, nor economics and class conflict, nor nutritional needs, nor technology, nor symbolism. But they all have a place in the study of food. In place of grand theories, we prefer finding the explanation that suits the question at hand. Just as tools are appropriate to tasks, so are explanatory principles. As we avoid grand unifying theories, we also reject the idea of an arc of history that moves from the past into a predictable future. The history of foodways is not a set of evidence from which we can extrapolate rules that will then allow us to make claims about what the future of food will be like. North Americans embraced sushi in the 1980s, which surprised many observers, but this does not mean that they (or a similar group of eaters, elsewhere in the world) will embrace another novel form of protein, such as laboratory-grown or "cultured" meat, today.[1] But if we do not believe in grand arcs of history, we are nevertheless interested in the future of food.

Food has always been full of the future. Communities have to plan for meals to come, whether this means storing the harvest for the winter, or prognosticating about population shifts and agricultural policy.[2] As we finished writing this book, the future of food looked precarious, both because of the climate crisis, and because of the global growth of resource-intensive diets. The modern Western diet, so heavy on meat, has globalized, while the world's population has increased dramatically. Available farmland and water are diminishing and seem likely to continue to diminish as our century ticks on. Scientists who track the depletion of major aquifers around the world are concerned, because groundwaters are withdrawn to irrigate crops faster than they are replenished; the agricultural sector is the single greatest consumer of water worldwide.[3] Within this wide matrix of threat, specific crops are in danger: eaters may need to give up beloved foods, like the banana; drinkers may lose cherished beverages, such as coffee. We may need to change our diets proactively in order to shrink industrial agriculture's long environmental shadow. And the area of industrial agriculture that seems most obviously wasteful is industrial meat production, which helped to make meat cheap in the developed world. Meat does not "scale up" well, and we are all living with the environmental consequences.[4]

Do we need a future of technology or a future of neo-agrarianism? Conversations about the future of food often founder between these apparent options. Since the late eighteenth century, and notably in the mid-twentieth century and the early twenty-first, some have argued that new agricultural techniques, and new technological tools, will provide a future of plenty for all. Others have argued that technological modernity, from industrialized farming to mass urbanization to remarkable population growth, created the very problems technologists now propose to solve. The answer, they say, lies not in new technologies but in a return to smaller-scale, non-industrial agriculture.

Rachel Laudan has written one of the most thoughtful defenses of industrialized food production, entitled "A Plea for Culinary Modernism" and first published in 2001.[5] It is easy to bash McDonald's and other fast food outlets, Laudan wrote, but such easy targets obscure the great gains secured by industrial food production over the past hundred and fifty years. Food is now safer and more abundant than ever before. Global agriculture feeds more mouths than ever before. The story about the agricultural past told by "culinary Luddites," Laudan wrote, gets many things wrong. To treasure local, natural, and "organic" foods, and place great value on hours spent in the kitchen doing things the hard way, is all quite novel, and often a perspective born of privilege. Indeed, before industrialization food was scarce when harvests were bad; it was geographically limited (unless you were rich enough to afford imported foods); and sometimes, it was infested with weevils. Natural, unprocessed food rotted quickly. For the ancient Greeks, Laudan wrote, "Happiness was not a verdant Garden of Eden abounding in fresh fruits, but a securely locked storehouse jammed with preserved, processed foods."[6] Laudan argued against too black-and-white an approach to food, and called for "an ethos that does not prejudge, but decides case by case when natural is preferable to processed, fresh to preserved."[7]

Laudan did not intend to defend industrial agriculture against all criticisms, and she acknowledged that the critics get something right. Simply put, industrial agriculture endangers our natural environment. Not only does it create pollution, it also endangers species by specializing in genetically un-diverse crops. Big agribusiness favors plant varieties well suited to vast scales of production and processing.[8] But genetic diversity in a species can help it to cope with threats such as disease, or to adapt to changing conditions, such as the shifting temperatures and weather produced by climate change. The banana industry, for example, relies heavily on the Cavendish, a variety of banana propagated through rhizomatic cuttings rather than sexually. Because of this propagation strategy (notably, a strategy used by the vast majority of banana farmers, for all varieties), Cavendish plants are essentially clones. They display little genetic diversity and have few mechanisms for adapting to disease. The Cavendish may collapse, taking most of an industry with it—unless banana growers can induce another variety of banana to scale up, without using the same propagation strategy. Naturally, big agribusiness companies recognize these problems, and seek solutions, but the sheer scale of industrial agricultural enterprise makes it difficult to change course.

Our industrial-agricultural condition presents us with ironies: many of us have the time to enjoy pleasurable kinds of food work, like baking our own bread, precisely because industry has taken up time-consuming tasks like grinding wheat into flour. Most of us do not have to labor as our ancestors did in order to eat. We should recognize these gains, but we should also look to the security of our food system, to our natural environment itself, and to the genetic diversity of the key species we count on. To place our trust in industrial modernity and its scalar effects, or to reject modernity wholesale, is mere ideology, and inadequate to the challenges ahead.

The very fragility of our industrial food system makes food history and food anthropology important resources. They are not predictive fields, but they document past and present possibilities for practice, and offer clues about how we might adapt ourselves to changing circumstances. Our ways of eating, and the plants and animals we have eaten, began as adaptations to local conditions. *Chapulines* (fried grasshoppers) in Oaxaca, and *maeng da* (giant water bugs) in Thailand, are reminders of the range of animal protein people eat around the world, reminders that the contours of edibility are diverse, and can shift. What do you consider offal, the parts of animals unworthy of your plate? Your definition of meat probably depends on the local food culture of your family, and on the standards of the larger community in which you live. What does the word "dumpling" mean to you, anyway? A piece of dough steamed in a pot along with other ingredients, or an envelope of dough folded around a savory package of vegetables and meat? Fluffy or chewy? Our strategies of provisioning, of roasting and boiling, of fermenting and pickling, are based on skill and received wisdom, and they are also maps of our social lives, little fractal parts of a larger culinary culture. Think of the simple thing a knife does: it divides our ingredients. The knife divides in order to share.

Notes

Introduction

1. See Egbert J. Bakker, *The Meaning of Meat and the Structure of the Odyssey* (Cambridge, UK: Cambridge University Press, 2013).

2. John Berger, *Ways of Seeing* (London: BBC, 1972).

3. On washing dishes as part of life in an active kitchen, see Peter Miller, *How to Wash the Dishes* (New York: Penguin Random House, 2020).

Chapter One

1. Charles Darwin, *The Descent of Man, and Selection in Relation to Sex* (London: Penguin Books, 2004 [1871]), chapter 5.

2. For one argument about prehistoric fire use and its relationship with hominid evolution see Richard Wrangham, *Catching Fire: How Cooking Made Us Human* (New York: Basic Books, 2010); for a contrary view see Alianda M. Cornélio, et al., "Human Brain Expansion during Evolution Is Independent of Fire Control and Cooking," *Frontiers in Neuroscience* 10 (2016): 167.

3. See, for example, Michael Pollan, *The Botany of Desire: A Plant's-eye View of the World* (New York: Random House, 2001).

4. For one classic study of such rituals see George Frazier, *The Golden Bough: A Study in Magic and Religion* (London: Palgrave, 2016).

5. Claude Lévi-Strauss, *The Raw and the Cooked: Mythologiques Volume I*, trans. John and Doreen Weightman (New York: Harper & Row, 1969).

6. On structuralism see Terence Hawkes, *Structuralism and Semiotics* (London: Routledge, 1977).

7. See Fiona Marshall and Elisabeth Hildebrand, "Cattle Before Crops: The Beginnings of Food Production in Africa," *Journal of World Prehistory* 16, no. 2 (June 2002): 99–143.

8. See Stanley Brandes, "Maize as a Cultural Mystery," *Ethnology* 31 (1992): 331–36.

9. James C. Scott, *Against the Grain: A Deep History of the Earliest States* (New Haven: Yale University Press, 2017). For criticisms of Scott, see Jedediah Britton-Purdy, "Paleo Politics," *The New Republic*, November 1, 2017, and Samuel Moyn, "Barbarian Virtues," *The Nation*, October 5, 2017.

Chapter Two

1. On rations as the materialization of a fine line between state coercion and state benefits, see Alexander H. Joffe, "Alcohol and Social Complexity in Ancient Western Asia," *Current Anthropology* 46, no. 2 (April 1998): 275–303.

2. Fernand Braudel, "History and the Social Sciences: The Longue Durée," trans. Immanuel Wallerstein, in *Review (Fernand Braudel Center)* 32, no. 2, *Commemorating the Longue Durée* (2009): 171–203, 179.

3. Oddone Longo, "The Food of Others," in *Food: A Culinary History*, ed. Jean-Louis Flandrin and Massimo Montanari (New York: Columbia University Press, 1999), 156.

4. See Pierre Briant, *From Cyrus to Alexander: A History of the Persian Empire*, trans. Peter T. Daniels (Winona Lake, IN: Eisenbrauns, 2002).

5. See János Harmatta, "Three Iranian Words for 'Bread,'" *Acta Orientalia Academiae Scientiarum Hungaricae* 3, no. 3 (1953): 245–83.

6. On Persian feasting patterns in general see Kaori O'Connor, *The Never-Ending Feast: The Anthropology and Archaeology of Feasting* (London: Bloomsbury, 2015), chapter 3.

7. On the Persian origins of Turkish Delight and the technique of using powdered nuts to thicken sauces, see Reay Tannahill, *Food in History* (New York: Stein and Day, 1973), 175.

8. See, for example, Briant, *From Cyrus to Alexander*.

9. See Rachel Laudan, *Cuisine and Empire: Cooking in World History* (Berkeley: University of California Press, 2013), 64.

10. Laudan, *Cuisine and Empire*, 70–71.

11. On the dietary patterns of Mediterranean Celts during the Roman period see Benjamin Peter Luley, "Cooking, Class, and Colonial Transformations in Roman Mediterranean France," *American Journal of Archaeology* 118, no. 1 (January 2014):

33–60. And see Michael Dietler, *Archaeologies of Colonialism: Consumption, Entanglement, and Violence in Ancient Mediterranean France* (Berkeley: University of California Press, 2010).

12. See J. J. Tierney, "The Celtic Ethnography of Posidonius," *Proceedings of the Royal Irish Academy. Section C: Archaeology, Celtic Studies, History, Linguistics, Literature* 60 (1959): 189–275, 247.

13. On the *annona* see Tannahill, *Food in History*, 85–87.

14. Similarly, an antecedent to today's Japanese sushi is *funazushi*, made by fermenting fish layered in salt for up to four years. In this process, the fish do not lose their shape, but the bones and internal organs become soft. This is still made as a delicacy, especially on the shores of Lake Biwa near Kyoto, seemingly antithetical to the idea that sushi must be made of hyper-fresh fish.

15. See Laudan, *Cuisine and Empire*, 81.

16. Pliny the Elder, *Natural History Volume III, Book 8–11*, trans. H. Rackham, Loeb Classical Library 353 (Cambridge, MA: Harvard University Press, 1940), 146–47.

17. See Tony King, "Diet in the Roman World: A Regional Inter-site Comparison of the Mammal Bones," *Journal of Roman Archaeology* 12 (1999): 168–202.

18. See Sally Grainger, "The Myth of Apicius," *Gastronomica* 7, no. 2 (Spring 2007): 71–77.

19. See Cicero, *De officiis* 1.150.

20. Cited in Robert Hughes, *Rome* (New York: A. Knopf, 2011), 7.

21. On parrot eating through history, see Bruce Boehrer, "The Parrot Eaters: Psittacophagy in the Renaissance and Beyond," *Gastronomica* 4, no. 3 (Summer 2004): 46–59.

22. See Lin Yutang, "The Chinese Cuisine," in *My Country and My People* (New York: Reynal & Hitchcock, 1935).

23. See Laudan, *Cuisine and Empire*, 92.

24. K.C. Chang, "Introduction," in *Food in Chinese Culture: Anthropological and Historical Perspectives*, ed. K.C. Chang (New Haven: Yale University Press, 1977), 11.

25. See Walter Scheidel, "From the 'Great Convergence' to the 'First Great Divergence': Roman and Qin-Han State Formation and Its Aftermath," Princeton/Stanford Working Papers in Classics, 2007.

26. On millet and rice cultivation in China see Kenneth Kiple, *A Moveable Feast: Ten Millennia of Food Globalization* (Cambridge, UK: Cambridge University Press, 2007): 41–42.

27. Kiple, *A Moveable Feast*, 43.

28. See Ying-shih Yü, "Food in Chinese Culture: The Han Period (206 B.C.E.–220 C.E.)," in Ying-shih Yü with Josephine Chiu-Duke and Michael S. Duke, *Chinese History and Culture: Sixth Century B.C.E. to Seventeenth Century* (New York: Columbia University Press, 2016).

29. See E. N. Anderson, *The Food of China* (New Haven: Yale University Press, 1988), 7.

30. Anderson, *The Food of China*, 44.

31. Anderson, *The Food of China*, 31.

32. From the *Chuang Tzu*. This translation by Derek Lin can be found at http://dereklin.com and https://taoism.net/carving-up-an-ox.

33. See David R. Knechtges, "A Literary Feast: Food in Early Chinese Literature," *Journal of the American Oriental Society* 106, no. 1 (January-March, 1986): 49–63, 52.

34. See Emily S. Wu, "Chinese Ancestral Worship: Food to Sustain, Transform, and Heal the Dead and the Living," in *Dying to Eat: Cross-Cultural Perspectives on Food, Death, and the Afterlife*, ed. Candi K. Cann (Lexington: University Press of Kentucky, 2018).

35. See Anderson, *The Food of China*, 11.

36. Anderson, *The Food of China*, 15.

Vignette Three

1. *The Phnom Penh Post,* January 23, 2022.

Chapter Three

Epigraph: see Larry D. Benson, ed., *The Riverside Chaucer* (Oxford: Oxford University Press, 2008), lines 379–84. In modern English, this reads "A Cook they had with them for the occasion//To boil the chickens with the marrow-bones/ And tart flavoring, and spice./Well could he appreciate a draught of London ale./ He could roast, and boil, and broil, and fry/Make stew, and well bake a pie.

1. On food as a constant theme in Chaucer, see Jayne Elisabeth Archer, Richard Marggraf Turley, and Howard Thomas, "'Soper at Oure Aller Cost': The Politics of Food Supply in the Canterbury Tales," *The Chaucer Review* 50, no. 1–2 (2015): 1–29. And see also Shayne Aaron Legassie, "The Pilgrimage Road in Late Medieval English Literature," in *Roadworks: Medieval Britain, Medieval Roads*, ed. Valerie Allen and Ruth Evans (Manchester: Manchester University Press, 2015).

2. See John Keay, *The Spice Route: A History* (Berkeley: University of California Press, 2006), 4.

3. See Fred C. Robinson, "Medieval, the Middle Ages," *Speculum* 59, no. 4 (October 1984): 745–56; on the idea of "the Dark Ages," see Theodore E. Mommsen, "Petrarch's Conception of the 'Dark Ages,'" *Speculum* 17, no. 2 (April 1942): 226–42. There is always a great deal of debate about when to set the boundaries for each period.

4. See Massimo Montanari, *Medieval Tastes: Food, Cooking, and the Table* (New York: Columbia University Press, 2015), chapter 15, "The Pilgrim's Food."

5. On Christianity as the basis of a cuisine, see Rachel Laudan, "Christian Cuisines," in *Cuisine and Empire*, especially 168–69.

6. See Caroline Walker Bynum, *Holy Feast and Holy Fast: The Religious Significance of Food to Medieval Women* (Berkeley: University of California Press, 1988), 38.

7. St. Augustine, Sermon 272, "On the Nature of the Sacrament of the Eucharist."

8. See Phyllis Pray Bober, *Art, Culture & Cuisine: Ancient and Medieval Gastronomy* (Chicago: University of Chicago Press, 1999), 253.

9. See Léo Moulin, "La bière, une invention médiévale," in *Manger et boire au Moyen Age: Actes du colloque de Nice*, ed. Denis Menjot (Paris: Les Belles Lettres, 1984).

10. See William Bostwick, *The Brewer's Tale: A History of the World According to Beer* (New York: W. W. Norton, 2015).

11. On such establishments see Justin Colson, "A Portrait of a Late Medieval London pub: The Star Inn, Bridge Street," in *Medieval Londoners: Essays to Mark the Eightieth Birthday of Caroline M. Barron*, ed. Elizabeth A. New and Christian Steer (Chicago: University of Chicago Press, 2019).

12. See Katherine L. French, "Gender and Changing Foodways in England's Late-medieval Bourgeois Households," *Clio: Women, Gender, History* 40 (2014): 42–62.

13. See Martha Carlin, "'What say you to a piece of beef and mustard?': The Evolution of Public Dining in Medieval and Tudor London," *Huntington Library Quarterly* 71, no. 1 (March 2008): 199–217.

14. See Barbara A. Hanawalt, "The Host, the Law, and the Ambiguous Space of Medieval London Taverns," in *Medieval Crime and Social Control*, ed. Barbara A. Hanawalt and David Wallace (Minneapolis: University of Minnesota Press, 1998).

15. See George Dameron, "Feeding the Medieval Italian City-State," *Speculum* 92, no. 4 (October 2017): 976–1019.

16. See Herman Pleij, *Dreaming of Cockaigne: Medieval Fantasies of the Perfect Life*, trans. Diane Webb (New York: Columbia University Press, 2003).

17. See Kathy L. Pearson, "Nutrition and the Early-Medieval," *Speculum* 72, no. 1 (January 1997): 1–32.

18. See Rachel Laudan, "The Birth of the Modern Diet," *Scientific American* (August 2000): 11–16.

19. See Bober, *Art, Culture & Cuisine*, 261.

20. For one overview focused on the English case, see Bruce M. S. Campbell and Mark Overton, "A New Perspective on Medieval and Early Modern Agriculture: Six Centuries of Norfolk Farming c. 1250–c. 1850," *Past & Present* 141 (November 1993): 38–105.

21. See Christopher Bonfield, "The First Instrument of Medicine: Diet and Regimens of Health in Late Medieval England," in *A Verray Parfit Praktisour: Essays Presented to Carole Rawcliffe*, ed. Linda Clark and Elizabeth Danbury (Woodbridge, UK: Boydell & Brewer, 2017).

22. See Laudan, *Cuisine & Empire*, 176, and Wolfgang Schivelbusch, *Tastes of Paradise: A Social History of Spices, Stimulants, and Intoxicants,* trans. David Jacobson (New York: Vintage, 1992).

23. Mace is nutmeg's lacy cover, separated from the matrix seed and used on its own as a spice and medicine; the fruit surrounding both mace and nutmeg is often made into jam.

24. See "Sir Thopas's Tale" in Chaucer, *The Canterbury Tales.*

25. See Clifford A. Wright, "The Medieval Spice Trade and the Diffusion of the Chile," *Gastronomica* 7, no. 2 (Spring 2007): 35–43.

26. See Keay, *The Spice Route,* 9.

27. Giles Milton, *Nathaniel's Nutmeg* (New York: Farrar, Straus and Giroux, 1999).

28. Quoted in Jack Turner, *Spice: the History of a Temptation* (New York: Knopf, 2008), 39.

29. Paul Freedman, ed., *Food: The History of Taste* (London: Thames and Hudson, 2007), 246.

30. See Keay, *The Spice Route,* 139.

31. See Henri Pirenne, *Economic and Social History of Medieval Europe,* trans. I. E. Clegg (New York: Harvest/Harcourt Brace & World, 1966), 141.

32. See Schivelbusch, *Tastes of Paradise.*

Chapter Four

1. Alfred Crosby, *The Columbian Exchange* (New York: Greenwood Press, 1972).

2. Charles C. Mann, *1491: New Revelations of the Americas Before Columbus* (New York: Knopf, 2005).

3. On Indigenous agriculture and land use see Mann, *1491*, and see also: David L. Lentz, ed., *Imperfect Balance: Landscape Transformations in the Pre-Columbian Americas* (New York: Columbia University Press, 2000); Robert A. Dull, "Evidence for Forest Clearance, Agriculture, and Human-Induced Erosion in Precolumbian El Salvador," *Annals of the Association of American Geographers* 97, no. 1 (March, 2007): 127–41. On the complexities of paleoethnobotany in this context see Christopher T. Morehart and Shanti Morell-Hart, "Beyond the Eco-fact: Toward a Social Paleoethnobotany in Mesoamerica," *Journal of Archaeological Method and Theory* 22, no. 2 (June 2015): 483–511.

4. Here we use the modern term Aztec for convenience, acknowledging that the people we call Aztecs called themselves by their region of origin; for example, Mexica or Tlatelolca.

5. Mann, *1491*, 18.

6. John Gerard, *Gerard's Herball* (Boston: Houghton Mifflin, 1969 [1597]), 276.

7. For one view of the potato's effects on world history, with a strong emphasis on Europe, see William H. McNeill, "How the Potato Changed the World's History," *Social Research* 66, no. 1 (Spring 1999): 67–83.

8. Crosby, *The Columbian Exchange*, 182.

9. See Mann, *1491*, 254.

10. Joanna Davidson, *Sacred Rice: An Ethnography of Identity, Environment and Development in Rural West Africa* (Oxford: Oxford University Press, 2016), 18 ff.

11. Davidson, *Sacred Rice*.

12. Davidson, *Sacred Rice*, chapter 1, especially p. 4.

13. See Judith A. Carney, *Black Rice* (Cambridge, MA: Harvard University Press, 2001).

14. Michael Twitty, *Rice* (Chapel Hill: University of North Carolina Press, 2021), 3.

15. Jessica B. Harris, "Out of Africa: Musings on Culinary Connections to the Motherland," in *Black Food: Stories, Art and Recipes from Across the African Diaspora*, ed. Bryant Terry (New York: Ten Speed Press, 2021), 27.

16. Harris, "Out of Africa," 28.

Chapter Five

1. See Maxine Berg, "Consumption in Eighteenth and Early Nineteenth-century Britain," in *The Cambridge Economic History of Modern Britain, Volume 1,*

Industrialization, ed. Roderick Floud and Paul Johnson (Cambridge, UK: Cambridge University Press, 2004), 365.

2. See Gregson Davis, "Jane Austen's *Mansfield Park:* The Antigua Connection," in *Antigua Conference Papers* (University of California at Davis, 2004), https://www.open.uwi.edu/sites/default/files/bnccde/antigua/conference/papers/davis.html.

3. See Sidney Mintz, *Sweetness and Power: The Place of Sugar in Modern History* (New York: Viking Penguin, 1985), 101.

4. Mintz, *Sweetness and Power*, 185.

5. Mintz, *Sweetness and Power*, 174.

6. See Mark Pendergrast, *Uncommon Grounds: The History of Coffee and How it Transformed the World* (New York: Basic Books, 1999), 8.

7. See Jürgen Habermas, *The Structural Transformation of the Public Sphere: An Inquiry into a Category of Bourgeois Society*, trans. Thomas Burger (Cambridge, MA: MIT Press, 1989).

8. See Merry I. White, *Coffee Life in Japan* (Berkeley: University of California Press, 2012).

9. White, *Coffee Life in Japan*, 73-74.

Vignette Six

1. Theodor W. Adorno, *The Jargon of Authenticity*, trans. Knut Tarnowski and Frederic Will (London: Routledge and Kegan Paul, 1973).

Chapter Six

1. Isabella Beeton, *Mrs. Beeton's Book of Household Management* (London: S. O. Beeton Publishing, 1861), 169.

2. William Makepeace Thackeray, *Vanity Fair* (New York: Vintage Books, 1950 [1848]), 21-22.

3. John Williams, 1841, cited on his mission in the South Seas in Lizzie Collingham, *The Hungry Empire* (London: The Bodley Head, 2017), 189.

4. Collingham, *The Hungry Empire*, 193.

5. Simon Schama, *The Embarrassment of Riches* (New York: Alfred Knopf, 1987).

6. Bernard Germain de Lacepede, cited in Laudan, *Cuisine and Empire*, 228.

7. Van Voi Tran, "How 'Natives' Ate at Colonial Exhibitions in 1889, 1900, and 1931," *French Cultural Studies* 26, no. 2 (2015): 163-75.

8. Sylvie Durmelat, "Introduction: Colonial Culinary Encounters and Imperial Leftovers," *French Cultural Studies* 26, no. 2 (2015): 119, with reference to Rebecca Spang, *The Invention of the Restaurant: Paris and Modern Gastronomic Culture* (Cambridge, MA: Harvard University Press, 2000).

9. Angela Giovanangeli, "'Merguez Capitale': The Merguez Sausage as a Discursive Construction of Cosmopolitan Branding, Colonial Memory and Local Flavour in Marseille," *French Cultural Studies* 26, no. 2 (2015): 231–43.

Chapter Seven

Epigraph: Arthur Young, *The Farmer's Tour Through the East of England* (1771), in D.B. Horn and Mary Ransome, eds., *English Historical Documents, Vol. X*, 1714–1783 (Oxford: Oxford University Press, 1969): 440–43.

1. Robert Allen, *Enclosure and the Yeoman* (Oxford: Clarendon Press, 1992).

2. Allen, *Enclosure and the Yeoman*, 1.

3. On the origin of the restaurant in the eighteenth century see Jean-Robert Pitte, "The Rise of the Restaurant," in Flandrin and Montanari, *Food*, and Spang, *The Invention of the Restaurant*.

4. On these food riots see E.P. Thompson, "The Moral Economy of the English Crowd in the 18th Century," *Past & Present* 50 (February 1971): 76–136.

5. T.S. Ashton, *The Industrial Revolution* (Oxford: Oxford University Press, 1954), 161.

6. Flandrin and Montanari, *Food*, 351.

7. Steven Kaplan, *The Bakers of Paris and the Bread Question: 1700-1775* (Durham, NC: Duke University Press, 1996).

8. David Clark, *Urban Geography* (London: Croom Helm, 1982).

9. Laudan, "The Birth of the Modern Diet."

10. Philip Hyman and Mary Human, "Printing the Kitchen: French Cookbooks, 1480-1800," in Flandrin and Montanari, *Food*, 394-401.

11. What follows is drawn largely from G.J. Leigh's comprehensive *The World's Greatest Fix: A History of Nitrogen and Agriculture* (Oxford: Oxford University Press, 2004).

12. Leigh, *The World's Greatest Fix*, 10-22.

13. William Croakes, *The Wheat Problem: Based on Remarks Made in the Presidential Address to the British Association at Bristol in 1898, Revised, with an Answer to Various Critics* (London: J. Murray, 1898).

Chapter Eight

1. On microorganisms such as yeast and the relationship between industrial production using microorganisms and artisanal food craft-practice, see Heather Paxson, *The Life of Cheese: Crafting Food and Value in America* (Berkeley: University of California Press, 2012).

2. Reyner Banham, "The Crisp at the Crossroads," *New Society*, July 9, 1970), 77.

3. On fast food see Eric Schlosser's *Fast Food Nation: The Dark Side of the All-American Meal* (New York: Houghton Mifflin, 2001).

4. Michael Pollan, *In Defense of Food: An Eater's Manifesto* (New York: Penguin 2008).

5. See Emiko Ohnuki-Tierney, "McDonald's in Japan: Changing Manners and Etiquette," in *Golden Arches East: McDonald's in East Asia,* ed. James Watson, 2nd ed. (Stanford, CA: Stanford University Press, 2006), 161–82.

6. For the mission statement of Slow Food, see www.slowfood.org.

7. See Nicola Twilley, "The Coldscape," in *Cabinet* 47 (Fall 2012): 78–87.

8. Joe Strummer and the Mescaleros, "Bhindi Bhagee," *Global a Go-Go* (2001).

9. Stuart Hall, "The Local and the Global: Globalization and Ethnicity," in *Culture, Globalization and the World-System: Contemporary Conditions for the Representation of Identity*, ed. Anthony D. King (Minneapolis: University of Minnesota Press, 1997), 19–40.

10. Arjun Appadurai, "How to Make a National Cuisine: Cookbooks in Contemporary India," *Comparative Studies in Society and History* 30, no. 1 (January 1988): 3–24.

11. Jeffrey Pilcher, "Tamales or Timbales: Cuisine and the Formation of Mexican National Identity, 1821–1911," *The Americas* 53, no. 2 (Oct. 1996): 193–216.

12. See Jeffrey T. Schnapp, "The Romance of Caffeine and Aluminum," *Critical Inquiry* 28, no. 1 (Autumn 2001): 244–69.

13. Pre-contact in Hawai'i means before the arrival of Captain James Cook in 1778, after which Western influences made deep inroads into Hawai'ian culture and worsened dietary health among Hawai'ians.

Chapter Nine

1. Nozaki Hiromitsu, *Japanese Kitchen Knives: Essential Techniques and Recipes* (Tokyo: Kodansha International, 2009): 14–15.

2. Bee Wilson, *Consider the Fork: A History of How We Cook and Eat* (New York: Basic Books, 2012).

3. See Margaret Visser, *The Rituals of Dinner: The Origins, Evolution, Eccentricities, and Meaning of Table Manners* (New York: Penguin, 1991).

4. See Mary Douglas, *Purity and Danger: An Analysis of Concepts of Purity and Taboo* (London: Routledge, 1984) and Stephen Bigger, "Victor Turner, Liminality and Cultural Performance," *Journal of Beliefs and Values* 30, no. 2, 2009: 209–12.

5. "At meat her manners were well taught withal/No morsel from her lips did she let fall/Nor dipped her fingers in the sauce too deep/But she could carry a morsel up and keep/The smallest drop from falling on her breast./For courtliness she had a special zest./And she would wipe her upper lip so clean/That not a trace of grease was to be seen/Upon the cup when she had drunk; to eat/She reached a hand sedately for the meat" ("The Prioress's Tale," in Chaucer, *The Canterbury Tales*.)

6. On all these issues, see Visser, *The Rituals of Dinner*.

Conclusion

1. See Benjamin Aldes Wurgaft, *Meat Planet: Artificial Flesh and the Future of Food* (Oakland: University of California Press, 2019).

2. See Warren Belasco, *Meals to Come: A History of the Future of Food* (Berkeley: University of California Press, 2006), the only book-length study of the history of imagining and predicting the future of food.

3. For one broad overview, see Jay Famiglietti, "A Map of the Future of Water," for the Pew Charitable Trusts: https://www.pewtrusts.org/en/trend /archive/spring-2019/a-map-of-the-future-of-water. And for a recent study considering possible future water scarcity by 2050, see X. Liu, et al., "Global Agricultural Water Scarcity Assessment Incorporating Blue and Green Water Availability under Future Climate Change," *Earth's Future* 10 (2022), e2021EF002567, https:// doi.org/10.1029/2021EF002567. Science journalist Erica Gies has written on the relationship between infrastructure and water, with an eye towards water futures, in her book *Water Always Wins: Thriving in an Age of Drought and Deluge* (Chicago: University of Chicago Press, 2022).

4. Much has been written on the problems of industrial meat production. Two landmark works are Francis Moore Lappé, *Diet for a Small Planet* (New York: Ballantine, 1971) and Orville Schell, *Modern Meat* (New York: Vintage, 1985). In 2006, a report released by the Food and Agriculture Organization (FAO) of the United Nations, entitled *Livestock's Long Shadow*, presented the problem of

industrial animal agriculture in dire terms, accounting for its contributions to climate change. The study originally estimated that the industry produces 18 percent of annual anthropogenic greenhouse gas emissions; subsequent work by FAO reduced that estimate to 14.5 percent.

5. Rachel Laudan, "A Plea for Culinary Modernism: Why We Should Love New, Fast, Processed Food," *Gastronomica* 1, no. 1. (2001): 36–44.

6. Laudan, "Plea," 38.

7. Laudan, "Plea," 43.

8. See Dan Saladino, *Eating to Extinction: The World's Rarest Foods and Why We Need to Save Them* (New York: Penguin, 2021).

Bibliography

Adorno, Theodor W. *The Jargon of Authenticity.* Translated by Knut Tarnowski and Frederic Will. London: Routledge & Kegan Paul, 1973.

Allen, Robert. *Enclosure and the Yeoman.* Oxford: Clarendon Press, 1992.

Anderson, E. N. *The Food of China.* New Haven: Yale University Press, 1988.

Appadurai, Arjun. "How to Make a National Cuisine: Cookbooks in Contemporary India." *Comparative Studies in Society and History* 30, no. 1 (January 1988): 3–24.

Archer, Jayne Elisabeth, Richard Marggraf Turley, and Howard Thomas. "'Soper at Oure Aller Cost': The Politics of Food Supply in the Canterbury Tales." *The Chaucer Review* 50, no. 1–2 (2015): 1–29.

Bakker, Egbert J. *The Meaning of Meat and the Structure of the Odyssey.* Cambridge, UK: Cambridge University Press, 2013.

Banham, Reyner. "The Crisp at the Crossroads." *New Society,* July 9, 1970.

Beeton, Isabella. *Mrs. Beeton's Book of Household Management.* London: S. O. Beeton Publishing, 1861.

Belasco, Warren. *Meals to Come: A History of the Future of Food.* Berkeley: University of California Press, 2006.

Benson, Larry D., ed. *The Riverside Chaucer.* Oxford: Oxford University Press, 2008.

Berg, Maxine. "Consumption in Eighteenth and Early Nineteenth-century Britain." In *The Cambridge Economic History of Modern Britain, Volume 1, Industrialization,* edited by Roderick Floud and Paul Johnson, 357–86. Cambridge, UK: Cambridge University Press, 2004.

Berger, John. *Ways of Seeing.* London: BBC, 1972.

Bigger, Stephen. "Victor Turner, Liminality and Cultural Performance." *Journal of Beliefs and Values* 30, no. 2 (2009): 209–12.

Bober, Phyllis Pray. Art, Culture & Cuisine: Ancient and Medieval Gastronomy. Chicago: University of Chicago Press, 1999.

Boehrer, Bruce. "The Parrot Eaters: Psittacophagy in the Renaissance and Beyond." Gastronomica 4, no. 3 (Summer 2004): 46–59.

Bonfield, Christopher. "The First Instrument of Medicine: Diet and Regimens of Health in Late Medieval England." In A Verray Parfit Praktisour: Essays Presented to Carole Rawcliffe, edited by Linda Clark and Elizabeth Danbury, 99–120. Woodbridge, UK: Boydell & Brewer, 2017.

Bostwick, William. The Brewer's Tale: A History of the World According to Beer. New York: W.W. Norton, 2015.

Brandes, Stanley. "Maize as a Cultural Mystery." Ethnology 31 (1992): 331–36.

Braudel, Fernand. "History and the Social Sciences: The Longue Durée." Translated by Immanuel Wallerstein. Review (Fernand Braudel Center) 32, no. 2, Commemorating the Longue Durée (2009): 171–203.

Briant, Pierre. From Cyrus to Alexander: A History of the Persian Empire. Translated by Peter T. Daniels. Winona Lake, IN: Eisenbrauns, 2002.

Britton-Purdy, Jedediah. "Paleo Politics." The New Republic, November 1, 2017. https://newrepublic.com/article/145444/paleo-politics-what-made-prehistoric-hunter-gatherers-give-freedom-civilization.

Bynum, Caroline Walker. Holy Feast and Holy Fast: The Religious Significance of Food to Medieval Women. Berkeley: University of California Press, 1988.

Campbell, Bruce M.S., and Mark Overton. "A New Perspective on Medieval and Early Modern Agriculture: Six Centuries of Norfolk Farming c. 1250–c. 1850." Past & Present 141 (November 1993): 38–105.

Carlin, Martha. "'What say you to a piece of beef and mustard?': The Evolution of Public Dining in Medieval and Tudor London." Huntington Library Quarterly 71, no. 1 (March 2008): 199–217.

Carney, Judith A. Black Rice: The African Origins of Rice Cultivation in the Americas. Cambridge, MA: Harvard University Press, 2001.

Chang, K.C., ed. Food in Chinese Culture: Anthropological and Historical Perspectives. New Haven: Yale University Press, 1977.

Clark, David. Urban Geography. London: Croom Helm, 1982.

Collingham, Lizzie. Curry: A Tale of Cooks and Conquerors. New York: Vintage Press, 2005.

———. The Hungry Empire. London: The Bodley Head, 2017.

Colson, Justin. "A Portrait of a Late Medieval London pub: The Star Inn, Bridge Street." In Medieval Londoners: Essays to Mark the Eightieth Birthday of

Caroline M. Barron, edited by Elizabeth A. New and Christian Steer, 37–54. Chicago: University of Chicago Press, 2019.

Cornélio, Alianda M., et al. "Human Brain Expansion during Evolution Is Independent of Fire Control and Cooking." *Frontiers in Neuroscience* 10 (2016).

Crosby, Alfred. *The Columbian Exchange*. New York: Greenwood Press, 1972.

Dameron, George. "Feeding the Medieval Italian City-State." *Speculum* 92, no. 4 (October 2017): 976–1019.

Darwin, Charles. *The Descent of Man, and Selection in Relation to Sex*. London: Penguin Books, 2004.

Davidson, Joanna. *Sacred Rice: An Ethnography of Identity, Environment and Development in Rural West Africa*. Oxford: Oxford University Press, 2016.

Davis, Gregson. "Jane Austen's *Mansfield Park*: The Antigua Connection." In *Antigua Conference Papers*. Davis: University of California at Davis, 2004. https://www.open.uwi.edu/sites/default/files/bnccde/antigua/conference/papers/davis.html.

Dietler, Michael. *Archaeologies of Colonialism: Consumption, Entanglement, and Violence in Ancient Mediterranean France*. Berkeley: University of California Press, 2010.

Douglas, Mary. *Purity and Danger*. London: Routledge, 1984.

Dull, Robert A. "Evidence for Forest Clearance, Agriculture, and Human-Induced Erosion in Precolumbian El Salvador." *Annals of the Association of American Geographers* 97, no. 1 (March, 2007): 127–41.

Durmelat, Sylvie. "Introduction: Colonial Culinary Encounters and Imperial Leftovers." *French Cultural Studies* 26, no. 2 (2015): 115–29.

Flandrin, Jean-Louis, and Massimo Montanari, eds. *Food: A Culinary History*. New York: Columbia University Press, 1999.

Frazier, George. *The Golden Bough: A Study in Magic and Religion*. London: Palgrave, 2016.

Freedman, Paul, ed. *Food: The History of Taste*. London: Thames and Hudson, 2007.

French, Katherine L. "Gender and Changing Foodways in England's Late-medieval Bourgeois Households." *Clio: Women, Gender, History* 40 (2014): 42–62.

Gerard, John. *Gerard's Herball*. Boston: Houghton Mifflin, 1969 [1597].

Gies, Erica. *Water Always Wins: Thriving in an Age of Drought and Deluge*. Chicago: University of Chicago Press, 2022.

Giovanangeli, Angela. "'Merguez Capitale': The Merguez Sausage as a Discursive Construction of Cosmopolitan Branding, Colonial Memory and Local Flavour in Marseille." *French Cultural Studies* 26, no. 2 (2015): 231–43.

Grainger, Sally. "The Myth of Apicius." *Gastronomica* 7, no. 2 (Spring 2007): 71–77.

Habermas, Jürgen. *The Structural Transformation of the Public Sphere: An Inquiry into a Category of Bourgeois Society.* Translated by Thomas Burger. Cambridge, MA: MIT Press, 1989.

Hall, Stuart. "The Local and the Global: Globalization and Ethnicity." In *Culture, Globalization and the World-System: Contemporary Conditions for the Representation of Identity,* edited by Anthony D. King, 19–40. Minneapolis: University of Minnesota Press, 1997.

Hanawalt, Barbara A. "The Host, the Law, and the Ambiguous Space of Medieval London Taverns." In *Medieval Crime and Social Control,* edited by Barbara A. Hanawalt and David Wallace, 204–23. Minneapolis: University of Minnesota Press, 1998.

Harmatta, János. "Three Iranian Words for "Bread."" *Acta Orientalia Academiae Scientiarum Hungaricae* 3, no. 3 (1953): 245–83.

Harris, Jessica B. "Out of Africa: Musings on Culinary Connections to the Motherland." In *Black Food: Stories, Art and Recipes from Across the African Diaspora,* edited by Bryant Terry. New York: Ten Speed Press, 2021.

Hawkes, Terence. *Structuralism and Semiotics.* London: Routledge, 1977.

Horn, D. B., and Mary Ransome, eds. *English Historical Documents, Vol. X, 1714–1783.* Oxford: Oxford University Press, 1969.

Hughes, Robert. *Rome.* New York: A. Knopf, 2011.

Hyman, Philip, and Mary Human. "Printing the Kitchen: French Cookbooks, 1480–1800." In Flandrin and Montanari, *Food,* 394–401.

Joffe, Alexander H. "Alcohol and Social Complexity in Ancient Western Asia." *Current Anthropology* 46, no. 2 (April 1998): 275–303.

Kaplan, Steven. *The Bakers of Paris and the Bread Question: 1700–1775.* Durham, NC: Duke University Press, 1996.

Keay, John. *The Spice Route: A History.* Berkeley: University of California Press, 2006.

King, Tony. "Diet in the Roman World: A Regional Inter-site Comparison of the Mammal Bones." *Journal of Roman Archaeology* 12 (1999): 168–202.

Kiple, Kenneth. *A Moveable Feast: Ten Millennia of Food Globalization.* Cambridge, UK: Cambridge University Press, 2007.

Knechtges, David R. "A Literary Feast: Food in Early Chinese Literature." *Journal of the American Oriental Society* 106, no. 1 (January-March 1986): 49–63.

Lappé, Francis Moore. *Diet for a Small Planet.* New York: Ballantine, 1971.

Laudan, Rachel. "The Birth of the Modern Diet." *Scientific American* (August 2000): 11–16.

———. "A Plea for Modernist Cuisine: Why We Should Love New, Fast, Processed Food." *Gastronomica* 1, no. 1 (2001): 36–44.

———. *Cuisine and Empire: Cooking in World History*. Berkeley: University of California Press, 2013.

Legassie, Shayne Aaron. "The Pilgrimage Road in Late Medieval English Literature." In *Roadworks: Medieval Britain, Medieval Roads*, edited by Valerie Allen and Ruth Evans, eds., 198–219. Manchester: Manchester University Press, 2015.

Leigh, G. J. *The World's Greatest Fix: A History of Nitrogen and Agriculture*. Oxford: Oxford University Press, 2004.

Lentz, David L., ed. *Imperfect Balance: Landscape Transformations in the Pre-Columbian Americas*. New York: Columbia University Press, 2000.

Lévi-Strauss, Claude. *The Raw and the Cooked: Mythologiques Volume I*. Translated by John and Doreen Weightman. New York: Harper & Row, 1969.

Lin Yutang. "The Chinese Cuisine." In *My Country and My People*, 317–25. New York: Reynal & Hitchcock, 1935.

Liu, X., et al. "Global Agricultural Water Scarcity Assessment Incorporating Blue and Green Water Availability under Future Climate Change." *Earth's Future* 10 (2022), e2021EF002567, https://doi.org/10.1029/2021EF002567.

Longo, Oddone. "The Food of Others." In Flandrin and Montanari, *Food*, 153–93.

Luley, Benjamin Peter. "Cooking, Class, and Colonial Transformations in Roman Mediterranean France." *American Journal of Archaeology* 118, no. 1 (January 2014): 33–60.

Mann, Charles C. 1491: *New Revelations of the Americas Before Columbus*. New York: Knopf, 2005.

Marshall, Fiona, and Elisabeth Hildebrand. "Cattle Before Crops: The Beginnings of Food Production in Africa." *Journal of World Prehistory* 16, no. 2 (June 2002): 99–143.

McNeill, William H. "How the Potato Changed the World's History." *Social Research* 66, no. 1 (Spring 1999): 67–83.

Miller, Peter. *How to Wash the Dishes*. New York: Penguin Random House, 2020.

Milton, Giles. *Nathaniel's Nutmeg*. New York: Farrar, Straus and Giroux, 1999.

Mintz, Sidney. *Sweetness and Power: The Place of Sugar in Modern History*. New York: Viking Penguin, 1985.

Mommsen, Theodore E. "Petrarch's Conception of the 'Dark Ages.'" *Speculum* 17, no. 2 (April 1942): 226–42.

Montanari, Massimo. *Medieval Tastes: Food, Cooking, and the Table*. New York: Columbia University Press, 2015.

Morehart, Christopher T., and Shanti Morell-Hart. "Beyond the Ecofact: Toward a Social Paleoethnobotany in Mesoamerica." *Journal of Archaeological Method and Theory* 22, no. 2 (June 2015): 483–511.

Moulin, Léo. "La bière, une invention médiévale." In *Manger et boire au Moyen Age: Actes du colloque de Nice (15–17 octobre 1982)*, edited by Denis Menjot, 13–31. Paris: Les Belles Lettres, 1984.

Moyn, Samuel. "Barbarian Virtues." *The Nation*, October 5, 2017. https://www.thenation.com/article/archive/barbarian-virtues.

Nozaki, Hiromitsu. *Japanese Kitchen Knives: Essential Techniques and Recipes*. Tokyo: Kodansha International, 2009.

Ohnuki-Tierney, Emiko. "McDonald's in Japan: Changing Manners and Etiquette." In Watson, *Golden Arches East*, 161–82.

O'Connor, Kaori. *The Never-Ending Feast: The Anthropology and Archaeology of Feasting*. London: Bloomsbury, 2015.

Paxson, Heather. *The Life of Cheese: Crafting Food and Value in America*. Berkeley: University of California Press, 2012.

Pearson, Kathy L. "Nutrition and the Early-Medieval." *Speculum* 72, no. 1 (January 1997): 1–32.

Pendergrast, Mark. *Uncommon Grounds: The History of Coffee and How it Transformed the World*. New York: Basic Books, 1999.

Pilcher, Jeffrey. "Tamales or Timbales: Cuisine and the Formation of Mexican National Identity, 1821–1911." *The Americas* 53, no. 2 (October 1996): 193–216.

Pirenne, Henri. *Economic and Social History of Medieval Europe*. Translated by I. E. Clegg. New York: Harvest/Harcourt Brace & World, 1966.

Pitte, Jean-Robert. "The Rise of the Restaurant." In Flandrin and Montanari, *Food*, 471–80.

Pleijj, Herman. *Dreaming of Cockaigne: Medieval Fantasies of the Perfect Life*. Translated by Diane Webb. New York: Columbia University Press, 2003.

Pliny the Elder. *Natural History Volume III, Books 8–11*. Translated by H. Rackham. Loeb Classical Library 353. Cambridge, MA: Harvard University Press, 1940.

Pollan, Michael. *The Botany of Desire: A Plant's-eye View of the World*. New York: Random House, 2001.

———. *In Defense of Food: An Eater's Manifesto*. New York: Penguin 2008.

Robinson, Fred C. "Medieval, the Middle Ages." *Speculum* 59, no. 4 (October 1984): 745–56.

Saladino, Dan. *Eating to Extinction: The World's Rarest Foods and Why We Need to Save Them*. New York: Penguin, 2021.

Schama, Simon. *The Embarrassment of Riches*. New York: Alfred Knopf, 1987.

Scheidel, Walter. "From the 'Great Convergence' to the 'First Great Divergence': Roman and Qin-Han State Formation and Its Aftermath." Princeton/Stanford Working Papers in Classics, 2007.

Schell, Orville. *Modern Meat*. New York: Vintage, 1985.

Schivelbusch, Wolfgang. *Tastes of Paradise: A Social History of Spices, Stimulants, and Intoxicants*. Translated by David Jacobson. New York: Vintage, 1992.

Schlosser, Eric. *Fast Food Nation: The Dark Side of the All-American Meal*. New York: Houghton Mifflin, 2001.

Schnapp, Jeffrey T. "The Romance of Caffeine and Aluminum." *Critical Inquiry* 28, no. 1 (Autumn 2001): 244–69.

Scott, James C. *Against the Grain: A Deep History of the Earliest States*. New Haven: Yale University Press, 2017.

Spang, Rebecca. *The Invention of the Restaurant: Paris and Modern Gastronomic Culture*. Cambridge, MA: Harvard University Press, 2000.

Tannahill, Reay. *Food in History*. New York: Stein and Day, 1973.

Thackeray, William Makepeace. *Vanity Fair*. New York: Vintage Books, 1950 [1848].

Thompson, E. P. "The Moral Economy of the English Crowd in the 18th Century." Past & Present 50 (February 1971): 76–136.

Tierney, J. J. "The Celtic Ethnography of Posidonius." *Proceedings of the Royal Irish Academy. Section C: Archaeology, Celtic Studies, History, Linguistics, Literature* 60 (1959): 189–275.

Tran, Van Voi. "How 'Natives' Ate at Colonial Exhibitions in 1889, 1900, and 1931." *French Cultural Studies* 26, no. 2 (2015): 163–75.

Turner, Jack. *Spice: the History of a Temptation*. New York: Knopf, 2008.

Twilley, Nicola. "The Coldscape." *Cabinet* 47 (Fall 2012): 78–87.

Twitty, Michael. *Rice*. Chapel Hill: University of North Carolina Press, 2021.

Visser, Margaret. *The Rituals of Dinner: The Origins, Evolutions, Eccentricities and Meaning of Table Manners*. New York: Penguin, 1991.

Watson, James L., ed. *Golden Arches East: McDonald's In East Asia*. Palo Alto, CA: Stanford University Press, 1997.

White, Merry. *Coffee Life in Japan*. Berkeley: University of California Press, 2012.

Wilson, Bee. *Consider the Fork: A History of How We Cook and Eat*. New York: Basic Books, 2012.

Wrangham, Richard. *Catching Fire: How Cooking Made Us Human*. New York: Basic Books, 2010.

Wright, Clifford A. "The Medieval Spice Trade and the Diffusion of the Chile." *Gastronomica* 7, no. 2 (Spring 2007): 35–43.

Wu, Emily S. "Chinese Ancestral Worship: Food to Sustain, Transform, and Heal the Dead and the Living." In *Dying to Eat: Cross-Cultural Perspectives on Food, Death, and the Afterlife*, edited by Candi K. Cann, 17–35. Lexington: University Press of Kentucky, 2018.

Wurgaft, Benjamin Aldes. *Meat Planet: Artificial Flesh and the Future of Food*. Berkeley: University of California Press, 2019.

Yü, Ying-shih. "Food in Chinese Culture: The Han Period (206 B.C.E.–220 C.E.)." In Ying-shih Yü, with Josephine Chiu-Duke and Michael S. Duke, *Chinese History and Culture: Sixth Century B.C.E. to Seventeenth Century*. New York: Columbia University Press, 2016.

Index

Adorno, Theodor, 132
Adzuki beans, 21, 56
Africa, "Scramble for," 135
African foodways, 144–145
  See also Rice, African; Merguez
    sausages; *Nem*
Africans, enslaved in the Americas,
  foodways of, 103–4, 186–7
Agriculture, 11–26
  animal, 12–13, 19–21, 23
  earliest sites, 18–19
  etymology, 11
  origins, 11–26
  population pressure theory as
    explanation 17–18
  possible politics, 24–26
  process rather than choice, 17
  See also Agricultural Revolution;
    Agriculture, Industrial; Enclosure
Agriculture, Industrial, 54, 155–160,
  165, 206–9
  environmental effects, 206–9
Agricultural Revolution, 157–160
  decline of meat eating during,
    158–159
  relationship with Industrial
    Revolution, 156–160

Akashiyaki (octopus balls), 27–9
  See also *Takoyaki*
Alexander the Great, 40–1, 49
"American" culinary identity, 186–9
  European colonial influences,
    187
  African slavery, 187
  U.S. colonial and imperial holdings,
    187–9
  Hawai'i as a case study, 188–9
Anthropology, cultural, 6–7
  observation, 6–7
  compared with historical research,
    6–7
Anthropology, sensory, 65
Anthropology, structural, 14
Apicius, Marcus Gavius, 46, 85, 161
Arab influence on medieval European
  food, 69
St. Augustine, baking analogy, 71
Austen, Jane (author of *Mansfield
  Park*), 117
Authenticity, 129–132, 184
Aztecs, 98, 120

Bananas, 13, 98, 178, 206, 208
Banham, Reyner, 173

Beans, 20, 21, 31, 43, 45, 56, 72, 77, 98,
    132, 163, 164, 187, 205
Beer, 72–4, 114–115, 166
    Benedictine monks as makers of, 73
    gruit in brewing, 74
    historical relationship with bread,
    72
    hops in brewing, 73–4
    Martin Luther and, 74
    medieval Church and beer
        brewing, 73–4
    women as makers of, 73
Beeton, Isabelle ("Mrs. Beeton"),
    133–4, 136
Berger, John, 3
Berra, Yogi, 191
Bialetti stovetop espresso machine,
    185
Black Death, effects of, 79, 81–2
Bolivia, 93
Bové, José, 176–7
Braudel, Fernand, 33
Bread, 36–8, 41–4, 49–50, 52, 70, 71,
    83–4, 97, 131, 159, 166–7, 173, 192
    French, in Vietnam, 192
    historical relationship with beer, 72
    as measure of quality of diet, 159,
    161
    naan, 38
    Persian words for; Persian baking
        techniques 37–8
    Roman, 41–4
    scooping with, 202
    white, 166–7
Bricolage, 168–170
British East India Company, 113–114,
    116, 134, 136
British Raj, 114, 134–78

Calorie(s), 13, 14, 16, 19, 31, 77, 80,
    100, 119, 166–167, 174, 180

Cambodia (Ratanakiri Province),
    62–6
Compostela, Santiago de, 69–70
Canned foods; canning, 147, 149, 154,
    171, 172
Canterbury Tales, 67, 79, 82, 84, 203
Carême, Marie-Antoine (Antonin),
    145
Carver, George Washington, 105
Chang Ch'ien, 53
Chhaang (barley or millet beer), 99
Chicha (corn beer), 99
Chapulines, 209
Charlemagne, influence on agricul-
    ture of, 79
Chaucer, Geoffrey, 67, 69, 71, 79, 82,
    203
Chili, 20, 26, 89–91, 92–3, 96, 134, 143,
    182,
Chinese cleaver (*tou*), 199, 201
Chocolate, 110–1, 120–3
    in Japan, 122
    in *mole*, 123
    Mexican origins of, 120
    military uses, 122
    Quakers in, 121
Cockaigne, 77–78
Coconuts, 102, 163, 186, 188
Coffee, 1, 6, 62, 98, 123, 124–128,
    129–131, 163, 178, 185, 186, 206
    Coffee houses, 125–126
    and politics, 126
    and "public sphere" theory of
        Jürgen Habermas, 126
    in Ethiopia 128
    in Japan, 127–128
    origins of, 124
    in Panama, 129–130
Colonialism vs. Imperialism, 135
Columbian Exchange, 43, 88, 92–105,
    186

Columbus, Christopher, 88, 93, 95
Columella, 163
Confucianism, 59
Cookbooks, 7, 46, 82, 141, 153–4,
    161–2, 182–186
    in India, 183–4
    and Italian Futurism 185–6
    as markers of cultural identity,
        184
Corn, 1, 3, 5, 13, 22, 26, 31, 32, 42, 93, 97,
    98–9, 184
    in Europe, 99–100
    origins of modern, 98–9
    See also Nixtamalization
Crisps, 172, 173
    See also Potato Chips
Croissants, 168–170
Crookes, Sir William, 165
Crosby, Alfred, 92
Crusades, the, 75–6
Curry, 133, 191
Curry Powder, 133, 136, 138

Darwin, Charles, 11
De re Coquenaria, 46
Dessert, 37, 53, 78, 118, 188, 190
    in Europe, origins of, 118
    in modern French cuisine, 161
    Persian, 37
Dickens, Charles, 153
Dutch East and West India Compa-
    nies, 139–140
Dutch Empire, 139–143
    and Dutch cuisine, 141–3
    Dutch-Portuguese rivalry, 140
    golden Age, 140
Dutch still life paintings, 142–3
Dumplings, 50, 83, 90, 209

Eggs, 1, 2, 12, 19, 27, 28, 38, 43, 45, 77,
    90, 148,

Empire, 30–61, 95, 98, 114, 120,
    133–146
    Defined, 30
Enclosure (of agricultural land),
    150–152, 158–9
Escoffier, Auguste, 145

Fan and t'sai, 52, 200, 202
Fantani, Duccio, 8–10
Fasting, 71
Fertile Crescent, 19, 35, 56
Fertilizer, 157, 163–6
    artificial, and population growth,
        166
Fire (in early hominid cooking), 11
Fisher, Mary Frances Kennedy, 1–2
Food riots, 155–6
French Empire, 143–6
    colonial and imperial holdings, 144
French cuisine, international
    influence of, 160–1
French fries, 174
Fruit leather, 82–3
Fufu, 201
Future of Food, 206–209
Futurists, Italian (and The Futurist
    Cookbook), 185–6

Galen; Galenic medicine, 60, 81, 118
Gama, Vasco da, 93
Gambia, The, 104
Garum, 44–5
Gauls (indomitable*), 41, 43, 48
Geechee-Gullah foodways, 104
Genetically modified foods, 171–2,
    176
Geng, 53
Glasse, Hannah, (author of Art of
    Cookery), 162
Globalization, 26, 90, 172, 176–7, 183
Gochujang, 90–91

Goat(s), 2, 21, 23, 35, 46, 77, 124, 131, 160

Guano, 140, 165

Haber, Fritz, 165–166
Hall, Stuart, 183
Halva, Persian origins of, 39
Han Dynasty China, 50–61
  agricultural projects, 54–5
  culinary diversity, 51
  population and diet 61
Hands, eating with, 202–3
Hogarth, William, 114–115
Honey, 32, 37, 39, 40, 43, 45, 49, 53, 69, 72, 79, 162
Hsi, Shu 50
Humboldt, Alexander von, 165
Hunting and gathering, 11–17, 21

Ice boxes and food preservation, 147–9
Imperialism vs. Colonialism, 135
Inca, 94, 95, 98
Industrial Revolution, 150–167, 174
Industrialization, 115, 152–5, 157, 159, 166, 169, 172–3, 186, 207
  and social inequality, 152–3
  defined, 152

Jook, 91

Kare raisu (curry rice), 191
Kashrut (kosher law), 71
Kimchi, 89–91,
Knife-making, Japanese, 194–6, 198–200
Knife-making, Stock removal, 196–8
Knives, 194–200, 209
Korean Food, 89–91, 93
Korean Food, idea of, 89–91

Laudan, Rachel, 207–8
Lévi-Strauss, Claude, 14, 21, 169
Liminal act, eating as a, 202

Maeng da (giant water bugs), 209
Magellen, 93, 96
Maize, see Corn
Malthus, Thomas Robert, 17–18
Mamaliga (Romanian porridge), 100
Manioc, 97, 100
Marco Polo, 83, 93, 94
Marinetti, Filippo, 185
Maya, 98, 120
McDonald's, 174–5, 176, 177, 207
  in non-Western countries, 175
  protests against, 177
Meat, 2, 4, 13, 19, 28, 35, 37, 40, 41, 42, 45, 47, 52, 53, 54, 57, 60, 64, 67, 70, 71, 72, 77, 78, 81, 87, 98, 100, 104, 133, 145, 159, 161, 175, 178, 185, 198, 199, 200, 201, 202, 209
  prestige and charisma of, 2
  "cultured," 206
  in the Western Diet, 206
  not "scaling up" well, 206
Medieval European peasant diet, 77
Medieval European agriculture, general conditions of 79–81
Medieval banquets 78–9
Pharmacopeia, medieval, 81–2
Medieval Christianity, food in, 70–2
Menus as educational texts, 190
Merguez sausages 143–4, 146
Milk, 1, 19, 26, 35, 38, 42, 43, 53, 71, 113, 116, 122, 148, 149
Millet, 21, 52, 53, 55, 56, 70, 99, 187
Modern migration and culinary change, 181–3
Modernization (defined), 152
Modernization of cuisine, 160–3

Moluccas, or "Spice Islands," 85, 86, 88, 93, 94, 95
Mulligatawny Soup, 133-134, 136, 138, 142
Mung beans, 21

Napkins in Western dining and in Japan, 203-4
Nem, Vietnamese and Senegalese, 191-3
Nepal, 110
Nescafe (ritual uses of), 110
Nitrogen; nitrogen fixation, both natural and artificial, 155, 163-6, 177
Nutrients, complimentary, 31-2
Nixtamalization, 22, 99
Noodles, 50, 52, 83-4, 90, 146, 186, 188, 200
    origins, 83
Nutmeg, 65, 84-86, 96, 120, 139
Nuts, 16, 35, 38, 39, 40, 43, 45, 49, 65-6, 97, 118, 142, 143
    nut trees, 97
    toxic 23
    used to thicken Persian sauces 212, fn. 7
Nutritional science, modern, 179-181

Okra, 104, 181, 187
Organic food, 9, 171, 175, 207

Packaging, Industrial, 173
Paraguay, 93
Parrots, edible, 49
Peanuts, 92-3, 104-105, 163, 186, 187
Peaches, 45, 56, 79, 98
Pepper, 40, 43, 45, 56, 62-3, 65, 66, 85, 86, 88, 96, 134, 141, 143
Pepys, Samuel, on spice pirates, 86-7

Persian Empire, 33-41
    baking 37
    cosmology, 38
    cuisine, Greek views of, 33-34, 40-41
    sweet tooth, 37
Pilgrims, medieval Christian, 67-72
Pineapple, 104-6, 187, 188
Pirates, Spice, 65, 86-7
Pizza, 92, 131, 132, 168, 169
Plato, as critic of eating too well, 41
Pollan, Michael, 174, 175
Polo, Marco, 83, 93, 94
Polynesian trade and foodways, 101-2, 188
Pope, Alexander, "The Rape of the Lock," 112-113
Portugal, 92-3, 127, 139-140
Potatoes, 13, 92, 97, 101, 172, 173, 188, European reactions to, 101
Potato chip, 173
    See also Crisps
Priestley, Joseph (and discovery of dinitrogen gas), 164

Rachis, shatterproof, as element of crop domestication, 22-3
Refrigeration, 177-9
    See also Ice Boxes
Restaurants, 29, 74-5, 89-91, 174, 176, 182-3, 186, 204
    and anthropological fieldwork, 190-3
    as bellwethers of culinary change, 154
    origins 74
Rhodes, Cecil, 135
Rice, 1, 13, 20, 21, 22, 31 32, 39, 52, 53, 55, 56, 69, 90, 91, 102-4, 130, 133, 138, 142, 145, 173, 175, 188, 191, 192, 200, 202, 205

African, 102–4
  necessity in a Japanese meal, 175
Roman Empire, 41–50
  annona system, 42
  banquets, 48–50
  banquets having nothing to do with
    orgies, 50
  cooking and social class in, 43–4
  porridge (*puls*) in, 42
  roads (as legacy) 67
  sauces of, 45
  views on frugality and luxury,
    46–8
  see also Garum
Rutherford, Daniel, 164

Sakai, knife-makers of, 194–6
Scarperia; knife-makers of, 200
Scott, James, 24
Sheng-Chih, Fan, 55–6
Silk Road, 76, 83–84
  food cultures along the, 83–4
Simha, Adam, 196–8
Slow Food, 177
Smell, sense of, 64–5
Social beverages, 110–128
  See also Chocolate; Coffee; Tea
"Soul Food" generalization, 104
Soybean(s), 13, 21, 56, 90
  in Han Chinese diet, 56
Soy Sauce, 51, 53, 142
Spice(s), 9, 27, 28, 29, 43, 65, 68, 76,
    84, 85, 86–8, 95, 96, 139, 140
  India as a source of, 85
  modernity explained by, perhaps,
    88
  Spice Islands (see also Moluccas),
    85, 86, 88, 93, 94, 95
  spice route of Columbus, 95
  spice trade, medieval, 84–88
Spirit Safes in distilling, 107–9

Staple foods (especially grains), 22,
    25, 30–61, 84, 92, 99, 100,
    102–104
  limited range eaten in modernity,
    13, 166
Stir fry cooking, 186, 199–200
Structuralism, 14
Strummer, Joe, 181
Sugar 4, 13, 37, 39, 40, 45, 53, 69,
    70, 73, 79, 87, 110, 111, 113,
    115, 116, 117–119, 121, 122, 123,
    128, 131, 137, 140, 149, 161,
    162, 163, 171, 172, 186, 187,
    188–9
  absence from the Roman table, 45
  and class, 119
  as opiate of masses, 119
Sugarcane, 13, 56, 98, 187
Supermarkets, 171–3, 179
Swallow (African food form), 100
Swift, Jonathan, 23

Taste, sense of, 64–5
Taste, diacritical, 48
Takoyaki (octopus balls) 27–29
  See also *Akashiyaki*
Taoism, 58–59
Taverns and inns in the medieval
    world, 74–5
Tea, 51, 57, 110–117, 118, 119, 120,
    121, 123, 124, 125, 126, 127,
    128, 131, 136, 137, 140, 163,
    186
  vs. coffee in Britain, 115–116
  grown in Darjeeling, Assam, and
    Ceylon (Sri Lanka), 114
  and industrialization, 115
  as a meal, 116
Thackeray, William (author of *Vanity
    Fair*), 133–134
"Three Sisters," 20, 98

Tong, Lu, 112, 114
Tupi-Guarani People, 100, 105

Utensils; cultural significance; as affordances or "ways" of eating, 201–4
Venice (as transformed by spice trade), 87–88
Vitamins, 22, 180–1

Weber, Max, 152
Webster, Thomas (artist of "A Tea Party"), 113
"Western Diet," 172
Wheat, 13, 19, 21, 22, 31, 32, 35, 36, 37, 38, 39, 43, 44, 45, 52, 55, 56, 69, 70, 73, 84, 97, 100, 111, 158, 165, 173, 185, 186, 200, 208

transmitted to the metabolism by pasta, 185
Whisky (or "whiskey"), 107–9
Whisky, Japanese, 107–9
Wine, 7, 36, 37, 43, 44, 45, 53, 56, 70, 71, 72, 74, 78, 98, 145
Wok, 53, 61, 199, 201

Xenophon, 38

Yin and Yang, 60
Young, Arthur, 150, 163
Yutang, Lin, 50

Zhou, Zuang zi (author of "Carving up an Ox"), 57–9
Zoroastrianism, 36

Founded in 1893,
UNIVERSITY OF CALIFORNIA PRESS
publishes bold, progressive books and journals
on topics in the arts, humanities, social sciences,
and natural sciences—with a focus on social
justice issues—that inspire thought and action
among readers worldwide.

The UC PRESS FOUNDATION
raises funds to uphold the press's vital role
as an independent, nonprofit publisher, and
receives philanthropic support from a wide
range of individuals and institutions—and from
committed readers like you. To learn more, visit
ucpress.edu/supportus.